Justice and the Parables of Jesus

Justice and the Parables of Jesus

Interpreting the Gospel Stories through Political Philosophy

Yung Suk Kim

NEW YORK • LONDON • OXFORD • NEW DELHI • SYDNEY

T&T CLARK

Bloomsbury Publishing Inc, 1359 Broadway, New York, NY 10018, USA
Bloomsbury Publishing Plc, 50 Bedford Square, London, WC1B 3DP, UK
Bloomsbury Publishing Ireland, 29 Earlsfort Terrace, Dublin 2, D02 AY28, Ireland

BLOOMSBURY, T&T CLARK and the T&T Clark logo are trademarks of Bloomsbury Publishing Plc

First published in the United States of America 2026

Copyright © Yung Suk Kim, 2026

For legal purposes the Acknowledgments on p. viii constitute an extension of this copyright page.

All rights reserved. No part of this publication may be: i) reproduced or transmitted in any form, electronic or mechanical, including photocopying, recording or by means of any information storage or retrieval system without prior permission in writing from the publishers; or ii) used or reproduced in any way for the training, development or operation of artificial intelligence (AI) technologies, including generative AI technologies. The rights holders expressly reserve this publication from the text and data mining exception as per Article 4(3) of the Digital Single Market Directive (EU) 2019/790.

Bloomsbury Publishing Inc does not have any control over, or responsibility for, any third-party websites referred to or in this book. All internet addresses given in this book were correct at the time of going to press. The author and publisher regret any inconvenience caused if addresses have changed or sites have ceased to exist, but can accept no responsibility for any such changes.

Library of Congress Cataloging-in-Publication Data
Names: Kim, Yung Suk author
Title: Justice and the parables of Jesus: interpreting the Gospel stories through political philosophy / Yung Suk Kim.
Description: 1. | New York: T&T Clark, 2026. | Includes bibliographical references and index.
Identifiers: LCCN 2025031818 (print) | LCCN 2025031819 (ebook) | ISBN 9780567725363 hardback | ISBN 9780567725370 ebook | ISBN 9780567725387 pdf
Subjects: LCSH: Jesus Christ–Parables | Social justice–Biblical teaching | Political science–Philosophy
Classification: LCC BT375.3 .K55 2026 (print) | LCC BT375.3 (ebook)
LC record available at https://lccn.loc.gov/2025031818
LC ebook record available at https://lccn.loc.gov/2025031819

ISBN: HB: 978-0-567-72536-3
PB: 978-0-567-72535-6
ePDF: 978-0-567-72538-7
eBook: 978-0-567-72537-0

Typeset by Deanta Global Publishing Services, Chennai, India
Printed and bound in the United States of America

For product safety related questions contact productsafety@bloomsbury.com.

To find out more about our authors and books visit www.bloomsbury.com and sign up for our newsletters.

Contents

Acknowledgments		viii
1	Introduction	1
	What Is a Parable?	2
	Political Context of the Parables of Jesus	3
	Divine Justice, Parables, and the Rule/Reign of God	5
	Political Reading of Jesus and the Parables	6
	Format and Use of the Book	7
2	Justice and Parables	11
	Theories of Political Philosophy	12
	Justice and Parables	22
3	Distributive Justice and Parables	35
	The Parable of the Vineyard Laborers	35
	The Parable of the Rich Man and Lazarus	44
	Conclusion	48
	Questions for Discussion	49
4	Attributive Justice and Parables	53
	The Parable of the Talents	54
	The Parable of the Treasure	60
	The Parable of the Pearl	64
	Conclusion	67
	Questions for Discussion	68
5	Procedural Justice and Parables	71
	The Parable of the Seed Growing Secretly	72
	The Parable of the Wheat and Weeds	77
	Conclusion	82
	Questions for Discussion	83

6	Social Justice and Parables	85
	The Parable of the Pharisee and the Tax Collector	86
	The Parable of the Leaven	92
	Conclusion	96
	Questions for Discussion	97
7	Racial Justice and Parables	99
	The Parable of the Good Samaritan	101
	The Parable of the Mustard Seed	108
	Conclusion	115
	Questions for Discussion	115
8	Restorative Justice and Parables	119
	The Parable of the Father and Two Sons	121
	The Parable of the Unmerciful Slave	128
	Conclusion	133
	Questions for Discussion	134
9	Compensatory Justice and Parables	137
	The Parable of the Unjust Steward	138
	Conclusion	145
	Questions for Discussion	146
10	Retributive Justice and Parables	149
	The Parable of the Unjust Judge and Widow	151
	The Parable of the Tenants	156
	Conclusion	163
	Questions for Discussion	164
11	Global Justice and Parables	167
	The Parable of the Rich Fool	169
	The Parable of the Lost Sheep	175
	Conclusion	180
	Questions for Discussion	180
12	Environmental Justice and Parables	183
	The Parable of the Sower	184
	Conclusion	191
	Questions for Discussion	193

13	Conclusion	195
	Summary of Justice and Parables	196

Bibliography	201
Index	210
About the Author	214

Acknowledgments

My journey exploring the parables of Jesus began early in my teaching career, where I had the privilege of regularly teaching courses on these profound stories at the Samuel DeWitt Proctor School of Theology, Virginia Union University. I am deeply thankful to my students for their enthusiasm, participation, and the enriching conversations we shared. Their engagement has been invaluable in shaping my understanding and appreciation of the parables. I also express my gratitude to Virginia Union University for its unwavering support and the warm environment it provides, enabling me to thrive as an educator. I feel truly blessed to teach such wonderful students, supported by Dean John Guns, a dedicated faculty and staff.

In 2018, I delivered a special lecture on parables and justice at Hanshin University Graduate School of Theology in Seoul, Korea. I appreciate Professor Chul Chun for arranging this event. This lecture experience planted the seed for this long-term book project. I extend my heartfelt thanks to the faculty and students who attended and provided insightful feedback. I also would like to express my heartfelt gratitude to Professor Sung Uk Lim at Yonsei University for his kind invitation to deliver a lecture on the parable of the Good Samaritan in 2024. This opportunity not only deepened my understanding of the text but also enriched my perspective on its relevance in today's world. Dr. Lim's support and encouragement have been invaluable to my work. I also thank Dr. Sejong Chun for his support by traveling from afar to support me at the lecture.

In 2019, I conducted a three-day Bible study series in Grove City, Pennsylvania, following an invitation from Bishop Moore of the Western Pennsylvania Conference of the United Methodist Church. This opportunity not only allowed me to share my insights but also enabled me to connect with the community in a meaningful way. In 2024, I was honored to be invited by the American Baptist Church of the South Conference to lead another Bible study. I am especially thankful to Rev. James Harrison for his warm hospitality and support throughout this event. These interactions with genuine individuals have significantly fueled my passion and research endeavors, inspiring me to continue my work with renewed energy and dedication.

I also wish to acknowledge the Journal of *Currents in Theology and Mission* for publishing my essays, "Justice Matters, but Which Justice?" and "Reading Mercy in the Parables of Jesus." These publications allowed me to refine my ideas further. I appreciate Dr. Craig Nessan as part of the journal editorship, along with the contributions of other members, especially Professor Troy Troftgruben at Wartburg Theological Seminary.

Special thanks go to Pastor Beanie Kelly for inviting me in 2025 to lead a Bible Study session titled "Justice and Parables" at Shady Grove UMC in Glen Allen, Virginia. It was a privilege to share my insights with such an engaged community.

This book would not have been possible without the trust and guidance of Dr. Richard Brown, senior editor, Bloomsbury. He facilitated rounds of peer reviews that provided crucial feedback, allowing me to refine my manuscript. I also extend my thanks to the anonymous reviewers whose insights shaped this work. Their thoughtful critiques and encouragement were instrumental in its development.

I am profoundly appreciative of my academic community and colleagues, whose support and collaboration were crucial throughout my research and writing process. Academic endeavors are never solitary, and I am grateful to be surrounded by such a supportive network. I would like to extend my heartfelt gratitude to several colleagues who have been instrumental in my journey. Dr. Robert Wafawanaka at Virginia Union University embodies a humbling spirit and serves as a constant source of inspiration. I am truly grateful for his kindness and resourcefulness in so many ways.

I would like to extend my heartfelt gratitude to Demetrius Williams, my colleague and friend at the University of Wisconsin-Milwaukee. In 2024, he invited me to lead a clergy workshop during the local conference of the Baptist churches, which was a transformative experience that significantly energized my research. Additionally, he graciously allowed me to preach at his church, an opportunity that rejuvenated my spirit and reignited my motivation to delve deeper into my work. I am truly thankful for his support and encouragement.

I also wish to recognize my colleagues who supported me during my recent trips to Korea for lectures. Dr. Jin Seong Woo provided me with the opportunity to share my insights on biblical interpretation and its connection to preaching, which was a rewarding experience. I am thankful to Professor Kyung Mi Park at Ewha Womans University for inviting me to engage with her students in the classroom, fostering enriching discussions. Additionally, I express my appreciation to Professor Hee-Kyu Heidi Park at Ewha Womans University, with whom I co-led a special lecture event in Jeonju city. Our time together was not only productive but also enjoyable, marked by her gentle spirit and the delightful dinner we shared.

During my travels to Korea, I had a wonderful opportunity to refresh my scholarship and find inspiration for my research and writing. I want to express my gratitude to Professors Kyoung Shik Min and Hak Chul Kim at Yonsei University for their generous hospitality and the enjoyable time we shared together. I am thankful to Rev. Jin-ho Kim and Professor Jae Hyung Cho for their kindness and the time they spent with me. If I have overlooked anyone, please forgive me.

Lastly, I would not be where I am today without the unwavering support and love of my family—Yongjeong, my wife; my three daughters (Hyerim, Hyekyung, and Hyein) and their spouses (Jason, Jinho, and Stephen). They are my anchor and inspiration, and I am deeply grateful for their presence in my life. I also include my granddaughter, Hana, in this group of supporters.

1

Introduction

Numerous books explore the parables of Jesus, generally falling into two categories: those offering theological interpretations, often focusing on soteriology or Christology, and those examining the parables within the historical context of Jesus's life.[1] A recent trend emphasizes social justice and contemporary relevance.[2] This book contributes to that trend by interpreting the parables through the lens of political philosophy, examining fundamental questions of politics, liberty, justice, and rights, among others. Given the parables' setting in first-century Palestine under Roman rule, a political philosophy approach, with its central concern for justice, is relevant.

This book applies ten types of justice—distributive, attributive, procedural, social, restorative, compensatory, retributive, global, racial, and environmental—to the interpretation of the parables, engaging with contemporary justice issues. While it does not suggest that the parables directly address these contemporary concerns, the book proposes a framework for interpreting them through a justice lens. This approach prompts readers to pose justice-related questions about Jesus's parables.

Conserving our planet and protecting human safety amid climate change and pandemics are crucial concerns wherever we live. Justice is fundamental to all aspects of life. The parable of the sower highlights the importance of cultivating fertile ground, a metaphor for preparing the earth that emphasizes environmental justice. The Parable of the vineyard laborers speaks to distributive justice, advocating for fair resource distribution and equitable job opportunities. The parables of the mustard seed and leaven invite us to rethink the transformative potential of the marginalized. How should we view race—as something to overcome or celebrate—in our increasingly diverse world? How can we achieve a just and equitable understanding of ourselves and others?

Ultimately, readers are challenged to interpret the parables' contemporary relevance. The open-ended nature of the parables facilitates this interpretation.

We face unprecedented global crises—pandemics, wars, rising suicide rates, and escalating conflicts across nations, political systems, and social groups. How can we speak of heaven while justice remains elusive? This book explores this question and others, seeking the meaning of justice within the parables, applying a justice lens to their interpretation, and discussing contemporary justice issues in all their complexity.

What Is a Parable?

A parable (*parabolē*) is "a story cast alongside life," reflecting various aspects of existence in society and challenging readers to see things differently.[3] The parable serves as a mind-opener for recognizing the deeper, radical reality of God's justice in the world.[4] Gordley observes: "In short, the parables invite us to live in mercy—to live with compassion and love in light of the reality of what Jesus called the 'kingdom of God.'"[5] A parable employs subversive language that challenges readers to reconfigure their understanding of God's rule in a world full of mercy and justice. Thus, the parable includes metaphorical links between God's rule and elements in the world. Hultgren states: "A parable is a figure of speech in which a comparison is made between God's kingdom, actions, or expectations and something in this world."[6] Similarly, Green describes a parable this way: "A parable is a narrative metaphor—a metaphor in motion—that, by the peculiar working of its juxtaposed elements, startles the mind into fresh awareness."[7] In Dodd's words, the parable, as a metaphor taken from nature or common life, arrests "the hearer by its vividness or strangeness" and leaves "the mind in sufficient doubt as to its precise application to tease the mind into active thought."[8] Taken together, this kingdom language is collaborative, as Crossan observes: "God's kingdom is here, but only insofar as you accept it, enter it, live it, and thereby establish it."[9] In other words, a new reality of God's justice will not come to fruition unless the audience participates in the invitation of God's good news or rule. Mk 1:15 ensures that a new time and the reign of God will not become a reality without a change of mind (*metanoia*).

Jesus was a great storyteller who conveyed many parables relating to personal life, socioeconomic matters, social maladies, and communal life. These are not stories that strengthen societal norms; they are subversive tales that shatter the familiar thoughts and habits that dominate individuals and society. Parables exemplify Jesus's concerns for justice, and through them, we may reach the heart of his teaching about the rule and reign of God.[10]

As noted above, a parable is neither a spiritual (allegorical) story that refers to otherworldly matters nor an apocalyptic tale highlighting only the future kingdom of God.[11] Instead, a parable addresses the present life conditions in which people are devastated by various forms of misfortune, social ills, and societal injustices. A parable is not a literal story but a metaphorical narrative that compares the rule and reign of God with individuals or elements in nature. For example, in the parable of the sower, the ideal world is compared to the sower who sows seeds indiscriminately and ultimately faces a great harvest. In the parable of the mustard seed, the ideal world and humanity are likened to the small mustard seed, which holds intrinsic value and grows enough to benefit people and birds. The parable helps hearers and readers reimagine a world filled with love, justice, mercy, peace, and reconciliation.

Political Context of the Parables of Jesus

Jesus was born into a world of chaos and injustice, partly due to the Roman Empire's merciless rule, which suppressed the poor, and partly due to the corrupt leaders and elites of Jewish society.[12] His life was modest as he was born to poor parents. His hometown was Nazareth in Galilee, and his mother was Mary. His adoptive father was Joseph, who was a *tektōn* (woodworker or stonemason), which means living day by day working on construction sites. According to Mark, Jesus is also a *tektōn*, described as "the son of Mary and brother of James and Joses and Judas and Simon" (Mk 6:3), while in Matthew, he is referred to as "the son of a *tektōn*" (Mt. 13:55).[13] Textual critics believe that Jesus is identified as a *tektōn* because the more difficult reading is typically preferred when determining which version is earlier. Mark is bold and straightforward in describing Jesus as a *tektōn*, but Matthew finds it difficult to present it that way; hence, the change to "the son of a *tektōn*." This adjustment is consistent with Matthew's theology and portrayal of Jesus. In Matthew, Jesus's birth carries royal imagery, told gloriously, with the wise men from the East visiting and worshiping him. However, it would be natural for Jesus to become a *tektōn*, following his father Joseph's trade.

At the time Jesus lived in Nazareth, both Joseph and Jesus likely sought work in Sepphoris, a large Hellenistic metropolitan city where significant building projects were underway, just a few miles north of Nazareth. It is presumed that Jesus observed a stark contrast between his hometown and Sepphoris. When Jesus was born, the first emperor of the Roman Empire was Augustus, who was referred to as "the son of God" and claimed to bring "peace and security" to the empire and its subjects. However, his empire was built on war and violence. While the elites of Rome and its puppet governments enjoyed many exclusive benefits of wealth and fame, the masses lived in abject conditions.

In this Roman world, as described above, justice meant that people stayed in their places and followed the roles assigned to them by society. Roman society was hierarchically structured, and the dominant philosophy of Stoicism undergirded the Roman Empire's hierarchical unity, suggesting that people must accept their social positions. The body, as a metaphor, is understood as a hierarchical organism. Just as body parts work together to maintain the unity of the whole, people are expected to do the same without protesting or complaining. In this system, the emperor is referred to as "the first one" (*Princeps*). All people and subjects are bound to serve the singular power of Rome and its majesty. Justice in the Roman Empire meant accepting the hierarchical system and patron-client relationships.[14] Within this framework of justice, individuals are judged by birth, social status, ethnicity, gender, and economic class. Opportunities are reserved for a few elites and their children, while economic inequalities and social discrimination are rampant, leading to widespread social maladies and despair.

Growing up in Nazareth and experiencing poverty and injustice, Jesus rethought God and reimagined a world of justice. He told parables within this political, social, and economic context, where people barely survived and had lost hope for the future. The parables address a wide range of issues concerning justice, including human dignity, equality, freedom, and socioeconomic justice. Some parables originate from the agricultural environment and compare the reign of God with nature, such as the Sower, the Seed Growing Secretly, the Wheat and Weeds, the Mustard Seed, and the Leaven. These parables evoke the peaceful character of life while challenging people to follow the rhythms and flow of nature. Through them, we can unpack the importance of human dignity, equality, and fair opportunities for all.

Some parables directly address social and economic justice, including the Vineyard Laborers, the Rich Fool, and the Rich Man and Lazarus. Others focus on community behavior and justice, such as the Unmerciful Slave, the Lost Sheep, and the Father and Two Sons. Still more deal with social issues and justice, including the Good Samaritan, the Unjust Judge and Widow, and the Pharisee and the Tax Collector. Another group addresses personal behavior and vocation, illustrated by the Pearls, the Treasure, and the Talents. The parables of Jesus encompass a wide array of personal, communal, and social themes, with justice as the major concern.[15] This book explores narrative parables whose origins trace back to Jesus, interpreting them through the lens of justice.[16]

Divine Justice, Parables, and the Rule/Reign of God

Divine justice is an inclusive term that encompasses all forms of justice derived from God's character and work, as presented in the Hebrew Scriptures. While this term is similar to God's righteousness, it is more closely related to the active aspect of humanity in following God's righteousness.

God is characterized by righteousness; therefore, both people and the world must follow the path of justice. The book of Isaiah describes this path as one where every valley is raised, every mountain is made low, uneven ground is leveled, and rough places are made plain (Isa. 40:4). God's righteousness is the source of everything, including justice. In Amos 5:24, justice and righteousness are mentioned separately to emphasize their importance: "But let justice roll down like waters, and righteousness like an ever-flowing stream." While righteousness reflects God's nature, justice pertains to social justice and its manifestation in people's lives within society. If there is no justice in society, there can be no true religion or God's salvation. Likewise, Jesus declares that the time (*kairos*) has been fulfilled and that the reign of God has come near (Mk 1:15), implying that the radical, just rule of God against all forms of evil, whether in individuals, society, or the Roman Empire, must be realized.

Jesus advocates for God's righteousness in his ministry (Mt. 6:33). To this end, he teaches about the reign of God, often through parables, heals the sick, and challenges normative worldviews and traditions. The central topic of the parables is *basileia tou theou*, often translated as "the kingdom of God." However, a more accurate connotation is "the rule or reign of God," as it refers to God's activity of justice and love in the world rather than to a physical place or time. This concept is a significant theme of Jesus's public ministry, emphasizing the importance of advocating for justice on behalf of the weak and marginalized.

The rule or reign of God is present in all aspects of human life, including religion, economics, and politics. Jesus's teachings revolve around this rule in the current world, which is actualized through justice. Justice serves as the foundation of God's rule, demonstrating God's righteousness. This theme is consistent in both the Old Testament and Jesus's teachings. God is righteous, loving, merciful, and faithful, constantly engaging with the world through his prophets and agents.

Political Reading of Jesus and the Parables

Scholars interpret the parables of Jesus as part of his challenge against the dominance of elites and imperial powers. Howard Thurman's *Jesus and the Disinherited* explores the social implications of Jesus's teachings, highlighting how the parables bring hope and justice to the oppressed.[17] He emphasizes the radical nature of Jesus's message for those facing social and economic oppression. Similarly, John Howard Yoder's *The Politics of Jesus* considers the parables as critiques of power, empire, and unjust systems, presenting a new vision of community based on justice, peace, and equity.[18] Walter Wink echoes Yoder's perspective, examining how Jesus's teachings, including the parables, confront systems of domination and power in his book *The Powers That Be*.[19] He argues that the parables reveal the intersection of spiritual and political realities and that Jesus's vision of the kingdom of God offers an alternative to violent, coercive power structures. Ched Myers's *Binding the Strong Man* argues that Jesus's parables critique the empire while advocating for justice and inclusion.[20] In a slightly different context, Elisabeth Schüssler Fiorenza, in her book *In Memory of Her*, contends that the parables often contain subversive messages that challenge patriarchal structures and promote social justice and inclusivity, connecting the teachings of Jesus to broader struggles for justice, particularly concerning gender and power.[21]

Some scholars focus on analyzing Jesus's parables in political contexts and relate them to justice, questioning imperial power and social structures. In his book *Parables as Subversive Speech*, William R. Herzog II interprets the parables as politically charged criticisms of the social and economic injustices of their time.[22] He believes that Jesus used parables to reveal the oppressive nature of the Roman Empire and the ruling class, educate the oppressed, and challenge power dynamics.

Matthew Gordley's book, *Social Justice in the Stories of Jesus*, argues that Jesus's parables challenge societal norms and present a different vision of community where justice, equality, and care for the vulnerable are central.[23] Gordley also examines how these teachings can be applied in our world, providing insights into how Jesus's stories continue to inspire social justice movements. The book emphasizes the relevance of Jesus's messages in addressing contemporary issues such as poverty, inequality, and systemic injustice.

Christopher Marshall's *Compassionate Justice* delves into the concept of restorative justice using two of Jesus's parables: the parable of the Unforgiving Slave (Mt. 18:23-35) and the parable of the Good Samaritan (Lk. 10:25-37).[24] Marshall argues that these parables provide valuable insights into how justice should be perceived and practiced, emphasizing restoration, mercy, and compassion over retribution. He draws connections between these ancient narratives and contemporary discussions in criminal justice, advocating for a system that prioritizes healing and restoring relationships rather than solely punishing offenders.

Richard Ford's *The Parables of Jesus & The Problems of the World* interprets the parables as stories that challenge existing power structures and promote justice and equity.[25] Ford argues that Jesus used the parables to incite social change and confront unjust systems. This book helps link the parables with broader social movements for justice, making it especially relevant for those interested in political theology.

The aforementioned books are powerful resources that deepen our understanding of the parables of Jesus within a political context, encouraging readers to engage meaningfully with contemporary social issues.

This book continues in the spirit of political reading and demonstrates a strong commitment to justice. What sets it apart is its comprehensive exploration of justice in various forms, including distributive justice, social justice, and global and environmental justice. While other works may focus primarily on specific aspects of justice, this book integrates these diverse themes to offer a holistic perspective on how Jesus's teachings can inform and inspire action in today's multifaceted social and political landscapes.

By examining the intersectionality of these justice categories, the book aims to equip readers with the tools necessary to advocate for change across different spheres of life—be it community organizing, policy-making, or environmental stewardship. In doing so, it not only honors the radical nature of Jesus's message but also challenges readers to reimagine their roles in promoting justice and equity in the world.

Format and Use of the Book

The book is organized into ten main chapters, each focusing on a different type of justice. There is one or two related parables for each chapter. Readers can choose any chapter to read first, depending on their interests. Environmental justice is addressed last, but this does not mean it is less important than the others. The book also covers historically new types of justice: racial justice and global justice. Racial justice is a prevalent issue intertwined with religion and political ideologies, and it remains a global concern as many forms of violence still occur around the issue of racism. Global justice is also crucial because issues such as climate change and global poverty are more pressing now than ever before.

The main chapters of the book consist of translations, interpretations of the parables, and engagement with them through the relevant type of justice. After interpreting the parables, we will engage with them concerning the relevant type of justice, raising critical questions. Finally, we will relate contemporary issues of justice to the given parable.

Each chapter ends with discussion questions, providing an opportunity for readers to review the chapter and deepen their understanding by answering them. These questions will also be useful for small group discussions within a class or various group study settings.

I hope this book serves as an ongoing storybook that presents challenges related to our daily lives, influenced by various issues in our world. The stories of Jesus were told and will continue to be retold as we engage with them in a world where we still struggle to understand justice in all areas of our lives. While the times of Jesus are strikingly different from our own, this does not mean we cannot comprehend them; we can still learn from these stories.

However, we should avoid generalizing Jesus's stories to fit our narratives. We should not limit ourselves to interpreting these stories solely in an allegorical sense, as if we are not experiencing life in this world. Despite the significant challenges posed by the lack of information available from first-century Roman Palestine, we can appreciate the rich treasures found in the stories told by Jesus.

It is our responsibility to retell our own stories by engaging with the stories of Jesus. Through this process, this book invites readers to view life through the lens of justice.

Notes

1 To name a few books concerning the theological interpretation of the parables: Barbara Reid, *Parables for Preachers A, B, C* (Collegeville, MN: Liturgical, 1999); Mary Ann Getty-Sullivan, *Parables of the Kingdom: Jesus and the Use of Parables in the Synoptic Tradition* (Collegeville, MN: Liturgical, 2007). For books about the

historical Jesus's teaching of the parables, see Robert Funk, Bernard B. Scott, et al., *The Parables of Jesus* (Sonoma, CA: Polebridge, 1988); John D. Crossan, *In Parables: The Challenge of the Historical Jesus* (Sonoma, CA: Polebridge, 1992); Bernard B. Scott, *Re-Imagine the World: An Introduction to the Parables of Jesus* (Sonoma, CA: Polebridge, 2001); William R. Herzog II, *Parables as Subversive Speech: Jesus as Pedagogue of the Oppressed* (Louisville, KY: Westminster John Knox, 1994); Luise Schottroff, *The Parables of Jesus* (Minneapolis, MN: Fortress, 2006). Concerning methods of parable interpretation, see Ruben Zimmermann, *Puzzling the Parables of Jesus: Methods and Interpretation* (Minneapolis, MN: Fortress, 2015). Regarding the Jewish interpretation of Jesus's parables, see Amy-Jill Levine, *Short Stories by Jesus: The Enigmatic Parables of a Controversial Rabbi* (New York, NY: HarperOne, 2014). See also Brad H. Young, *The Parables: Jewish Tradition and Christian Interpretation* (Grand Rapids, MI: Baker Academic, 1998).

2 See for example: Matthew E. Gordley, *Social Justice in the Stories of Jesus: The Ethical Challenge of the Parables* (Pittsburgh, PA: Wiley Blackwell, 2024); Richard Q. Ford, *The Parables of Jesus and the Problems of the World: How Ancient Narratives Comprehend Modern Malaise* (Eugene, OR: Cascade, 2016); Christopher D. Marshall, *Compassionate Justice: An Interdisciplinary Dialogue with Two Gospel Parables on Law, Crime, and Restorative Justice* (Eugene, OR: Cascade, 2012); Emerson B. Powery, *The Good Samaritan: Luke 10 for the Life of the Church* (Grand Rapids, MI: Baker Academic, 2022).

3 Marcus Borg, *Jesus: The Life, Teaching, and Relevance of a Religious Revolutionary* (New York: HarperCollins, 2008), 259.

4 Howard Thurman, *Sermons on the Parables* (Maryknoll, NY: Orbis, 2002), 8.

5 Matthew Gordley, *Social Justice in the Stories of Jesus*, 6.

6 Arland J. Hultgren, *The Parables of Jesus: A Commentary* (Grand Rapids, MI: Eerdmans, 2000), 3.

7 Barbara Green, *Like a Tree Planted* (Collegeville, MN: Liturgical, 1997), 10.

8 C.H. Dodd, *The Parables of Jesus* (New York: Charles Scribner, 1961), 16.

9 John D. Crossan, *The Power of Parable: How Fiction by Jesus Became Fiction about Jesus* (New York: HarperOne, 2012), 127.

10 Michael Cook, "Jesus' Parables and the Faith that Does Justice," *Studies in the Spirituality of Jesuits* 24, no. 5 (1992): 3–4.

11 David Gowler, *What Are They Saying about the Parables?* (New York: Paulist, 2000), 28–40.

12 See Yung Suk Kim, *Resurrecting Jesus: The Renewal of New Testament Theology* (Eugene, OR: Cascade, 2015), 27–47.

13 Though the birth narrative in Matthew and Luke states that Mary's conception is by the Holy Spirit, what that means from another perspective is that Jesus's biological father is unknown.

14 Regarding complexities in economic relationships between classes and consequential implications, see Anthony Keddie, *Class and Power in Roman Palestine: The Socioeconomic Setting of Judaism and Christian Origins* (Cambridge: Cambridge University Press, 2019). There is no one clear picture of the Roman economy, class, and power relations; but the bottom line is that Romans "provoked resentment regardless of whether or how much taxes increased, for taxation was incessantly burdensome" (130).
15 Yung Suk Kim, *Jesus's Truth: Life in Parables* (Eugene, OR: Resources, 2018).
16 Yung Suk Kim, "Justice Matters, But Which Justice? In the Case of Jesus' Parables," *Currents in Theology and Mission* 46, no. 3 (2019): 41-3.
17 Howard Thurman, *Jesus and the Disinherited* (Boston, MA: Beacon, 1996).
18 John Howard Yoder, *The Politics of Jesus* (Grand Rapids, MI: Eerdmans, 1994).
19 Walter Wink, *The Power That Be: Theology for a New Millennium* (Manhattan, NY: Harmony, 1999).
20 Ched Myers, *Binding the Strong Man* (Maryknoll, NY: Orbis, 2008).
21 Elisabeth Schüssler Fiorenza, *In Memory of Her: A Feminist Reconstruction of Christian Origins* (Louisville, KY: WJKP, 1994).
22 William Herzog, *Parables as Subversive Speech*.
23 Matthew Gordley, *Social Justice in the Stories of Jesus*.
24 Christopher Marshall, *Compassionate Justice*.
25 Richard Ford, *The Parables of Jesus and the Problems of the World*.

2

Justice and Parables

Jesus's parables can be analyzed through the lens of political philosophy as any human society grapples with questions of justice. While the culture, society, and politics of first-century Palestine and the broader Roman world differ significantly from those of today, we still share a common humanity with them. Although Jesus did not explicitly engage with modern concepts of political philosophy, we can examine his parables to explore questions of justice that are relevant to their social, political, and economic contexts. What is important is not only understanding the meaning of the parables in their historical context but also how readers engage with these stories from the perspective of justice.

Political philosophy addresses fundamental questions about power, authority, rights, justice, and the organization of society. It explores the role of justice in society, the distribution of resources, and the nature of freedom and equality.[1] The central questions are:

1. What is a just society?
2. How should resources, opportunities, and power be distributed among individuals and groups?
3. What is the purpose of the state?
4. What rights do individuals possess?
5. How should these rights be balanced against the needs or desires of the community?

As we can see, the central concept or issue of political philosophy is justice. Below, we will briefly explore contending theories of justice that seek to answer questions about what is just, how justice can be achieved, and what the principles of justice should be.[2]

Theories of Political Philosophy

Classical Liberalism

Classical liberalism emphasizes individual liberty, freedom, free markets, and small government. John Locke argues that individuals have inherent rights to life, liberty, and property.[3] In pursuit of these rights, the government's role is restricted to protecting them. Similarly, Adam Smith emphasizes free markets without government controls, believing that economic prosperity can best be achieved through the "invisible hand," a metaphor for consumers' self-interests driving economic growth.[4]

Classical liberalism is challenged by Kantian deontological ethics, which holds that moral decisions should not be influenced by personal interests or inclinations. Deontological ethics creates a moral system guided by reason-based, duty-driven principles that are not swayed by individual interests or goals in life. The decision-making agency is the autonomous self, embodying "pure practical reason" and remaining unaffected by external forces, personal agendas, or ideology.[5] People must act and make decisions based on the motive of duty rather than inclination, meaning they should do something because it is the right thing to do. This leads to the concept of the "categorical imperative," a universal law of justice that applies to all.

There are areas where classical liberalism and biblical teachings align, such as human dignity, moral agency, and personal responsibility. For example, biblical traditions emphasize human dignity based on being made in the image of God (Gen. 1:26-27). Moral agency and personal responsibility are highlighted in Deut. 30:19: "I call heaven and earth to witness against you today that I have set before you life and death, blessings and curses. Choose life so that you and your descendants may live" (cf. Josh. 24:15). There are also teachings about property rights and the importance of hard work: "You shall not steal" (Exod. 20:15); "Anyone unwilling to work should not eat" (2 Thess. 3:10); "A slack hand causes poverty, but the hand of the diligent makes rich" (Prov. 10:4).

Biblical ethics also challenges certain aspects of classical liberalism, particularly its emphasis on individualism over communal care and its approach to wealth and inequality. The relationship between these ideas varies based on how one interprets biblical teachings, whether one prioritizes personal freedom or communal justice. For instance, in Acts 2:44-45, early Christians are depicted as sharing their possessions. Isa. 1:17 also emphasizes the importance of defending the oppressed. Additionally, Jesus's teachings challenge the greed and competition that exacerbate poverty (see Mt. 6:25-34; 19:24; Jas. 5:1-6). Ultimately, many of Jesus's parables address injustices and inequalities among people.

Modern Libertarianism

Modern libertarianism inherits classical liberalism and advocates for minimal government intervention and maximization of individual liberty. Nozick's view of liberalism focuses on protecting individual liberty and property rights.[6] The government's role is to protect individuals from force or fraud and to guarantee a society where individuals' property rights are upheld. From this perspective, redistributing wealth is seen as a violation of individual property rights. The central argument is that people are entitled to their holdings as long as they acquire them justly through labor or voluntary exchange. However, this view of liberalism does not address inequalities in wealth and opportunity.

As noted above, libertarianism is a political philosophy that aims to create a society of free individuals with maximum liberties and rights. Libertarians believe in the importance of free markets and competition and tend to oppose government intervention in individuals' personal lives and the economy. This view of liberalism has limitations in securing a more equality-based society because some individuals may possess greater abilities and talents, giving them an advantage.[7] Rawls critiques meritocracy for its promotion of social and economic inequalities, arguing that one's abilities do not belong solely to that individual but rather are a common asset of society.

There are different branches of libertarianism, including the laissez-faire branch, which advocates for complete freedom for individuals and markets, and the fairness branch, which focuses on ensuring fairness in the market and society while reducing social and economic inequalities. John Rawls advances the concept of equality to encompass fairness among individuals, developing a theory known as "the hypothetical contract."[8] This theory emphasizes the importance of equal liberties for all citizens as well as social and economic equality. He argues that justice should be conceived as fairness and that individuals should make decisions behind a "veil of ignorance," unaware of their social status or abilities, to ensure impartiality.[9] Under this condition, inequalities are permissible only if they benefit the least advantaged members of society—this theory is known as the "difference principle."[10] Rawls's theory aims to provide equal basic liberties for all citizens and derives its philosophical grounding from social contract theory.[11]

As noted earlier, freedom, or liberty, is a vital aspect of justice because it allows individuals to think and act independently. However, this freedom comes with the responsibility not to harm others. On a positive note, liberty encourages people to advocate for the freedom of others. For Jesus, freedom means being liberated from oppressive conditions and working to support the freedom of others. It is also a gift from God that bestows human dignity and creativity. Biblical freedom is primarily oriented toward serving the common good rather than individual interests. Similarly, Paul's view of freedom aligns with this concept, and the Gospels emphasize the importance of freedom in the context of service. Jesus and the New Testament do not focus solely on individual freedom or rights as seen in modern democracies.

Utilitarianism

Utilitarianism posits that justice is established by maximizing happiness for the greatest number of people.[12] This perspective holds that justice entails prioritizing overall happiness or utility, even if it means sacrificing the well-being of a minority. According to this view, an action or policy is just if it results in the greatest benefit for the largest number of individuals. Jeremy Bentham, who founded this approach to justice, argued that the purpose of life is to maximize pleasure and minimize pain.

However, a critique of utilitarianism is that it tends to overlook individual rights in favor of collective welfare, potentially justifying the sacrifice of minority well-being. The challenge lies in balancing individual rights and freedoms with the pursuit of the greater good. Utilitarianism is further challenged by libertarianism, which argues that individual freedom is non-negotiable, even if it comes at the expense of the happiness of the majority. To address these criticisms, John Stuart Mill proposed that individual freedom should be respected and that the pursuit of greater happiness should be viewed in the long term. By doing so, utilitarianism can avoid compromising individual rights while still striving toward the greatest happiness for the greatest number.

Since this consequentialist ethical theory aims to maximize overall happiness or pleasure, it contrasts with many biblical teachings that focus on the inherent value of individuals. The concept of "good" in utilitarianism differs from the biblical concept, which arises from God's nature and seeks justice for all people.

For example, Jesus emphasizes the impartiality of God's love and care for all, both the good and the evil (Mt. 5:43-48).

Communitarianism

Communitarianism emphasizes the importance of the common good and the moral obligations of people within society who strive to achieve collective prosperity for all.[13] Communitarianism posits that individuals are nurtured and flourish through their communities. Justice is linked with communal values and collective growth among all members of society. This view of justice critiques liberal individualism, which communitarians believe emphasizes individual rights too heavily.[14] However, the caution is that it may deemphasize universal values while focusing on specific communities.

The communitarian approach asserts that individuals are not separate from their communities or societies. This perspective contrasts with autonomous moral ethics (such as Kant's), libertarianism, and utilitarianism. According to the communitarian perspective, what is considered right or wrong is based on one's history, culture, and experiences, as one's identity is embedded in a personal and collective narrative of the past. This belief opposes moral individualism, which communitarians view as a radical perspective that rejects an individual's responsibility for both the past and others. Additionally, the communitarian approach critiques egalitarian liberals for not sufficiently emphasizing the importance of community and public moral engagement.

Classical philosophers from China, such as Confucius and Laozi, align with the communitarian approach. Confucius's concept of mutuality is well-known; he notes that the most important human virtue is to treat others as oneself, as he states: "Do not impose on others what you do not want for yourself."[15] This teaching is comparable to Jesus's Golden Rule (Mt. 7:12) and Rabbi Hillel's famous saying about the Torah: "What is hateful to you, do not do to others. That is the whole Torah; and the rest is commentary."[16] Laozi's sensibility is aligned with a holistic approach rooted in community. He notes, "If you regard the world as precious as your body, you are entrusted to work for the world. If you love the world as your body, you can take care of the world."[17]

Some biblical teachings support the communitarian approach. For example, the command to love one's neighbor, illustrated in the parable of the Good Samaritan, encourages communal living and shared responsibilities.

Additionally, prophetic traditions emphasize the importance of advocating for marginalized individuals in society to promote the common good for all.

Egalitarianism

Egalitarianism sees justice through the lens of equality. However, the concept of equality is varied. In circumstances beyond one's control, "luck egalitarianism" may be applicable, as justice requires compensating for disadvantages.[18] In other situations, justice ensures equal relationships between citizens ("relational egalitarianism").

We can further break down forms of equality. Formal or legal equality means that everyone should be treated the same under the law, regardless of differences such as race, gender, or wealth. This includes equal voting rights, legal protections, and access to political institutions. Equality of opportunity emphasizes the same starting point or opportunities and ensures that social, economic, and institutional barriers do not prevent individuals from achieving their potential.[19] For example, addressing social inequalities in education or healthcare is crucial. Equality of outcome means that individuals should experience similar outcomes in terms of wealth or resources, regardless of their starting position. This view of justice may require the redistribution of wealth and resources to remedy economic disparities through mechanisms such as progressive taxation or universal basic income.

While theories of equality are varied, the most essential features of equality involve treating every person fairly and without any form of discrimination. This means that everyone should be cared for and supported, irrespective of their gender, sexual orientation, race, ethnicity, or social status. Equality also means that everyone should be granted the same basic freedoms, human rights, and access to the resources necessary for a decent standard of living. In essence, equality promotes the values of fairness, compassion, and solidarity, which are core human qualities that we should all aspire to embrace.

Biblical teachings generally support the idea of egalitarianism. The God of the Hebrew Bible expresses concern for the marginalized and the foreigner. Jesus's understanding of God aligns with this, as he says in Matthew 5:45: "so that you may be children of your Father in heaven; for he makes his sun rise on the evil and on the good and sends rain on the righteous and on the unrighteous." Paul's ethics also reflect this view, as he states in Galatians 3:28: "There is no longer Jew or Greek; there is no longer slave or free; there is no longer male and female, for all of you are one in Christ Jesus."

Virtue Theory

According to Aristotle's virtue theory, the purpose of a person is to achieve a good life (*eudaimonia*), which is possible only by cultivating virtue. He argues that virtues like courage, justice, and temperance must be developed through repeated action. As people gather and live in society, they must contribute to the common good through their virtues. Aristotle's thinking is teleological in that a virtuous person can attain happiness and serve the common good. Resources are distributed according to virtue; however, virtue theory does not elaborate on freedom of choice, equality, or individual rights.

Confucius and Laozi both express a deep concern for ideal human virtues, emphasizing the importance of character development. While their philosophies differ in approach—Confucius focusing on social order and ethical behavior, and Laozi advocating for harmony with nature—they share foundational beliefs about human nature. They view humanity as inherently imperfect yet capable of improvement through the cultivation of key virtues such as love, humility, and wisdom. This shared understanding highlights the potential for personal and communal growth, suggesting that individuals can strive to become better versions of themselves through mindful practice and ethical living. Their teachings encourage a journey of self-cultivation that fosters deeper connections within the community and promotes a more harmonious society.

Biblical teachings and virtue theory share a common focus on the development of character, the role of moral exemplars, and the significance of community in shaping ethical behavior. However, biblical teachings uniquely root virtue in divine grace and the example set by Jesus, who emphasizes traits such as gentleness and mercy as essential characteristics of a righteous life (Mt. 5:3-12). The transformation of character is grounded in Christ (Rom. 12:2; 2 Cor. 3:18; Phil. 2:5-8), and virtues like love, humility, and faith are crucial to living a moral life (Gal. 5:22-23).

Intersections of Race, Gender, Class, and Sexuality

The growing interest in race, gender, class, and sexuality has rejuvenated our pursuit of justice, encompassing racial justice, gender equality, economic justice across social classes, and sexual equality. These interrelated issues highlight the complexity of social dynamics and the need for a holistic approach to justice. Theoretical frameworks such as critical race theory, feminism, Black radical thought, and intersectionality provide essential tools for analyzing how systemic inequalities manifest and affect individuals and communities.

For instance, critical race theory asserts that justice involves dismantling racial inequalities and systemic racism while challenging the notion that laws and institutions are neutral or colorblind.[20] This theory argues that racism is not merely individual prejudice but rather deeply embedded within legal, economic, and social structures. Consequently, achieving justice necessitates advocating for legal reforms and policies aimed at rectifying racial biases and countering racist ideologies. It calls for an examination of how these structures perpetuate inequities and a commitment to dismantling them to foster systems of equity and inclusion.

While critical race theory highlights racial discrimination, feminist theorists analyze the role of gender in political contexts, critique patriarchal structures, and advocate for gender equality.[21] Some feminists emphasize values such as care, empathy, and relationships in discussions of justice, challenging individualistic and rights-based frameworks that often overlook the importance of community and collective well-being.[22] It is crucial to recognize that gender intersects with other social categories, including race, class, and sexuality, leading to unique experiences of marginalization and privilege. This intersectionality enriches our understanding of justice by emphasizing the importance of addressing overlapping oppressions.

This multifaceted understanding of justice aligns with certain biblical teachings, which offer a foundation for advocating equality and human dignity. For example, the story of God's covenant with Abraham illustrates racial justice, as Abraham, initially an ordinary person, was called by God and blessed. This narrative emphasizes that all people, regardless of their background, are valued and included in God's redemptive plan. Moreover, the assertion that all individuals are created in the image of God, both male and female (Gen. 1:26-27), reinforces the inherent worth of every person and the call for equality.

Additionally, in Galatians 3:28, Paul envisions a beloved community in which there is no discrimination based on class, race, ethnicity, or gender. This radical vision challenges societal norms and urges believers to cultivate communities marked by acceptance, inclusivity, and mutual respect. Ultimately, this alignment of contemporary theories of justice with biblical teachings encourages a transformative approach to social issues, inviting us to work together toward a more just and equitable world for all.

Postcolonial Theories

Postcolonial theories of justice highlight the necessity of addressing justice in light of historical colonialism and its lingering effects. These theories argue that achieving true justice entails confronting global inequalities, poverty, and exploitation that have roots in colonial histories. By analyzing the sociopolitical dynamics of formerly colonized nations, postcolonial theorists contend that meaningful justice cannot be realized without acknowledging and addressing the systemic injustices inflicted by imperialism and global capitalism. This critique emphasizes the need for voices from historically marginalized communities to be included in discussions about justice and equity.

Postcolonial theory intersects with biblical teachings in its criticism of empire, advocacy for the oppressed, and affirmation of alternative identities. While postcolonial theory primarily focuses on critiquing structures of colonial domination and their lasting impacts on societies and cultures, biblical teachings also provide poignant insights into these matters. For example, contexts such as the Exodus (Exod. 3:7-10) illustrate God's concern for the oppressed, and prophetic literature (Amos 5:24; Isa. 10:1-2) reinforces the call for justice and righteousness. Additionally, the ministry of Jesus emphasizes themes of justice, oppression, and the inherent dignity of marginalized people (Lk. 4:18-19), reflecting a commitment to social equity.

Jesus notably challenges not only Roman rule but also the religious leaders who align themselves with oppressive systems, as seen in passages like Mt. 23:23-28 and John 18:36. His teachings advocate for a radical reorientation of societal values, underscoring the importance of compassion, justice, and inclusion. Furthermore, the Book of Revelation portrays the empire, symbolized as Babylon, as corrupt and destined for judgment (Revelation 18), serving as a cautionary reminder of the moral implications of imperial power and the promise of divine justice.

In conclusion, both postcolonial theories and biblical teachings urge a critical examination of power structures and advocate for the rights and dignity of those who have been historically oppressed. They invite us to seek justice that is not only restorative but also transformative, aiming for a reimagined society that values equity and inclusion for all.

Environmentalism

The environmental theory of justice underscores the fair distribution of environmental benefits and burdens, ensuring that all people live in a healthy environment. This theory posits that individual duties must encompass environmental responsibilities toward future generations and non-human life. Marginalized communities often bear the brunt of environmental hazards, facing disproportionate exposure to pollutants, inadequate access to clean water, and the consequences of climate change. Therefore, it is essential to advocate for environmental justice as a means of addressing these disparities and ensuring equitable access to resources.

Significant connections exist between environmental theory and biblical teachings, particularly in themes of stewardship, interconnectedness, and renewed responsibility for creation. The concept of stewardship is emphasized in passages such as Gen. 2:15, where humanity is tasked with caring for the Garden of Eden, and Psalm 24:1, which affirms that the earth and everything in it belongs to God. This sense of stewardship implies a moral obligation to protect and preserve the environment for future generations.

Interconnectedness is another crucial theme found in biblical texts. Job 12:7-10 illustrates the interconnectedness of all living beings, suggesting that humans should learn from nature and acknowledge their place within it. Psalm 104 celebrates the diversity of creation, highlighting the intricate relationships among different forms of life. Additionally, Lev. 25:1-7 provides a framework for sustainable land use and the importance of allowing the land to rest, thereby promoting ecological balance.

The call to renewed responsibility for creation is vividly articulated in passages like Isa. 11:6-9 and Rom. 8:19-22, which envision a restored creation where harmony prevails among all living beings. In Revelation 21:1, the promise of a new heaven and new earth underscores the hope for a transformed reality where justice and peace flourish, including in the environmental realm.

The biblical prophets also play a vital role in advocating for environmental justice. They condemn the exploitation of land and people, as seen in Isa. 5:8 and Amos 5:11-24, where the consequences of greed and social injustice are starkly outlined. Furthermore, these texts warn against the overuse and mismanagement of resources, as articulated in Prov. 30:8-9, which emphasizes the importance of moderation and respect for the earth's gifts. This lesson is particularly highlighted in the Parable of the Rich Fool (Lk. 12:13-31), where Jesus critiques the futility of accumulating wealth without regard for one's responsibilities to others and the environment. The parable serves as a poignant reminder that true richness lies not in material wealth but in generosity, stewardship, and ethical living.

In summary, the environmental theory of justice not only addresses contemporary ecological issues but also resonates deeply with biblical principles that advocate for a harmonious relationship between humanity and creation. By integrating these teachings, we can cultivate a more just and sustainable world for all.

Marxist Theory

Marxist theory argues that justice requires the abolition of class structures and the collective ownership of the means of production. Under socialism or communism, resources would be distributed according to need, not profit.[23] However, Marxist justice has been criticized for not providing clear mechanisms to ensure individual freedoms and prevent authoritarianism in socialist or communist regimes.

Marxism and biblical teachings share concerns about economic justice and the dignity of the oppressed, but they differ in their views on human nature, religion, and how justice is achieved. Many Christian theologians have drawn from Marxist critiques of capitalism while rejecting its atheistic and revolutionary elements, leading to movements like liberation theology, which seeks justice within a biblical framework. Examples of such teachings include advocacy for the poor and warnings against the dangers of wealth accumulation (Isa. 1:17; Amos 5:11-24; Lk. 6:20; Acts 2:44-45; Jam 5:1-6; Prov. 14:31). The Exodus story stands out as a powerful narrative against systems of oppression.

There are significant differences between Marxism and biblical traditions. Marxism promotes collective ownership of property and economic structures, while biblical traditions emphasize voluntary actions and moral transformation rather than state-enforced measures (cf. Acts 4:32-35). Another key difference lies in their views on human nature and religion. Marxism regards religion as an ideological tool used to pacify the oppressed, asserting that human nature is shaped by material conditions. In contrast, biblical traditions acknowledge that human nature is fallen but can be redeemed through divine grace. Justice, according to the Bible, is ultimately rooted in God's will rather than merely in economic frameworks (Mic 6:8).

. Faith and spiritual transformation, rather than class struggle, are central to social change in biblical teachings. These teachings promote justice through ethical living, nonviolent resistance, and divine guidance. For instance, Jesus calls for love of enemies (Mt. 5:44), and Paul encourages believers to seek justice without resorting to violence (Rom. 12:17-21). While Marxism is materialistic and atheistic, biblical teachings are centered on God. While Marxism views class struggle as essential for achieving justice, biblical teachings emphasize reconciliation and peace. Marxism relies on economic restructuring, whereas biblical teachings establish justice based on divine moral law.

Justice and Parables

As noted earlier, the central theme of the parables is the reign of God, where justice must be realized in various life situations. As people and society need various aspects of justice, there must be diverse types of justice that can be embedded in the stories of Jesus. This book will explore ten types of justice, using various parables as examples.

- Distributive Justice: Vineyard Laborers; Rich Man and Lazarus
- Attributive Justice: Talents; Treasure; Pearl
- Procedural Justice: Seed Growing Secretly; Wheat and Weeds
- Social Justice: Pharisee and the Tax Collector; the Leaven
- Restorative Justice: Father and Two Sons; Unmerciful Slave
- Compensatory Justice: Unjust Steward
- Retributive Justice: Unjust Judge and the Widow; Tenants
- Global Justice: Rich Fool; Lost Sheep
- Racial Justice: Good Samaritan; Mustard Seed
- Environmental Justice: Sower

While a particular parable may illustrate a specific type of justice, it simultaneously reveals other forms of justice as well. In other words, we should not assume that each parable is tied to only one type of justice. Even the same parable can be viewed through multiple lenses of justice. For example, the Parable of the Vineyard Laborers showcases various aspects of justice depending on the perspective taken, including distributive justice, attributive justice, global justice, racial justice, and environmental justice. From the vineyard owner's perspective, his focus is on distributive justice. In contrast, the early hires argue from the standpoint of attributive justice. When viewed through a global justice lens, the parable highlights the need for more job opportunities in underprivileged countries, especially since the last hires are treated fairly. From a racial justice perspective, it underscores the necessity for marginalized individuals to receive better treatment in the job market.

For heuristic purposes, this book categorizes parables into specific types of justice. While some parables may concentrate on a particular type, this does not mean that other types are entirely excluded. This method aims to help readers understand that the categorization of parables into different types of justice is heuristic, enabling diverse interpretations. Throughout the book, readers will discover the overlapping aspects of justice present in various parables. However, certain parables emphasize particular aspects of justice more than others.

Distributive Justice and Parables

Distributive justice is concerned with the fair allocation of resources, wealth, and opportunities within society. It seeks to address fundamental questions such as: How should goods and resources be distributed? What constitutes a fair or just distribution of wealth, income, or opportunities? These questions are critical in evaluating social equity and ensuring that all individuals have access to the means necessary for a dignified life.

Among various parables that illustrate the concept of distributive justice, we may examine the Parable of the Vineyard Laborers (Mt. 20:1-16) and the Parable of the Rich Man and Lazarus (Lk. 16:19-31). In the Parable of the Vineyard Laborers, the landowner pays all workers the same wage, regardless of the hours they worked. This prompts an examination of whether such equal pay is just. Is it fair for those who worked fewer hours to receive the same compensation as those who labored for a longer time? If this equal treatment is indeed considered just, we must inquire into the underlying principles of that justice. Does it stem from the landowner's desire to demonstrate generosity, or does it reflect a deeper moral obligation to treat all workers equally, irrespective of the time they spent working? This parable invites us to reflect on the values that guide our understanding of equitable compensation and the meaning of fairness in employment practices.

Similarly, in the Parable of the Rich Man and Lazarus, we confront pressing issues of responsibility and accountability regarding poverty and wealth. The narrative draws a stark contrast between the opulent life of the rich man and the dire conditions faced by Lazarus, the beggar at his gate. The question arises: who is ultimately responsible for Lazarus's poverty? Is it the rich man who ignores Lazarus's plight, or does systemic inequality play a role in perpetuating such disparate living conditions? This parable encourages us to reflect on the implications of wealth accumulation and the moral obligations that accompany the possession of resources. How should society respond to such disparities? The story highlights the need for compassion and action to address poverty, suggesting that those who are affluent have a responsibility to assist those in need.

Through these parables, distributive justice emerges as a pivotal theme, prompting us to consider not only how resources are distributed but also the ethical dimensions of our choices regarding wealth and poverty. They challenge readers to engage with the complexities surrounding economic justice and to reflect on their own responsibilities in contributing to a more equitable society.

Attributive Justice and Parables

Attributive justice refers to a concept in which individuals or groups are given their due based on their attributes, qualities, or status. This form of justice assigns goods, rights, or responsibilities according to criteria like merit, need, or capability. For instance, in a workplace setting, employees may receive rewards based on their performance or skills, whereas in a social context, aid might be distributed according to individual needs. The principle underlying attributive justice is often contrasted with distributive justice, which focuses more on the fair distribution of resources regardless of specific individual characteristics.

The Parable of the Vineyard Laborers prompts a debate regarding whether it promotes distributive justice or attributive justice. Some critics argue that the vineyard landowner exploits the early employees by providing equal pay to all, regardless of the hours worked. This perspective suggests that attributive justice is compromised, as those who worked longer feel unjustly treated. Conversely, others contend that the parable illustrates a form of distributive economic justice, aiming to highlight themes of generosity and equality in compensation.

Similarly, in the Parable of the Talents (Mt. 25:14-30), discussions arise around the nature of the master's character and whether he is good or exploitative. Does he reward the diligent slaves justly, or does he take advantage of their hard work for his own profit? These questions challenge our understanding of what constitutes fairness and merit in the allocation of resources and can lead to varying interpretations of the master's intent and the moral of the story.

Moreover, we can also examine the parables of the Treasure and the Pearls (Mt. 13:44-46), which emphasize the values of hard work, discernment, and ethical decision-making. These parables illustrate that the pursuit of one's goals requires effort and moral integrity, suggesting that the outcomes of attributive justice must also align with ethical principles. Collectively, these parables encourage critical reflection on how we define justice and the implications of our interpretations in real-life applications.

Procedural Justice and Parables

Procedural justice focuses on the fairness of the processes used to make decisions. It raises important questions about whether the rules are applied consistently and impartially. Even in situations where outcomes may be unequal, procedural justice emphasizes that the methods and procedures used in decision-making must be fair and transparent. This principle is crucial in fostering trust and legitimacy within any system of governance or organization. Democratic systems serve as prime examples of procedural justice from a theoretical perspective, as they aim to provide a framework in which all voices can be heard and decisions are made based on established rules and processes.

Among the various parables that illustrate themes of procedural justice, we may discuss the Parable of the Seed Growing Secretly (Mk 4:26-29) and the Parable of the Wheat and Weeds (Mt. 13:24-30). The Parable of the Seed Growing Secretly highlights the idea that the growth of the reign of God occurs through a natural, often unseen process, suggesting that just outcomes can emerge over time, even when the procedures may not be immediately visible or understood. Meanwhile, the Parable of the Wheat and Weeds emphasizes the importance of patience and discernment amid conflicting elements, showcasing the need for careful consideration in the decision-making process regarding good and evil.

Together, these parables underscore the significance of procedural justice in the realm of moral and ethical decision-making. They invite readers to reflect on the importance of fair processes in achieving just outcomes, reminding us that the integrity of the path we take toward justice is as vital as the destination itself. By examining these narratives, we can gain a deeper understanding of how procedural justice operates within various contexts and its implications for our interactions in society.

Social Justice and Parables

Social justice aims to create a fair society by addressing systemic inequality and discrimination based on race, gender, class, and various other factors. It seeks to challenge and reform societal structures that perpetuate these inequities, fostering an environment in which all individuals can thrive regardless of their background. Key questions arise in this discussion: How can societal structures be reformed to ensure justice for all groups? What measures can be taken to dismantle institutional barriers that hinder access to resources and opportunities?

To explore these themes, we will discuss the following parables: the Leaven (Mt. 13:33) and the Pharisee and the Tax Collector (Lk. 18:9-14). The Parable of the Leaven illustrates the transformative power of small, seemingly insignificant actions or elements when they are introduced into a larger system. Just as a small amount of leaven can permeate an entire batch of dough, individuals, especially those who are considered small, working toward social justice can effect meaningful change within their communities, demonstrating that every action counts in the larger quest for equity.

On the other hand, the Parable of the Pharisee and the Tax Collector addresses prejudices and narrow-mindedness, spotlighting the dangers of self-righteousness and exclusionary attitudes. In this parable, the contrasting prayers of the Pharisee and the tax collector reveal the complexity of judgment and societal hierarchy. The tax collector's humble acknowledgment of his shortcomings serves as a powerful reminder of the importance of empathy and compassion in the pursuit of social justice. It challenges us to recognize our own biases and to approach the quest for justice with humility, understanding that true transformation requires acknowledging one's flaws.

Together, these parables underline the essence of social justice, revealing both the potential for individual actions to create systemic change and the necessity of confronting personal biases in the pursuit of equity. They encourage us to reflect on our roles within society and inspire collective efforts to build a more just world for all.

Racial Justice and Parables

Racial justice is a critical component of the broader framework of social justice, aiming to ensure equitable treatment and opportunities for individuals of all races. According to critical race theory, race permeates all facets of society, including politics, education, and economic structures. This theory posits that addressing racial justice requires a comprehensive effort to dismantle policies, practices, and social norms that perpetuate racial discrimination and inequality.

The overarching goal is to rectify the historical and ongoing impacts of racism and create a society where race does not dictate one's access to resources, opportunities, or quality of life.

Achieving racial justice involves implementing anti-racist policies and fostering inclusive education that authentically represents diverse histories and experiences. It also entails reforming the criminal justice system to eliminate racial biases, ensuring that legal and punitive measures are applied fairly and equitably. Additionally, racial justice requires guaranteeing equal access to essential services and opportunities, such as employment, housing, and healthcare, to prevent racial disparities from perpetuating systemic disadvantages.

The parable of the Good Samaritan offers profound insights into racial justice by challenging societal notions of "neighbor" and extending the concept to encompass care and compassion without regard to ethnic or cultural boundaries. In this parable, it is the Samaritan—a member of a marginalized group—who demonstrates true neighborliness, urging listeners to transcend prejudice and embrace a universal ethic of empathy and solidarity.

Similarly, the parable of the Mustard Seed underscores the significance of diversity and agency among people. This narrative highlights the power of small beginnings or the potential of marginalized individuals, as the mustard seed grows into a large tree, providing shelter and sustenance to all. From a racial justice perspective, it emphasizes the value of diverse contributions and the transformative potential of the marginalized to foster a more inclusive and equitable society.

By examining these parables, we are encouraged to reflect on the moral imperatives of racial justice and to actively contribute to a world where racial equality is realized not merely as an ideal but as a tangible reality. They inspire a commitment to challenging and changing the social fabric to ensure that all individuals, regardless of race, can enjoy the freedoms and opportunities inherent in a just society.

Restorative Justice and Parables

Restorative justice focuses on repairing the harm caused by wrongdoing and restoring relationships between the victim, offender, and community.[24] It emphasizes accountability, empathy, and the opportunity for offenders to make amends for their actions, as well as facilitating the restoration for victims. Critics argue that restorative justice may be too lenient on offenders and question whether it is effective for all types of crimes, particularly violent offenses. This raises important questions about the balance between justice for victims and the rehabilitation of offenders.

In the Parable of the Father and Two Sons (Lk. 15:11-32), the central issue revolves around how to restore a fractured family. The narrative illustrates a journey of forgiveness and reconciliation as the younger son returns home after squandering his inheritance. The father's open arms symbolize unconditional love and acceptance, yet the story remains open-ended, inviting readers to explore various pathways toward reconciliation between the father and both sons. This ambiguity encourages a deeper reflection on the complex dynamics of family relationships and the necessary steps toward healing after betrayal.

We can also consider the Parable of the Unmerciful Slave (Mt. 18:21-35), which addresses the restoration of a slave who is unable to pay even a small debt to his fellow slave. This parable highlights the importance of mercy and forgiveness in the context of restorative justice. The master's initial compassion in forgiving the overwhelming debt emphasizes the notion of grace, while the unmerciful slave's refusal to extend that same grace to his fellow slave illustrates the dangers of a lack of empathy and understanding.

Together, these parables underscore the core tenets of restorative justice, emphasizing the potential for healing and transformation within relationships. They challenge us to consider how we can foster reconciliation not only within families but also in broader community contexts. By reflecting on the principles of accountability, empathy, and forgiveness illustrated in these stories, we can gain deeper insights into the processes necessary for genuinely restoring harmony and balance in our relationships. Ultimately, restorative justice invites us to engage in practices that promote healing and community solidarity, serving to strengthen the bonds among individuals and foster a more compassionate society.

Compensatory Justice and Parables

Compensatory justice focuses on compensating individuals who have been wronged or harmed, often through financial restitution or other forms of reparation. This approach to justice seeks to address the direct consequences of wrongdoing by ensuring that victims receive appropriate compensation for their losses, thereby aiming to restore them to their rightful position. Compensatory justice can take many forms, including monetary payments, service restitution, or the provision of resources that can alleviate the impact of the harm endured.

This view of justice extends beyond individual cases and encompasses a broader acknowledgment of historical injustices such as slavery, colonization, and systemic discrimination. In these contexts, compensation or reparations can serve to recognize and address the deep-rooted inequalities and traumas inflicted on marginalized communities over generations. It highlights the moral responsibility to rectify past wrongs and supports the idea that justice cannot be fully realized without acknowledging and addressing historical grievances.

The Parable of the Unjust Steward (Lk. 16:1-13) exemplifies the complexities associated with compensatory justice. In this narrative, the steward, who has been accused of squandering his master's resources, is faced with impending dismissal. In a bid to secure his future, he cleverly reduces the debts of his master's customers. While his actions are initially unjust, they serve as a means of remedying some of the wrongs done to the clients. This raises important questions about the nature of justice and the ethics of compensation—can questionable means lead to favorable ends, and does the act of compensating those wronged justify the steward's earlier misconduct?

The parable compels readers to reflect on the relationship between justice, accountability, and the necessity of making amends, even when the process may be morally ambiguous. It prompts discussions about the implications of compensatory actions, particularly how individuals and institutions can take responsibility for past harms while navigating the complexities of ethical behavior and reparation.

In summary, compensatory justice not only seeks to resolve present grievances but also calls for a thoughtful consideration of historical injustices. By examining narratives like that of the Unjust Steward, we gain insights into the delicate balance between restitution and morality, ultimately encouraging a more nuanced understanding of how justice can be achieved in both personal and societal contexts.

Retributive Justice and Parables

Retributive justice refers to the fair punishment of wrongdoers and how society responds to crimes and moral wrongs. This form of justice is grounded in the principle that individuals who commit offenses deserve to be punished in a manner that is commensurate with their actions. Theories of retribution vary widely; some advocate for punishment that is proportionate to the crime committed, asserting that fairness requires that the severity of the penalty reflects the severity of the wrongdoing. Others argue for a more rehabilitative approach, seeking to reform offenders rather than simply inflicting punitive measures, emphasizing the potential for personal growth and reintegration into society.

Additionally, some proponents of retributive justice emphasize the importance of deterrence, arguing that punishment serves to discourage future wrongdoing by instilling a sense of consequence. This perspective suggests that publicizing the repercussions of criminal behavior can serve to protect society by dissuading individuals from engaging in harmful actions.

We can see the idea of retributive justice illustrated in the parables of the Tenants (Mk 12:1-12) and the Unjust Judge and Widow (Lk. 18:1-8). In the Parable of the Tenants, the landowner sends slaves to collect his share of the harvest from the tenants, who respond by mistreating and ultimately killing them. The landowner's decision to take retribution against the tenants for their actions highlights the principle of accountability and the consequences of their wrongdoing, leading to the tenants facing severe punishment for their transgressions.

Similarly, the Parable of the Unjust Judge and Widow brings forth themes of persistence and the pursuit of justice. In this story, the widow continually appeals to the judge for justice against her adversary. Although the judge initially refuses to respond to her pleas, her relentless pursuit eventually compels him to grant her justice. This parable emphasizes the concept that justice should be served, highlighting both the moral obligation of those in power to respond justly and the accountability of societal structures to provide fair resolutions for grievances.

Together, these parables not only illustrate the principles underlying retributive justice but also raise questions about the nature of justice itself. They encourage readers to consider the balance between punishment and mercy, as well as the importance of ensuring that justice is served in a manner that is both fair and compassionate. Ultimately, retributive justice serves as a foundational concept within the broader discourse on ethics, morality, and the functioning of society.

Global Justice and Parables

Global justice deals with issues that stretch beyond national borders, aiming to establish justice on a global scale by addressing challenges such as poverty, war, human rights violations, and economic inequality. It encompasses a wide range of concerns, including international human rights, fair trade practices, global poverty alleviation, and the urgent need to combat climate change. The overarching goal of global justice is to create frameworks and policies that ensure fairness and equity for all people, regardless of their geographic location, promoting a more interconnected and just world.

Among various parables that resonate with themes of global justice, we may discuss the Parable of the Rich Fool (Lk. 12:13-31) and the Parable of the Lost Sheep (Mt. 18:12-14; Lk. 15:3-7). In the Parable of the Rich Fool, the wealthy man hoards his surplus, focusing solely on his own comfort and security without considering the needs of others. This lack of consideration underscores a critical issue in global justice: the responsibility of those with excess resources to contribute to the well-being of others, particularly the impoverished and disadvantaged. From a global perspective, this parable challenges us to reflect on how wealth and resources can be distributed more equitably across nations and communities.

Similarly, the Parable of the Lost Sheep invites reflection on the global challenge of seeking out and supporting those who are marginalized or vulnerable. The shepherd's dedication to finding the one lost sheep emphasizes the importance of attention and care for those who may be overlooked or left behind. From a global justice viewpoint, this parable highlights the moral imperative to extend our concern to "lost sheep" among poorer countries—nations and communities struggling with poverty, conflict, or neglect. It calls for international solidarity and concerted efforts to ensure that no one is abandoned or forgotten in the quest for justice.

Together, these parables prompt us to examine our roles and responsibilities within the global community. They encourage us to consider how our actions and decisions impact those beyond our immediate borders, reinforcing the idea that achieving true justice requires a collective commitment to address global disparities and promote equality for all.

Environmental Justice and Parables

Environmental justice seeks to ensure that environmental benefits, such as access to clean air, water, and green spaces, are distributed fairly across all communities, while environmental burdens, such as pollution and toxic waste, are not disproportionately placed on marginalized groups. This approach emphasizes that all people, regardless of race, ethnicity, or socioeconomic status, have the right to a healthy environment and that the inequitable distribution of environmental risks and resources is a critical area of concern.

Beyond human welfare, environmental justice advocates for a broader, more inclusive understanding that recognizes our interconnectedness with nature. This perspective encourages us to act as stewards of the environment, acknowledging our responsibility to care for not just human habitats, but also the natural world—including air, land, water, and ecosystems—and to preserve these for future generations.

The parable of the Sower offers profound insights into the importance of resource stewardship. This narrative can be viewed through the lens of environmental justice by highlighting the importance of nurturing and protecting our natural resources to ensure fruitful outcomes. By carefully tending the environment and considering the long-term impact of our actions, we align with the principles of environmental justice and sustainable stewardship. The parable encourages us to reflect on how we can cultivate practices that promote ecological balance and respect for the earth, ensuring that all communities can benefit from its bounty while safeguarding its health for generations to come.

Notes

1 See Jonathan Wolff, *An Introduction to Political Philosophy*, 4th edition (Oxford: Oxford University Press, 2023); Michael J. Sandel, *Justice: What's the Right Thing to Do?* (New York: Farrar, Straus and Giroux, 2009).
2 Regarding theories of justice, see "Justice," in *Stanford Encyclopedia of Philosophy*, accessed Oct 6, 2024. https://plato.stanford.edu/entries/justice/.
3 For John Locke's life and thoughts, see "John Locke," accessed Oct 6, 2024. https://plato.stanford.edu/entries/locke/.
4 See "Adam Smith's Moral and Political Philosophy," accessed Oct 6, 2024. https://plato.stanford.edu/entries/smith-moral-political/.
5 John Rawls, *A Theory of Justice* (Cambridge, MA: Belknap Press, 1971), 103–39.
6 See Robert Nozick, *Anarchy, State, and Utopia* (New York: Basic Books, 1974).
7 John Rawls, *A Theory of Justice*, 266.
8 John Rawls, *A Theory of Justice*, 140–66.
9 John Rawls, *A Theory of Justice*, 118.
10 John Rawls, *A Theory of Justice*, 65.
11 See "Contemporary Approaches to the Social Contract," accessed Oct 6, 2024. https://plato.stanford.edu/entries/contractarianism-contemporary/.

12 See "The History of Utilitarianism," accessed Oct 6, 2024. https://plato.stanford.edu/entries/utilitarianism-history/. See also "Jeremy Bentham," accessed Oct 6, 2024. https://plato.stanford.edu/entries/bentham. See also "John Stuart Mill," accessed Oct 6, 2024. https://plato.stanford.edu/entries/mill/.
13 See Alasdair MacIntyre, *After Virtue* (Notre Dame, IN: University of Notre Dame Press, 1981); Michael Walzer, *Spheres of Justice* (New York: Basic Books, 1983).
14 Michael J. Sandel, *Liberalism and the Limits of Justice* (Cambridge: Cambridge University Press, 1982), 3–30. See also Charles Taylor, "The Nature and Scope of Distributive Justice," in Charles Taylor, *Philosophy and the Human Sciences, Philosophical Papers*, vol. 2 (Cambridge: Cambridge University Press, 1985).
15 Analects of Confucius 15:24.
16 Shabbat 31a.
17 Dao De Jing 13.
18 "Justice," accessed Oct 6, 2024. https://plato.stanford.edu/entries/justice/.
19 John Rawls, *A Theory of Justice*.
20 See "Critical Philosophy of Race," accessed Oct 6, 2024. https://plato.stanford.edu/entries/critical-phil-race/.
21 Carol Pateman, *The Sexual Contract* (Stanford, CA: Stanford University Press, 1988); Iris Marion Young, *Justice and the Politics of Difference* (Princeton, NJ: Princeton University Press, 2022); bell hooks, *Feminism Is for Everybody: Passionate Politics* (New York: Routledge, 2014).
22 Carol Gilligan, *In a Different Voice: Psychological Theory and Women's Development* (Cambridge, MA: Harvard University Press, 2016). See also Susan M. Okin, *Justice, Gender, And the Family* (New York: Basic Books, 1991).
23 See "Karl Marx," accessed Oct 6, 2024. https://plato.stanford.edu/entries/marx/.
24 Howard Zehr, *Little Book of Restorative Justice: Revised and Updated* (New York: Good Books, 2015). See also John Braithwaite, *Restorative Justice & Responsive Regulation* (Oxford: Oxford University Press, 2002).

3

Distributive Justice and Parables

This chapter investigates the parables of the Vineyard Laborers (Mt. 20:1-16) and the Rich Man and Lazarus (Lk. 16:19-31), engages with the concept of distributive justice in these parables, and draws contemporary implications from them. On one hand, there will be a section interpreting these parables within the context of first-century Palestine. On the other hand, these parables will be examined through the lens of distributive justice. Each of the parables addresses specific aspects of distributive justice, which primarily concerns the fair distribution of resources, wealth, or income.

We may ask questions such as, "Is the vineyard owner's equal pay to all workers just? Who is responsible for Lazarus's poverty, and how should it be resolved?" All these questions involve theories of justice that deal with a fair or just distribution of income and resources. From the outset, distributive justice can be understood as follows: all people need fair treatment, with an emphasis on human dignity and equality. They must be cared for not only because they are equal as human beings but also because they all require sufficient income and resources, regardless of their social status, gender, ethnicity, or other social determinants.

For instance, in the Parable of the Vineyard Laborers, we see this type of justice at play, as the vineyard master ensures that all workers receive a basic income. This view of distributive justice is based on divine justice, as exemplified by Jesus, and aligns with egalitarianism or communitarianism, among other perspectives. As we will see later, this understanding of distributive justice differs from utilitarianism and extreme forms of libertarianism.

The Parable of the Vineyard Laborers

Mt. 20:1-16[1]

1 "For *the rule/reign of heaven* is like a landowner who went out early in the morning to hire laborers for his vineyard. 2 After agreeing with the laborers for

a denarius for the day, he sent them into his vineyard. 3 When he went out about nine o'clock, he saw others *without work* in the marketplace, 4 and he said to them, 'You also go into the vineyard, and I will pay you whatever is right.' So they went. 5 When he went out again about noon and about three o'clock, he did the same. 6 And about five o'clock he went out and found others standing around, and he said to them, 'Why are you standing here all day *without work*?' 7 They said to him, 'Because no one has hired us.' He said to them, 'You also go into the vineyard.' 8 When evening came, the owner of the vineyard said to his manager, 'Call the laborers and give them their pay, beginning with the last and then going to the first.' 9 When those hired about five o'clock came, each of them received a denarius. 10 Now when the first came, they thought they would receive more; but each of them also received a denarius. 11 And when they received it, they grumbled against the landowner, 12 saying, 'These last worked only one hour, and you have made them equal to us who have borne the burden of the day and the scorching heat.' 13 But he replied to one of them, 'Friend, I am doing you no wrong; did you not agree with me for a denarius? 14 Take what belongs to you and go; I choose to give to this last the same as I give to you. 15 Am I not allowed to do what I choose with what belongs to me? Or *is your eye evil* because *I am good*?' 16 So the last will be first, and the first will be last."²

Interpreting the Parable

This parable reflects the agrarian society in Galilee, where the owner of a vineyard hires day laborers to work in his vineyard and pays them for their efforts. Given the vivid scenes in the parable depicting the landowner's hiring practices (vv. 1–7) and the manager's payment of the laborer's wages (vv. 8–15), it is likely that this parable originated with Jesus.³ To interpret the parable, we must first consider the term *basileia ton ouranon* ("kingdom/reign of heaven") in verse 1, which appears thirty-one times in Matthew's Gospel. In contrast, *basileia tou theou* ("kingdom/reign of God") appears only five times. However, this difference does not necessarily mean that the former carries a unique or distinctive meaning, as if it points exclusively to a heavenly or otherworldly realm. Matthew's Gospel is often seen as a Jewish version of the Gospel; in it, God is considered too holy to be explicitly named. Thus, "God" is replaced by "heaven," which represents God's realm, as reflected in the Lord's Prayer: "Our Father in heaven" (6:9). Therefore, "the kingdom of heaven" is interchangeable with "the kingdom of God." It should not be associated solely with an otherworldly kingdom but rather with the godly or heavenly realm on earth.

Indeed, Matthew embraces and articulates the vision of the godly realm on earth, which effectively represents Jesus's tradition. In Mt. 5:43-48 (part of the Sermon on the Mount), Jesus emphasizes the impartial love for all—both good and evil—and instructs his disciples to love even their enemies. In verse 48, he states, "Be perfect, therefore, as your heavenly Father is perfect." Here, being perfect does not imply a status of sinless living but rather the radical activism of love for all people, regardless of who they are.

In 6:25-34, Jesus advises his disciples not to worry about worldly concerns, such as what to eat or wear, and cautions against stockpiling goods for the future. Instead, he teaches them to be content with their daily provisions while striving to manifest "the righteousness of God" (6:33). He urges them to prioritize: "But seek first the kingdom/reign of God and his righteousness, and all these things will be given to you as well" (6:33). Jesus's message ultimately points to God and his activity. His fundamental thesis is that God is steadfast and righteous, impartial to all, and that God's reign embodies justice. The present, imperative, active verb "seek" emphasizes a human endeavor to actualize this reign of God. Discipleship, therefore, entails actively seeking God's reign and righteousness. Similarly, in the Hebrew Bible, *tzedakah*, which means righteousness or justice, is one of the most frequently used terms to describe God. Micah 6:8 reads: "O mortal, what is good, and what does the Lord require of you but to do justice, to love kindness, and to walk humbly with your God?"

In Matthew's Gospel, Jesus thoroughly follows the tradition of Judaism rooted in the concept of God's reign and his righteousness. What distinguishes Jesus from other Jewish teachers is his radical interpretation of the law and its flexible application in context, as seen in the Sabbath debate (12:9-14). This does not imply that he was anti-Judaism; he was a devout Jew, practicing Jewish laws and loving the God of the Jews. However, his interpretation of God and the Scriptures often differed from those of other Jews in several areas, particularly as he taught in the Sermon on the Mount (chapters 5–7). One contentious issue was the Sabbath law. Jesus healed the sick on the Sabbath because he believed that doing good on such a holy day, which God blesses for everyone, is a matter of justice from his perspective. Likewise, he provides a new law: to treat others well, as he states, "In everything, do to others as you would have them do to you, for this is the Law and the Prophets" (7:12).

The other difference with Jesus lies in his understanding of the kingdom of God. While Jesus believes in the resurrection, a view shared by most Jews regarding the future messianic kingdom, his teaching differs from that of other Jews who emphasize the future completion of the kingdom. He proclaims the reign of God as a present reality while also awaiting the end. This emphasis is evident throughout Matthew's Gospel; until the end, the community or church of Matthew must patiently embrace God's love for all, including enemies. This principle is illustrated in the Parable of the Wheat and the Weeds, where Jesus warns against preemptive strikes against enemies. Only at the time of the last judgment (25:31-46) will the separation between good and evil take place, as conveyed by Jesus. Until then, the community's role is not to judge but to forgive and care for the marginalized, as seen in the Parable of the Unmerciful Slave. In summary, the reign of heaven or God signifies the realization of God's love and justice in the world.

In the Parable of the Vineyard Laborers, the heavenly realm or rule is likened to a vineyard owner. Carefully examining the relationship between these two is crucial, as it can profoundly impact our comprehension of the parable. Depending on our interpretation of this connection, our analysis of the parable may vary, resulting in either a positive or negative perception of their relationship. William Herzog construes it as a negative one, viewing the owner of the vineyard as an example of an exploitative master of day laborers.[4] He argues that the parable codifies "the agrarian world of rural Galilee and Judaea," revealing the oppressive and abusive practices in society.[5] However, codification can go in either direction—showing the positive aspects of a landowner or the negative aspects of him. While Herzog argues that this landowner represents a typical, exploitative master, it is important to note that, in Jesus's parables, similes and metaphors are often used positively in connection with the reign of God. In the parable of the Sower, God's rule is compared to a sower, whose role offers insights into the nature of God's reign in the world. In the parable of the Mustard Seed, God's reign is likened to a mustard seed, emphasizing the potential within God's rule. Similarly, in the parable of the Pearl, the reign of God is compared to a merchant whose radical decision to purchase a single, precious pearl signifies the importance of making significant choices regarding God's rule. People are encouraged to make similar decisions and take action.

In all these examples, God's reign is connected with the positive aspects of the metaphors used in the parables, even if those aspects are not easily noticeable because readers may not be ready to hear the countercultural, subversive language. For example, it is a revolutionary idea that God's reign is compared to a mustard seed or leaven because, in society, they are often considered trivial or worthless. Yet the truth is that God's reign values small beginnings and embraces lower-class people.

In the parable, "to be like" represents a form of simile and involves a metaphor. "God's reign," referred to as the target domain or tenor, is exemplified through metaphors such as a sower or a mustard seed, which are called source domains or vehicles. These metaphors are understood in radically unconventional ways that transcend the norms of society. Ultimately, it is the reader's task to construe the dissimilar link between the rule of God and the metaphor.

With this understanding of parable and metaphor, we must grapple with the relationship between the heavenly realm and the landowner in the Parable of the Vineyard Laborers. From the outset, we can identify the positive aspects of God's reign as reflected in this landowner. Since the parable is a genre of subversion, we can discern countercultural, provocative, or challenging elements within this story. The landowner is atypical; he differs from the usual masters in society who typically do not go to the market to hire workers.[6] Instead, they would send their managers to find laborers. These managers would oversee the work, controlling the employees from a distance. In contrast, the landowner in the parable personally goes out to the market to hire laborers for his vineyard five times a day, from early morning to late afternoon, even as late as one hour before the vineyard closes. He could have easily sent his manager to hire them, but he chooses to undertake this task himself.

We do not know why the landowner had to go out five times to hire laborers; he could have hired enough workers at once if he knew how many he needed. One possible scenario is that his vineyard was too large to find enough workers in just a few attempts. Each time he found laborers in the market, he sent them to his vineyard, as he implies when he sees others there: "Why are you standing here all day without work?" (20:6). They answered, "Because no one has hired us," which suggests that they could not find work earlier. Likely, they arrived late at the market for unknown reasons, such as illness or familial responsibilities, like caring for their elderly. Alternatively, they might have been waiting to be hired at another location without success. The typical master does not send laborers to their vineyard just for an hour's work, but this owner in the parable does so.[7]

Another atypical behavior is paying one denarius to all the workers, regardless of their hours worked. When he finds laborers in the market, he promises to pay them a denarius, a Roman silver coin—enough for a living wage for a day or sufficient to support a family for several days.[8] He also states he will pay "whatever is just or right" (*dikaios*). The owner is willing to provide a just wage—not an exploitative one—and his primary concern is to send laborers into the workplace as soon as possible. At the end of the workday, the manager is instructed to pay each laborer a denarius. The first-hired laborers expect to receive more upon seeing the last-hired receive a denarius, but they also receive the same wage and complain against the owner, stating they "have borne the burden of the day and the scorching heat" (20:12). At a superficial level, there seems to be an injustice for these workers. However, there is a deeper truth in the parable that may be difficult to recognize from a conventional perspective. We can note several points here.

First, the owner's response is both legal and moral. By hiring the laborers, he made a verbal contract with them for one denarius per day. His point is that he did not do wrong. Morally speaking, he claims he is good (*agathos*), perhaps because he cares for all by providing them with what they need—a basic income for daily life (cf. Exod. 16:16).[9] His statement does not necessarily imply that he can act unethically simply because he is rich or powerful. Rather, his concern is to allow them to work and pay them an acceptable wage.[10] Defending his actions, the owner asserts that their eyes are wicked (*ponéros*) because they lack compassion for the others who arrived late. Indeed, being among the last hired is not their fault; they may not have been hired early enough or might have arrived late due to unavoidable circumstances such as illness or familial duties.[11] Brad Young points out the issue of those who grumble: "From a religious perspective, the laborers should have been happy about the good fortune of their coworkers who, because of the generosity of the landowner, would now have enough provision for their families."[12] Furthermore, we wonder why the first-hired workers forgot to thank the owner for the opportunity to work and be paid. They accomplished their original expectations—to find work and receive compensation—but they lost perspective due to their tendency to compare themselves with others.

Second, there is no guarantee that the first-hired workers labored harder than others. Simply spending long hours in the scorching heat does not necessarily mean they worked diligently. A rabbinic parable from the Jerusalem Talmud in *Berakhot* 2.7 implies that a worker is compensated "not for the quantity of time served, but for the quality of work done."[13] Of course, in the Parable of the Vineyard Laborers, there is no clear indication that the last-hired worked harder either. However, the fact remains that working long hours does not always lead to superior quality work. It is possible that the last-hired workers exerted more effort than the others.

Third, and most importantly, the owner cares for all laborers equally, recognizing their need for a basic income to sustain their daily lives. His actions are fair and just in this regard. While fairness comes from his unbiased hiring of laborers, justice lies in his practice of paying the same daily wage to everyone. He could potentially lose money by compensating the later hires equally, but his primary concern is their well-being. Midrash Psalms emphasizes the importance of equal pay in terms of grace: "Solomon said to the Holy One, blessed be He: Master of the Universe, when a king hires good laborers who perform their work well and pays them their wage, what praise does he merit? When does he merit praise? When he hires lazy laborers and still pays them their full wage." The Parable of the Vineyard Laborers does not imply that the last hired were lazy; they were simply unemployed earlier because no one had hired them. The landowner deserves commendation for allowing these laborers to work and for offering them pay equal to that of others, which sets him apart from typical employers.

In summary, the Parable of the Vineyard Laborers illustrates the heavenly reign through the actions of a landowner who, from society's perspective, is atypical in his care for all laborers. He embodies goodness, not merely generosity, because he is dedicated to ensuring full employment and equal pay (a basic income) for everyone. By disrupting industry standards and paying all workers the same wage, he acknowledges their shared need for a basic livelihood. This exemplifies the challenging nature of the rule and reign of God.

Engaging Distributive Justice

The central concern about distributive justice in this parable is the unequal economic system, where most people lack landownership and are dependent on the wealthy landowners. These landowners, as an elite class, make significant profits by employing day laborers with limited bargaining power, thus maintaining their wealth. Their refusal to offer long-term contracts creates significant insecurity for the day laborers. The lack of job security, while advantageous to the owners who can maintain lower wages, leaves the laborers vulnerable. Many compete for work, accepting subsistence wages merely to survive.

In this parable, even if the landowner pays all laborers equally—a denarius, a fair daily wage—the inherent inequality persists; they remain trapped in a cycle of daily job seeking, with little hope for improvement. While a denarius might be considered generous, it is insufficient to address the diverse needs of the laborers; the sick require more for medical care, and larger families need greater support. This unequal system undermines distributive justice because the landowner's profits are not factored into resource distribution. However, the owner's equal pay, atypical in this context, aims for full employment. While arguably better than other masters, he falls short of representing true justice and should not be idealized.

The other thing is that the fairness of the verbal contracts is questionable, as laborers lack the power to negotiate wages. The owner's offer of a denarius appears fair given market conditions and societal expectations, especially considering the laborers' weak bargaining positions. However, his later promise to pay "whatever is right" to those hired later is ambiguous. While likely intended to mean a just wage (a denarius, given the context of the Greek word *dikaios*), this vagueness undermines the agreement's equity. The lack of explicit payment terms for the final group hired further complicates the issue.

The workers hired last did not anticipate a full day's wage, as they worked for only an hour. The owner's silence about payment, perhaps due to urgency, contrasts with his explicit agreement with early workers (using the Greek verb *symphōnéō*, implying mutual agreement). Despite limited bargaining power, the early workers freely accepted the denarius. Thus, legally, their complaints are unfounded; they received what was explicitly promised. However, morally, their lack of solidarity with later-arriving laborers is problematic.[14]

The owner's equal pay raises questions of justice. Libertarian perspectives argue that payment should be merit-based, yet there is no evidence that early hires worked harder. Egalitarian perspectives might view equal pay as just, providing basic needs, though overlooking varying needs among laborers (e.g., family size, illness). A communitarian perspective would emphasize the equal basic income's role in fostering community unity and solidarity. However, this requires the virtue of sympathy from the early workers toward those less fortunate. Even if not divinely inspired, the landowner's actions echo the principle of God's impartial provision (Mt. 5:45).

As noted above, the vineyard owner does not embody ideal distributive justice, but his commitment to full employment and equal pay distinguishes him. He ensures basic needs are met, with no one denied work or paid less than a minimum wage. His claim of goodness (*agathos*) stems from this equal treatment, including those hired late. This prioritization of the last, as highlighted in the Dao De Jing—"What is most straight seems devious; to yield means to be whole; to be bent means to be straight" (大直若屈, 枉則直, 枉則直, wǎng zé zhí, dà zhí ruò qū, wǎng zé zhí)—underscores justice's complexities in labor dynamics and power structures.[15]

This parable, while not presenting a perfect model of distributive justice, offers valuable insights into fairness, equality, and moral responsibility. It prompts critical reflection on societal structures impacting laborers' livelihoods, urging us to strive for a more just and equitable system for all.

Contemporary Implications

The Parable of the Vineyard Laborers serves as a reminder of the importance of implementing a basic income in our modern society, regardless of whether it is a poor or rich country. Income disparities and poor living conditions are global challenges. This basic income should cover the essential needs of a family, taking into account its size and related cost factors. Without such a measure, while individual incentives and great achievements may be recognized, it remains challenging to reach a consensus on the necessity of a basic income, the amount required, or the criteria for determining it.

Libertarians do not support this idea of a basic income because they believe in free and competitive markets. They also advocate for individual freedom and choice in economic activities, asserting that people can achieve their goals through hard work. However, the reality is that not all individuals start from the same starting point. Some have more inheritance, come from wealthy families, or possess better educational backgrounds. Even when beginning from a similar position, individual differences in abilities can still affect outcomes. Some people demonstrate greater intellectual capabilities, organizational strategies, social skills, and so on. This leads to a meritocratic-based justice system where the fastest runners win the race. However, one's abilities or talents are not solely their own; they are also influenced by their parents or by a higher power (God).[16] Therefore, this type of merit-based justice is considered unfair, as innate abilities or talents are seen as a shared asset of the community.[17]

To address the shortcomings of a meritocratic distribution system, John Rawls proposes "the difference principle."[18] According to this principle, income inequality is permissible only if it ensures that the needs of the disadvantaged are adequately met. In contrast, proponents of communitarianism advocate for a basic income, believing that economic justice for all requires a strong sense of community and solidarity.

Achieving a just society requires more than simply ensuring a fair distribution of income. Individuals also need meaningful work that engages them as active members of their communities, along with a deeper understanding of each other grounded in empathy. Furthermore, we must embrace a nuanced and compelling vision of justice—one that may seem complex but ultimately serves the greater good for everyone involved. The Dao De Jing (Chapter 45) supports this idea of justice: "What is most perfect seems incomplete, but its usefulness is endless. What is most full seems empty, but its usefulness is endless. What is most straight seems devious. The great skill seems clumsy. Great eloquence seems awkward. Restlessness overcomes cold, but calm overcomes heat. Clarity and stillness are the foundation of the world."[19]

Similarly, the Dao De Jing (Chapter 22) conveys paradoxical notions of justice, suggesting that opposites can lead to fulfillment.[20] Yielding signifies wholeness, bending indicates straightness, and emptiness hints at fullness. Those who embrace these dualities become wise and serve as beacons in the world. By avoiding self-promotion and competition, they achieve distinction and longevity. The saying "to yield means to be whole" emphasizes that striving for wholeness allows everything to flow naturally.

The moral challenge to individualism is this: How can one be happy when others are starving to death? It is morally problematic to feel free in the face of such stark inequalities. From a community-centered perspective, freedom is communal. When one person is starving, economic justice involves rescuing them from poverty. If one person suffers in a community, all members feel the impact. The Parable of the Vineyard Laborers illustrates the importance of mutual care and solidarity in society. This principle is part of divine justice, as reflected in both the Hebrew Bible and the New Testament.[21]

The Parable of the Rich Man and Lazarus

Lk. 16:19-31

19 "There was a rich man who was dressed in purple and fine linen and feasted sumptuously every day. 20 And at his gate lay a poor man named Lazarus, covered with sores, 21 and longed to satisfy his hunger with what fell from the

rich man's table; even the dogs would come and lick his sores. 22 The poor man died and was carried away by the angels to be Abraham's side. The rich man also died and was buried. 23 In Hades, where he was being tormented, he looked up and saw Abraham far away, with Lazarus by his bosom. 24 He called out to him, 'Father Abraham, have mercy on me and send Lazarus to dip the tip of his finger in water and cool my tongue, because I am in agony in these flames.' 25 But Abraham said, 'Child, remember that during your lifetime you received your good things, while Lazarus received evil things; but now he is comforted here, and you are in agony. 26 Besides all this, between you and us a great chasm has been fixed, so that those who might want to go from here to you cannot do so, and no one can cross from there to us.' 27 He said, 'Then, I beg you, father, to send him to my father's house—28 for I have five brothers—that he may warn them, so that they will not also come into this place of torment.' 29 Abraham replied, 'They have Moses and the prophets; they should listen to them.' 30 He said, 'No, father Abraham; but if someone from the dead goes to them, they will repent.' 31 He said to him, 'If they do not listen to Moses and the prophets, neither will they be convinced even if someone rises from the dead.'"[22]

Interpreting the Parable

The Parable of the Rich Man and Lazarus is not about the afterlife but rather about moral and economic life in the present. The parable of the Pharisee and Tax Collector is a folktale found across cultures, suggesting that one's life on earth has consequences in the afterlife. The purpose of this type of story is not to enter heaven or avoid hell, but rather to emphasize the importance of living a moral life in the here and now.[23]

Jesus is familiar with the Jewish tradition that emphasizes the importance of almsgiving in maintaining the covenantal community. For example, Deut. 15:11 reads: "Since there will never cease to be some in need on the earth, I therefore command you, 'Open your hand to the poor and needy neighbor in your land'" (see also Isa. 58:7).[24] The book of Tobit, a third-century BCE Jewish writing from the Second Temple Judaism, also contains the importance of almsgiving to the poor (Tob. 4:5-11).

In Luke, Jesus urges people to invite those who cannot repay their kindness, such as the poor, the crippled, the lame, and the blind (Lk. 14:12-14). He also gives similar instructions to his disciples, telling them, "Sell your possessions and give alms. Make purses for yourselves that do not wear out, an unfailing treasure in heaven, where no thief comes near and no moth destroys" (Lk. 12:33; cf. 18:22).

This parable raises important questions about distributive justice. Why does a poor man named Lazarus find himself at the rich man's gate without the means to secure daily sustenance? What circumstances led him there? Why does the rich man not care for Lazarus, and is he responsible for this neglect? How did the rich man acquire his wealth, and how did Lazarus fall into poverty?

Significantly, the parable distinguishes Lazarus as a poor man (*ptochos*) rather than a beggar (*prosaites*).[25] While we cannot ascertain his social life or living conditions before reaching the rich man's gate, the fact remains that he could not overcome extreme poverty on his own and depended on others for survival. Ultimately, he found himself at the rich man's gate, hoping to "satisfy his hunger with what fell from the rich man's table" (16:21). Yes, he was left alone, with only the dogs to lick his sores.

Regardless of the reasons for his poverty, it is unjust to witness Lazarus starving while the rich man enjoys a lavish party with his friends. Such a society displays a profound lack of justice in failing to care for him. Conversely, we question how the rich man acquired his wealth. If he abused or exploited the poor, his riches are tainted by injustice. This contrasts sharply with Zacchaeus, a wealthy chief tax collector introduced later in the Lukan narrative, who tells Jesus: "Look, Lord, half of my possessions, I will give to the poor; and if I have defrauded anyone of anything, I will pay back four times as much" (Lk. 19:8).

Even if the rich man achieved his success independently, he still has a moral duty to care for Lazarus, who is also a member of society. The name Lazarus is derived from the Hebrew name Eliezer, meaning "God helps" (Exod. 18:4). This suggests that God cares for Lazarus because he is also a child of Abraham. Abraham explains Lazarus's presence with him after death, stating that it is because Lazarus suffered in life and is now comforted as a child of God. Notably, there is no indication that Lazarus was saved by his faith or good works; he should have been treated with dignity on earth simply because he is a child of God, but that care did not happen.

Lazarus is now comforted because he suffered unnecessarily without assistance. As an equal member of society, he deserves protection from life's dangers. The rich man's fate in Hades underscores his failure to fulfill his duty to care for the poor when he had the opportunity. This suggests that our actions in this life hold significance. As Greg Carey observes, "Let us simply consider the possibility that it matters what we do in this life—specifically, how we relate to the poor—and it matters more than we might be willing to appreciate."[26]

Engaging Distributive Justice

The primary question regarding distributive justice, as we reflect on this parable, is where things went wrong to the extent that Lazarus had to beg for his life while the rich man lived in excess, hosting lavish parties for his friends daily. Was it Lazarus's fault, perhaps due to failed business ventures? Or did unforeseen circumstances, such as family illness or sudden, unmanageable debt, strip him of control over his life and family? If he became poor through his own mistakes, was it acceptable for him to resort to begging? Conversely, if his poverty was due to no fault of his own, why did he have to endure such suffering? In either scenario, begging represents a last resort, as it is no better than dying. Each day is filled with despair, and every moment brings shame.

As a member of society—and he was—Lazarus should have been rescued from his state of begging through the charity of his neighbors. Thus, it is evident that the system failed him.

Regarding the rich man, was he not morally responsible for Lazarus? Did he acquire his wealth by exploiting others, or did he do so through fair business practices? If he inherited his wealth from his parents, can he genuinely claim all his property as solely his own? Did he pay his fair share of taxes? Did he contribute sufficiently to the village fund, if one existed?

Libertarians argue that the wealthy have no obligation to help the poor, as they believe individuals receive rewards based on their hard work. They assert that the rich are free to act as they choose, without a moral duty to assist others. In their view, the poor must overcome their circumstances through their own efforts. Libertarians maintain that neither government nor religion should compel the wealthy to support the poor, as they regard freedom as the highest virtue.

However, critics question why the poor are not free from poverty and why those with wealth and freedom do not extend support to them. They argue that the principle of freedom should apply to everyone, not just the rich or select groups.

Egalitarian liberals address societal inequalities by advocating for special taxes on the wealthy to redistribute income. They prioritize equality among individuals and promote the fair distribution of resources.

In a similar vein, communitarianism emphasizes the importance of solidarity and mutual support in society, underscoring the need to assist the poor and viewing poverty as a communal issue. This perspective aligns closely with the teachings of Jesus, which challenge systems of exploitation and the abuse of power.

From this viewpoint, Lazarus deserves support from society and his neighbors, as he is also a member of that community. When such support is absent, God ultimately restores him to the privileged status of Abraham's child after death, sending divine warnings to the wealthy that they should live in a manner worthy of being called children of God.

Contemporary Implications

One of the most pressing issues in today's world is the widespread state of poverty. Many individuals must work two or three jobs just to make ends meet, often lacking adequate health insurance. The cycle of poverty frequently continues for their children and future generations. An immediate concern is how to provide financial support to these individuals, whether through welfare programs or emergency assistance. To generate the necessary funds, comprehensive tax code reforms must be implemented.

However, financial aid alone may not suffice, as the playing field is not level for the poor or marginalized, making it difficult for them to rise up the social ladder. In the United States, affirmative action has been introduced to enhance educational opportunities for underrepresented racial groups applying to colleges. As a result, minority students have gained access to higher education through this initiative. Advocates argue that such measures are essential for equalizing opportunities. However, critics contend that race-based admissions are unconstitutional and infringe on fundamental individual rights and freedoms. Thus, it is vital to explore additional strategies to level the playing field if affirmative action does not yield the desired results. Addressing these challenges is essential in our efforts to create a more equitable society.[27]

Conclusion

In this chapter, we analyzed two parables—the Vineyard Laborers and the Rich Man and Lazarus—and interpreted them through the lens of distributive justice. It is essential to note that these parables can also be understood from other justice perspectives, such as attributive justice or restorative justice. Furthermore, other parables may address issues of distributive justice as well.

I chose these two parables because they most clearly highlight concerns related to income inequality and social and economic disparities. From the two parables, we can see that Jesus values the equality of all people, regardless of their status. His teachings about the rule or reign of God apply to both individuals and society, as he speaks out against social and economic injustices and envisions a new world founded on justice and love. Jesus does not endorse excessive individualism that neglects responsibility toward the community.

In this regard, these parables resonate with John Rawls's approach to justice, which emphasizes both personal liberties and social and economic equality.[28] One area of alignment between Jesus's teachings and Rawls's ideas is in the concept of talents or possessions. Rawls views an individual's skills and inherited wealth as common assets of society, while Jesus teaches that everything ultimately belongs to God. However, while Rawls does not explore broader questions about the common good, Jesus raises ultimate, teleological questions through his parables, prompting readers to consider who we are as human beings and as children of God, as well as the purpose of our lives.

Ultimately, Jesus's parables encourage readers to reimagine a just society where the rule of God applies to everyone. In summary, Jesus does not endorse radical individualism or maximal liberties, nor does he advocate sacrificing the interests of the many for the few, as utilitarianism suggests. His ethical principles are universally applicable, akin to Kant's proposals, and even more radical than those of any philosopher or theorist, as he teaches us, "Love your enemies" (Mt. 5:44). Unlike Kant and Rawls, however, Jesus seeks the common good for all people through godly virtues. For Jesus, justice involves embracing the rule or reign of God—characterized by his mercy and love—through which people can live with dignity, freedom, and equality by transforming their hearts and minds.

Questions for Discussion

1. In the Parable of the Vineyard Laborers, is the owner abusive, or is he concerned about distributive justice in some respects? If the latecomers have disabilities, are they responsible for their circumstances? How would you describe the adjective *agathos* (good or generous) in light of

the owner's claim to possess this character? Is he intended to represent a figure of God?
2. Do you believe that equal pay for all workers constitutes economic justice, or could it be a means of exploiting powerless laborers?
3. In the parable of the Rich Man and Lazarus, is the rich man responsible for the poor man's misfortunes? Lazarus did not choose to be poor. While libertarians argue that individuals are not responsible for poverty, supporters of egalitarianism advocate for equality. According to Kantian ethics, helping the marginalized is an unnegotiable moral duty. What grounds do you have for pursuing justice in this narrative?
4. Does Luke criticize the rich man solely because of his wealth, or primarily because he fails to share his resources with the marginalized? Luke appears to promote "sharing ethics" over radical justice. How would you evaluate Luke's overall message?

Notes

1 Throughout this book, parable texts are from the NRSVue unless otherwise noted, and italics indicate my translation.
2 20:16 is considered to be Matthew's addition.
3 One notable characteristic of Jesus's parables is their vividness, which makes readers and listeners feel as if they are present with him. This parable is unusual and subversive, defying the expectations of its audience. The landowner's actions, such as going to the labor market five times and paying every worker the same wage, are difficult to comprehend within the context of his time. These characteristics suggest that this parable likely originated with Jesus.
4 William Herzog, *Parables as Subversive Speech*, 89–90. David Buttrick, *Speaking Parables: A Homiletic Guide* (Louisville, KY: WJKP, 2000), 114. Herzog and Buttrick read the vineyard owner as an exploitative master. See also Luise Schottroff, *The Parables of Jesus*, 211–12.
5 William Herzog, *Parables as Subversive Speech*, 84.
6 Matthew Gordley, *Social Justice in the Stories of Jesus*, 234–5. See also Van Eck Ernst and John Kloppenborg, *The Parables of Jesus the Galilean: Stories of a Social Prophet* (Eugene, OR: Cascade, 2016), 146–52.
7 Matthew Gordley, *Social Justice in the Stories of Jesus*, 236–7.
8 Douglas Oakman, "The Buying Power of Two Denarii," *Forum* 3 (1987): 33–8.
9 Michael Cook, "Jesus' Parables and the Faith that Does Justice," 26. See also Yung Suk Kim, "Reading Mercy in the Parables of Jesus," 18–21.

10 Amy-Jill Levine, *Short Stories by Jesus*, 197–219.
11 *Argos* in verses 3 and 6 mean "jobless status" or standing without work. It does not mean to be lazy. Those who were hired late were the marginalized. See Pablo Jiménez, "The Laborers of the Vineyard (Matthew 20:1-16): A Hispanic Homiletical Reading," *Journal for Preachers* 21, no. 1 (1997): 35–40. See also José Rodriguéz, "The Parable of the Affirmative Action Employer," *Apuntes* 8, no. 3 (1933): 51–9. Others argue that those who were hired late are lazy and that their coming late is their fault. See Joachim Jeremias, *The Parables of Jesus* (London: SCM, 1954), 26. See also Eduar Schweizer, *The Good News According to Matthew* (Louisville, KY: WJKP, 1975), 392.
12 Brad H. Young, *The Parables*, 78.
13 Amy-Jill Levine, *Short Stories by Jesus*, 213.
14 See Thomas Massaro, *Mercy in Action: The Social Teachings of Pope Francis* (Lanham, MD: Rowman & Littlefield, 2018), 34–55. See also Mary Kay Dobrovolny, "The Laborers in the Vineyard," in Matthew Gordley, *Social Justice in the Stories of Jesus*, 319–21. Latin American liberation theology emphasizes the preferential option for the poor. See Jon Sobrino, *No Salvation Outside the Poor: Prophetic-Utopian Essays* (Maryknoll, NY: Orbis, 2008), 14. See also Brooks Harrington and John Holbert, *No Mercy, No Justice: The Dominant Narrative of America Versus the Counter-Narrative of Jesus' Parables* (Eugene, OR: Cascade, 2019), 39–47; 237–40.
15 Dao De Jing 45, 22. The translation is mine.
16 John Rawls, *A Theory of Justice*, 266. See also Michael Sandel, *Justice*, 154.
17 Michael Sandel, *Justice*, 156.
18 Michael Sandel, *Justice*, 156.
19 Yung Suk Kim, *Dao De Jing*, accessed Mar 20, 2022. http://drkimys.blogspot.com/p/dao-de-jing_22.html.
20 Yung Suk Kim, *Dao De Jing*, accessed Mar 20, 2022. http://drkimys.blogspot.com/p/dao-de-jing_22.html.
21 One of the prominent themes in the Hebrew Bible is God's righteousness (*tsedaqah*) and God's love (*hesed*). Both concepts emphasize divine justice, highlighting the importance of caring for one another. Jesus also advocates for these ideals; for example, see Mt. 6:33.
22 While the authenticity of this parable is debated, 16:27-31 is considered Luke's creation. See Robert Funk, et al., *The Parables of Jesus*, 64.
23 Matthew Gordley, *Social Justice in the Stories of Jesus*, 258.
24 See Amy-Jill Levine, *Short Stories by Jesus*, 276.
25 Amy-Jill Levine, *Short Stories by Jesus*, 254–7. See also Yung Suk Kim, *Jesus's Truth*, 99–103.
26 Greg Carey, *Stories Jesus Told: How to Read a Parable* (Nashville: Abingdon, 2019), 93.

27 See James Cone, *Black Theology of Liberation* (Maryknoll, NY: Orbis, 1990). He argues that "no one is free until all are free" (88). He also says: "Christians can never be content as long as their sisters and brothers are enslaved. They must suffer with them, knowing that freedom for Jesus Christ is always freedom for the oppressed" (101).
28 John Rawls, *A Theory of Justice*, 266.

4

Attributive Justice and Parables

Attributive justice is the principle of rewarding individuals based on their efforts in a fair environment.[1] If this fairness is lacking, attributive justice cannot be achieved. A healthy society motivates individuals to strive for their best, ensuring they receive the outcomes they anticipate for their hard work. It is crucial to eliminate any barriers that obstruct fair competition among people. From this perspective, attributive justice does not advocate for a strict meritocracy where individuals retain all the benefits of their achievements solely for themselves; rather, fair competition encourages hard work and fosters a positive spirit.

This chapter will examine three parables—the Talents, the Treasure, and the Pearl—through the lens of attributive justice. However, interpreting these parables presents challenges. For instance, in the parable of the Talents, we lack essential information about the master's identity and character. Is he kind or cruel? Furthermore, the parable does not specify the abilities of the three slaves, nor does it explain the work done by the two who generated income.

These ambiguities hinder our ability to reach a definitive conclusion about justice. If we interpret the master as abusive or exploitative, attributive justice loses its relevance, as the slaves are merely working to serve him. In such a scenario, a more appropriate concept of justice would be distributive justice, given that the slaves are not compensated fairly for their labor.

Can we view the master in the parable as a positive character? The answer is yes, as this parable is situated within an eschatological context that emphasizes the urgency of taking action within a limited timeframe and using resources wisely. This parable appears in the eschatological discourse found in Mt. 24:1–25:46. In this context, the master in the Parable of the Talents can be compared to God's agent, similar to the vineyard owner in the Parable of the Vineyard Laborers (Mt. 20:1-16), where the owner is focused on ensuring full employment and fair wages for all workers.

In the parable of the Talents, the master is concerned about his property during his absence, which requires a strong work ethic and positive attitude from his slaves. However, master-slave relationships are inherently abusive, making the use of this metaphor problematic, even in religious discourse. Despite the challenges associated with such language, this parable emphasizes the importance of individuals' work ethic within an eschatological context. The master reprimands the slave who received one talent, not for failing to generate profits, but for lacking initiative.

In this parable, the kingdom of God is compared to a man going on a journey. As we noted in the Parable of the Vineyard Laborers, it is important to focus on the entity to which the kingdom of God is compared. While one could view the comparison of the kingdom to a man traveling as negative, given Jesus's frequent use of metaphors, such as in the parables of the leaven and the vineyard laborers, there are positive connotations associated with this imagery.

Thus, we must examine the Parable of the Talents closely to understand the man's responses. The master's perspective emphasizes the importance of diligent work over mere profit; he believes that hard work is necessary, even at the risk of failure. He contends that he is not a harsh man who exploits his slaves for failing to generate profits, but rather sees the fulfillment of one's responsibilities as vital, especially given the limited nature of time.

Similarly, we can interpret the parables of the Treasure and the Pearl through the lens of attributive justice. In the former, a man discovers a valuable treasure and invests everything to obtain it, illustrating the correct attitude toward future opportunities. Here, the kingdom of God is again likened to a man, prompting us to observe how he acts in light of the new reality of the kingdom. Likewise, in the parable of the Pearl, a merchant sells all his possessions upon finding a pearl of great value. In each of these parables, what is required due to the kingdom of God is a radical determination and action to embrace this new reality in one's life.

The Parable of the Talents

Mt. 25:14-30

14 "For it is like a man going on a journey, who summoned his slaves and entrusted his property to them. 15 To one he gave five talents, to another two,

However, within Matthew's community context, the term "talent" is more closely associated with the God-given duty of love. Each individual is bestowed with various gifts by God, and they are called to fully realize and utilize these gifts for the benefit of the community. By doing so, they need not worry about the future, as they prepare themselves for the day of Parousia. If they actively care for others—feeding the hungry and quenching the thirsty—they are, in essence, serving Jesus (Mt. 25:31-46). Therefore, the Parable of the Talents conveys a message that extends beyond mere eschatological preparation.

Considering the God-given talents of love, the primary failure of the one-talent slave lies not in his inability to generate profit but in his complete unwillingness to use his talent. Instead of taking a risk, he buried it in the ground, driven by fear of losing what he had. The master's concern was not about profits but the absence of effort. Even if the slave had tried and failed, he would not have faced punishment. What mattered most was that he never seized the opportunity to attempt anything at all.

From an anti-imperial perspective, the slave's action may be seen as a resistant voice against the master's exploitative practices, as he chooses not to cooperate with the profit-driven enterprise.[5] However, the context in Matthew suggests that the message aligns more with the idea of attributive justice. Moreover, a man embarking on a journey must possess good character, as previously noted. Ultimately, the point is that slaves are responsible for the work assigned to them.

As God loves and forgives the people in Matthew's community, they are called to fulfill God's work, which includes loving their enemies. They are expected to work diligently until the very end. Their efforts will be evaluated on the final day based on their love for their neighbors, as indicated in the passage about the final judgment (Mt. 25:31-46). Feeding the hungry is akin to feeding Jesus himself. Every member has a role in God's work, but the nature and extent of that work will differ. Those assigned more responsibilities are expected to contribute more. In summary, Brad Young insightfully emphasizes the stewardship of God's resources in his reflections on this parable:[6]

> Although the eschatological force of the master's return to give reward or punishment to his servants on the basis of their performance pervades the rich imagery of the plot of the parable, its primary message is on stewardship of God's graciously bestowed resources in the present. God is good, and the stewards of his divinely given abilities and assets must use them creatively and faithfully to achieve a maximum return on their master's investment.

Engaging Attributive Justice

The two slaves who received five and two talents are praised for successfully doubling the money entrusted to them through trading. Their efforts reflect sound and ethical business practices, driven by their master's trust in them.

It is important to understand that if the slaves had engaged in malpractice or dishonest behavior, their gains would be seen as immoral and not worthy of praise. Therefore, we should avoid a purely success-driven perspective. Even if the two slaves had put forth their best efforts but failed to achieve significant success, the master would not reprimand them for their genuine attempts.

The master distributes talents according to each slave's capabilities. He is wise and considerate, understanding his slave's strengths and not demanding more than they can handle. What he seeks is diligence in their assigned tasks. This sentiment echoes Confucius's sayings in Analects 13:25: "The noble person is easy to work for but difficult to please. If you try to please them by dubious means, they will not be happy. And in their employment of people, they assign them tasks commensurate with abilities."[7] The noble person is wise because they do not expect more than what people can realistically achieve.

When considering individual abilities, it is important to reflect on how they were acquired. Some may have been cultivated through effort, while others may have been inherited. Therefore, while celebrating their results, the slaves should not view their gains as solely their own; they must recognize that their achievements are not entirely self-made. Their successes should be shared with those who are less fortunate, particularly those who lack job opportunities or urgently need assistance due to an economic crisis.

Understood in this way, the parable does not imply that one can possess everything without sharing with others. This reflects a core value of communitarianism: the importance of solidarity within society. It is often difficult to distinguish between personal effort and inherent ability, making it challenging to claim success as entirely one's own. Personal efforts also depend on various factors, such as health and positive relationships within the community. In this sense, their success can be viewed as a manifestation of God's grace. Unlike in the parable, the real world does not guarantee success solely through effort.

The slave who received one talent failed to act with it. Driven by fear of loss, he returned the talent to his master without attempting to invest or grow it. He perceived his master as harsh, which further deepened his inaction and resulted in a missed opportunity for success. Likely haunted by past failures, he experienced a fear of punishment that stifled his ambition. However, he could have overcome this trauma by taking a risk with his talent. Had he committed to making the most of it, he might have experienced divine grace and developed his sense of agency, key components of self-worth and esteem. Such a daring attempt may not reflect the reality of his life if he is in a powerless situation. Therefore, it is also difficult to judge him.

Even if the slave had failed despite his best efforts, he would not have been scolded for trying his best. Ultimately, no one can help another person establish their agency if they remain passive. Yet, even in this failed situation, we are left to ponder why this unfortunate man, perhaps burdened by past trauma, was not given another chance. It is possible that his failure stemmed not only from his actions but also from the circumstances surrounding him.

In other words, his trauma is not solely his burden; others contributed to it. More importantly, his community has a collective responsibility to take care of those left behind in trauma. This highlights the theme of social or community responsibility, which is emphasized in both egalitarianism and communitarianism.

Contemporary Implications

Attributive justice concerns the assignment of praise or blame based on individual actions, choices, or character, presenting significant implications and challenges in contemporary society. In normal circumstances, "moral desert" suggests that good deeds should be rewarded and bad deeds punished. For instance, a hard-working employee deserves a raise, an outstanding student merits a scholarship, a dishonest student should face disciplinary action, and a perpetrator must receive an appropriate punishment. The Parable of the Talents illustrates the importance of encouraging and acknowledging hard work. People need to believe that their efforts will lead to success. In contrast, the passive slave who merely hid his talent exemplifies a moral failure.

At a deeper level, while attributive justice emphasizes individual accountability, its application in a diverse society often raises concerns about equity and the broader social context in which actions occur. One key issue is how responsible individuals are for their actions in the presence of structural inequities. When discrimination against minority groups is deeply entrenched—whether based on economic, racial, or gender disparities—it can limit opportunities and restrict the ability to make informed choices. Focusing solely on attributive justice may overlook these systemic factors, resulting in a "blame the victim" mentality. In such cases, individuals may be held accountable for their circumstances without considering the structural barriers that limit their options.

Furthermore, it is troubling when attributive justice emphasizes individual actions without considering the complex circumstances individuals may encounter, such as severe health issues, extreme stress, or mental health challenges. In these circumstances, people may make poor choices. Simplifying attributive justice to blame individuals is not beneficial for a healthy society. Instead of creating a rigid definition of "good" or "bad" actors and emphasizing punishment, communities should prioritize opportunities for rehabilitation. Those struggling with addiction often face blame instead of support, stemming from perceptions of moral failing. Such attitudes can lead to stigmatization and inadequate support structures for vulnerable populations, ultimately further marginalizing groups that require empathetic policies rather than punitive judgments.

Additionally, we must consider economic disparities and social welfare when judging individuals as deserving or undeserving of aid based on their perceived efforts or moral character. Some welfare policies restrict assistance to those labeled as "lazy," ignoring factors like economic crises or systemic barriers. Such approaches perpetuate cycles of poverty. We must also examine the criminal justice system and sentencing practices. Systemic biases, such as racial profiling and socioeconomic factors, complicate how blame is assigned. This focus often results in inequitable sentencing, where individuals from marginalized backgrounds receive harsher penalties due to unconscious biases rather than genuine differences in culpability.

The Parable of the Treasure

Mt. 13:44

44 "The kingdom of heaven is like treasure hidden in a field, which someone found and hid. Then in his joy, he went and sold all that he had and bought that field."

Interpreting the Parable

The parable of the Treasure appears only in Matthew and the Gospel of Thomas (109). Thomas elaborated on the earlier oral version of this parable, placing it within a Gnostic context. He removed unnecessary misunderstandings regarding the morality of the buyer, emphasizing his effort, such as plowing, to find the treasure and highlighting his money-lending business.[8]

Matthew's version of the parable is both complex and concise, presenting ambiguities about the buyer's motivations and actions. Some interpreters view the buyer as dishonest, arguing that he should have reported the treasure to the field's owner. While this interpretation has merit, the parable does not provide definitive evidence to conclude his guilt.[9]

We lack details about the treasure itself—specifically, its value to the buyer, how it compared to the perceptions of others, and the reasons for his joy upon discovering it. Additionally, we do not know why he sold everything he had to purchase the field or the specifics of his agreement with the seller. However, if his deal with the seller included all the movable items within the field, then his contract would be legally valid and socially acceptable.[10]

Moreover, Jesus's use of parables is characteristically abrupt, brief, and somewhat unusual. Unlike the merchant searching for pearls or other wealthy individuals, the ordinary man in this parable discovers something that holds great value. His act of finding and hiding the treasure is not necessarily dishonest; rather, it reflects his joy, which warrants further examination.

Jesus conveys this story in a fast-paced manner, intentionally omitting many details. He explicitly compares God's rule or reign to a hidden treasure in a field, implying that this is a positive and desirable thing. The buyer's actions symbolize the appropriate attitude toward God's rule—recognizing its value and taking the risk to acquire it at any cost. Notably, there is no indication that the buyer intends to sell the treasure. This contrasts with Thomas's version, in which the treasure is used to establish a money-lending business after being acquired through the purchase of the field.

Ultimately, the origin of the parable can be traced back to Jesus, as the story is both strange and radical, drawing from the everyday experiences of agricultural life. In the parable of the treasure, the rule or reign of God is likened to a treasure hidden in a field. This treasure represents something positive and valuable in God's work, but it is not material wealth like gold or silver; it may encompass scriptures, the word of God, the mission of God, or one's vocation.

The notion of a treasure hidden in a field suggests that it is not easily found without luck or additional effort. The term "hidden" does not imply that it can be concealed forever; instead, it serves as a metaphor indicating that valuable treasures can eventually be discovered. As Jesus states, "For nothing is hidden, except to be disclosed; nor is anything secret, except to come to light" (Mk 4:22; cf. Mt. 10:26; Lk. 8:17; 12:2).

Regarding the discovery of the treasure, the key question is: How was it found? One possibility is that it was discovered by accident. The individual noticed its value and chose to rebury it until he could legally purchase the field with the proper contract.[11] As mentioned before, this act of hiding does not constitute dishonesty, as he can acquire it legally through legitimate means.

The important point is that he "found" the value of something hidden in a field, suggesting that most people do not easily recognize its worth due to their focus on worldly and expensive matters. Not everyone can see its value, even if they stumble upon it, simply because they lack an interest in matters relating to God's reign or justice.

In this context, the individual should not be judged or blamed for not reporting his discovery to the owner or the public, as we do not know the nature of what he found. It may be something too old or damaged to identify the owner. Therefore, his next logical step would be to purchase the field with a proper contract that includes all movable items. Thus, the notion of the buyer's dishonesty is unfounded.

The issue at hand is not about the man's lack of integrity but rather his quick decision-making and willingness to take risks in acquiring a treasure that may not hold the same value for others. This treasure signifies something meaningful in his life; it could represent the rediscovery of purpose through God's grace. Such a treasure is invaluable and irreplaceable, varying significantly from person to person, which is why each discovery holds its importance.

Another possibility for how the treasure is discovered lies in the finder's deep hunger and thirst for the reign of God. Unlike the merchant in the parable of the pearl, he is not openly searching for something valuable. An analogy to Moses can help illustrate the significance of ordinary life and the search for meaning. After fleeing from Egypt, Moses spent forty years in the Midian desert, wandering as he shepherded Jethro's sheep and contemplating God's will for his life. His life may have seemed mundane, yet one day, he ventured beyond the desert's boundaries and encountered God at the burning bush. This moment became a revelation for him, leading to a new mission.

Something similar occurs with the man in the parable. He yearns to find something valuable in his ordinary, seemingly routine life, and the turning point arrives unexpectedly. Due to his focus, he notices something hidden in a field. This determination aligns with Jesus's teaching: "Ask, and it will be given to you;

search, and you will find; knock, and the door will be opened for you" (Mt. 7:7; see also Lk. 19:9-10).

Engaging Attributive Justice

To engage in attributive justice within this parable, we must consider whether man's discovery of the treasure is morally valid. I argue that Jesus focused not on the morality of the person who discovered and hid the treasure, but rather on the sudden realization of God's reign through the ordinary individual's radical action of purchasing the field at great cost.

This act transforms the hidden treasure into an asset, enabling him to participate actively in the reign of God on earth. The parable emphasizes the immediate reality of God's reign, which requires the finder's swift discernment, decision, and total commitment. Therefore, he is commended for his decision and action to manifest the reign of God in his life.

Recognizing the treasure's value, he makes rapid, sound decisions that deserve commendation. Life demands a series of good decisions, and even when the reign of God appears powerfully in the world, some people do not recognize or accept it. However, this man exemplifies commendable qualities through his character and virtues, including discernment and a refusal to be blinded by worldly standards. While God's grace may come to anyone, he recognizes the value of what he has found. The treasure is not something extravagant or coveted by others; it may be a different kind of treasure that some people overlook. His ability to discern this must be acknowledged, as he distinguishes the value of God's reign from selfish, worldly treasures.

Thus, he is commended not merely for his radical determination and action but also for his character development, which aligns with the focus of virtue ethics.[12] Often, we concentrate on consequences, but in this parable, we should recognize the man's cultivated traits, such as courage and devotion to God's reign. Confucius emphasizes the importance of human virtues like love, empathy, and modesty, stating, "It is the person who unfolds the way. It is not the way that unfolds the person" (人能弘道、非道弘人, rén néng hóng dào, fēi dào hóng rén).[13]

The man in the parable takes risks, selling everything he owns to obtain the treasure, thereby demonstrating courage. Selling all he possesses is risky because his haste might place him in a weaker position in any potential business contract. Moreover, he does not invest in the treasure to resell it for profit. The parable does not suggest this intention; instead, he seems genuinely happy to have found it, though the exact nature of the treasure remains unknown.

His discovery of the treasure symbolizes something positive and genuine about God's reign. While the treasure may hold great value for him, it may not have the same significance for others who lack interest in God's reign. This fresh revelation of new value underscores the importance of his risk-taking in making this value a reality in his life. By purchasing the field, he gains access to the treasure, transforming him into a new person who has found the treasure of God in the world.

Contemporary Implications

One of the biggest challenges in our world today is the lack of moral values in decision-making and actions, leading to a distorted perception of worth in oneself and society. People often judge worth based on social status, wealth, or reputation. This culture drives individuals to pursue success by accumulating skills and achievements, striving to excel in competition. Others wait for success to come through luck, investing everything in risky ventures. Society tends to label those who succeed, particularly in economic terms, as "good" people who deserve accolades, while those who do not fit this mold are often viewed as mediocre or inferior.

In this environment, individuals are conditioned to perceive success as defeating others or making swift, high-stakes decisions for personal gain. However, there is a critical need to redefine our values. True worth should not stem from materialism, power, or wealth, but rather from a joyful pursuit of justice and love, advocating for marginalized communities and promoting God's reign in all areas of life. Embracing this way of life requires bold decisions and a willingness to take risks.

The Parable of the Pearl

Mt. 13:45-46

45 "Again, the kingdom of heaven is like a merchant in search of fine pearls; 46 on finding one pearl of great value, he went and sold all that he had and bought it."

Interpreting the Parable

The origin of the parable of the Pearl, like the parable of the Treasure, traces back to Jesus. This parable follows immediately after the parable of the Treasure, and its focus is similar. Both parables share common themes, such as finding a treasure or pearl, selling all one has, and purchasing the treasure or pearl. The significant difference, however, lies in the man's motivation and status. In the parable of the Pearl, the man is a merchant of pearls, a professional and affluent trader.

Readers are aware that the rule or reign of God in the parable of the Pearl is compared to a merchant (*emporos*), similar to a wholesaler.[14] This comparison differs from the parable of the Treasure, where the focus is on a treasure hidden in a field. While merchants are often portrayed negatively in biblical traditions (Gen. 37:28; Isa. 23:8; Amos 8:6; Ezek 38:13; John 2:16; Rev 18:3), the merchant in this parable transforms due to his diligent search for fine pearls and his discovery of something new in the rule or reign of God.[15]

Typically, the merchant works for profit, buying many fine pearls, storing them in a warehouse, and selling them at a higher price later. However, one day, amid his usual travels, he encounters "one pearl of great value." This moment is not a sudden revelation; rather, it occurs after many days of seeking. When he sees this pearl, he is moved to sell all he has to acquire it. At this moment, he is no longer an ordinary businessman, as the standard practice is to trade multiple fine pearls for higher profits. It appears he has decided to abandon this business model; now, this one pearl is everything to him, and he cannot part with it because it is far too precious. This transformation signifies that he must embrace this pearl and live with it. Amy-Jill Levine observes the importance of identity change:

> Whether what he does is risky or wise, foolhardy or dedicated, he has gained a pearl of enormous value. In gaining, he has not only fulfilled a desire he did not know he had; he has also changed his identity. He had been looking for fine pearls, but he bought only one. By finding that pearl of ultimate worth, the merchant stops being a merchant. Thus he redefines himself, and we must see him anew as well.[16]

The implications of this parable for attributive justice are somewhat similar to those of the parable of the Treasure. However, a significant difference lies in the merchant's diligent seeking (*zeteo*), which is lacking in the parable of the Treasure. This verb, *zeteo*, is used in Mt. 6:33, where Jesus tells his disciples, "Seek the reign of God and his righteousness."[17] In the parable, the object of seeking must be the rule or reign of God, which necessitates a deliberate action of pursuit. This same verb appears in Mt. 7:7-8: "Seek (*zeteite*), and you will find;

knock, and the door will be opened for you. For everyone who asks receives, and everyone who searches finds, and for everyone who knocks, the door will be opened." Due to his persistent search for fine pearls, the merchant eventually discovers one pearl of great value that changes his life. He sells all he has to buy this singular pearl.

Engaging Attributive Justice

The merchant in the parable is a seasoned expert in the pearl trade, dedicated to his business endeavors. His pursuit of fine pearls demonstrates a deep understanding of the market and a commitment to quality. Although we do not know his character, charitable contributions, or community reputation, one thing is clear: he is a professional in his field. The notion of expertise implies that maintaining accurate and consistent records is essential for success.

The merchant's accomplishments are not attributed to luck but rather to his relentless business efforts. After many days of searching, he discovers one pearl of great value. This moment serves as an "aha" revelation, representing the culmination of his labor and the realization that true treasures come to those who seek them diligently.[18]

Similarly, exceptional performance or outstanding results often stem from substantial effort, prolonged searching, or continuous practice. There are no shortcuts to success, and the merchant's unwavering diligence illustrates this truth.

Upon discovering the magnificent pearl, the merchant makes a bold and immediate decision to acquire it by selling all he possesses. This pivotal moment underscores his profound desire for the pearl, signifying that he cannot envision life without it. His choice reflects a readiness to sacrifice everything in pursuit of something of greater value.

Embracing this newly acquired pearl illustrates his commitment to the treasure. Rather than viewing the pearl as a mere opportunity for profit, he chooses to invest in it. This radical decision signifies a transformative investment in his future and alignment with the divine.

By putting all his resources into this one extraordinary pearl, he may find himself poorer. However, his joy is immense due to the fulfillment and richness derived from his newfound life in God's reign. This story conveys the profound truth that true wealth lies not in material possessions but in the treasures we choose to embrace.

In conclusion, the merchant's journey highlights the importance of expertise, hard work, radical decision-making, and the ultimate joy that comes from living in harmony with one's values. His story encourages us to seek what truly matters and to be willing to invest wholly in our passions and discoveries.

Contemporary Implications

One's worth or self-esteem is not determined by material possessions or fame. It is essential to work diligently in one's chosen field, whatever it may be. Through hard work, new revelations may arise, presenting opportunities for deeper meaning in life. At such pivotal moments, individuals might make bold decisions, take risks, and embark on new careers, even when faced with numerous challenges. This choice can lead to a renewed sense of identity for those who pursue a different path. This newfound identity can enhance self-esteem and inspire further dedication to achieving that identity.

Starting a second career alongside an already successful one is a courageous act. Regardless of the outcome, no one is in a position to judge, as the individual is pursuing a new life and meaning. Just as the merchant's life changed forever upon discovering a valuable pearl, we, too, must embrace our opportunities for transformation.

Ultimately, it is our personal decisions that shape our identities; no one else can make those choices for us. The concept of a "pearl of great value" may look different for everyone, but the joy of discovering a meaningful vocation is universal. We should continuously seek the guiding principles of our beliefs and strive to find our own unique pearls.

Conclusion

In this chapter, we have explored the three parables through the lens of attributive justice, which focuses on rewards or punishments based on one's work. These parables certainly advocate for a strong work ethic centered on the reign of God. The Parable of the Talents encourages individuals to give their best, even at the risk of losing everything. The emphasis is not on making profits but on sincere efforts.

The slaves who received five and two talents did their best and achieved commendable results. However, they must also recognize that their achievements are not solely their own; their abilities were entrusted to them.[19] They bear the responsibility of supporting others who have not been given as much.

In contrast, the slave who received one talent failed to take any action. From a traditional perspective on attributive justice, this presents a wasted opportunity to generate more profit or yield. He missed the chance to contribute to economic development or build social capital. However, we must also consider that his failure may stem from past trauma. He may have experienced harsh treatment due to previous setbacks, leading him to protect himself from potential tragedy.

If this trauma influenced his behavior, he cannot be fully held accountable for his actions. This raises the question: Can the community as a whole take steps to assist him? Here, the principles of communitarian justice come into play.

In the parable of the Treasure, the central theme revolves around making bold decisions upon discovering a hidden treasure in a field, taking risks associated with purchasing the field along with the treasure. Such actions deserve commendation because God's reign requires boldness, even when it entails significant costs. The man in this parable is an ordinary individual, which highlights that moments of revelation can happen to anyone who understands the true value of a treasure. This treasure does not have to be something expensive. The key point is his ability to recognize this value, similar to the concept of the reign of God.

In the parable of the Pearl, the main point is similar to the parable of the Treasure, with the key distinction being that the protagonist is a merchant, an atypical and radical figure. As an expert and businessman, he sought fine pearls, and one day, upon discovering a pearl of great value, he made the bold decision to purchase it and embrace a new life with it. This choice does not guarantee him worldly success or an easy path; rather, it signifies a commitment that may lead to greater challenges, as he has invested everything in this one pearl. However, his new life will provide him with joy and a sense of self-worth. Ultimately, one's value is not determined by material possessions or fame, emphasizing the importance of value ethics.

Questions for Discussion

1. Does the Parable of the Talents portray the master as an abusive figure, or does he embody qualities of a good master?

2. Did the slave who received one talent make a wise decision by resisting the master's pressure to generate profits? Should he be held accountable for his failure to act, especially if he had previously faced unreasonable trauma or failure?
3. In the parable of the Pearl, the merchant sought fine pearls and ultimately purchased one of great value after selling all he owned. Is this decision typical or reasonable, considering he does not intend to resell it for profit? Is he destined for poverty due to his choice?
4. What does the one pearl of great value represent? Does the merchant find fulfillment in his decision?

Notes

1 Yung Suk Kim, "Justice Matters, But Which Justice?" 41–3.
2 "Enter into the joy of your master" in v. 21 and 23 is also considered Matthew's creation. See Robert Funk, et al., *The Parables of Jesus*, 54–5.
3 The parable proper begins in v. 13 and appears in v. 15–24. Otherwise, v. 12, 14, 25–7 is considered Lukan redaction. See Robert Funk, et al., *The Parables of Jesus*, 54–5.
4 John B. Carpenter, "The Parable of the Talents in Missionary Perspective: A Call for an Economic Spirituality," *Missiology* 25 (1997): 167; A. M. Hunter, *The Parables of Then and Now* (London: SCM, 1971), 96–7; A. J. Hultgren, *The Parables of Jesus*, 278–9; Bernard Scott, *Hear the Parable: A Commentary on the Parables of Jesus* (Minneapolis, MN: Fortress, 1989), 234; Davies and Dale Allison, *A Critical and Exegetical Commentary on the Gospel According to Matthew*, Vol. 3 (London: T & T Clark, 1997), 402–3. See also Joachim Jeremias, *The Parables of Jesus*, 61–2.
5 For example, see Justin Ukpong, "The Parable of the Talents (Matt 25:14-30): Commendation or Critique of Exploitation? A Social-Historical and Theological Reading," *Neotestamentica* 46, no. 1 (2012): 205 (190–207). See also Richard Rohrbaugh, "A Peasant Reading of the Talents/Pounds: A Text of Terror?" *Biblical Theology Bulletin* 23, no. 1 (1993): 32–9. Luise Schottroff, *The Parables of Jesus*, 223–4.
6 Brad Young, *The Parables*, 97.
7 "Analects of Confucius," accessed March 16, 2025. http://www.acmuller.net/con-dao/analects.html#div-14.
8 Gospel of Thomas, accessed Oct 27, 2024. https://www.gospels.net/thomas.

9 John Dominic Crossan, *Finding Is the First Act: Trove Folktales and Jesus' Treasure Parable* (Eugene, OR: Wipf & Stock, 2008), 91–2. Bernard B. Scott, *Hear Then the Parable*, 402.
10 Brad H. Young, *The Parables*, 217–18.
11 In Matthew's context, buying a field (*agros*) may be comparable to a mission place or the world at large, where God's compassion must be implanted and made known to all people. The reign of God is like a mustard seed being sown in "his field" in Matthew, which evokes the image of the mission field for him.
12 "Virtue Ethics," accessed March 15, 2025. https://plato.stanford.edu/entries/ethics-virtue/.
13 "Analects of Confucius," accessed March 16, 2025. http://www.acmuller.net/con-dao/analects.html#div-16.
14 Amy-Jill Levine, *Short Stories by Jesus*, 130.
15 Amy-Jill Levine, *Short Stories by Jesus*, 127–50.
16 Amy-Jill Levine, *Short Stories by Jesus*, 138.
17 Amy-Jill Levine, *Short Stories by Jesus*, 136–7.
18 Here, as we saw in the parable of the Treasure, cultivating virtues such as love and persistence is important. Ultimately, the truth or way can be discovered and realized through hard work and effort, as Confucius suggests: "It is the person who unfolds the way; it is not the way that unfolds the person." See "Analects of Confucius," accessed March 16, 2025. http://www.acmuller.net/con-dao/analects.html#div-16.
19 The winner of the competition should not hold all the fruit of his or her work because one's gifts or abilities are not one's own. So, one must contribute to the well-being of others in society. John Rawls's theory of "the difference principle" addresses this issue in that surplus created by the winner may be redistributed to those who are less fortunate. See John Rawls, *A Theory of Justice*, 65.

5

Procedural Justice and Parables

Procedural justice focuses on the fairness of processes within personal lives, institutions, and society. It emphasizes the need for equal and fair opportunities for all individuals. For example, hiring procedures should be transparent and well-defined, ensuring that discrimination based on social factors such as class, race, or gender is eliminated. This principle aligns closely with social justice, which seeks to create a community and society free from discrimination.

To ensure fairness, it is crucial to level the playing field. Individuals with disabilities may be granted additional time for tests, recognizing their unique challenges. Additionally, job qualifications should be clearly outlined to avoid ambiguity. This brings up an important question: What truly qualifies someone for a specific position? Should it depend on merit, moral character, or potential?

Many of Jesus's parables explore themes of procedural justice, emphasizing fairness, transparency, and impartiality. The Parable of the Vineyard Laborers primarily addresses distributive justice, yet it raises questions about procedural and attributive justice concerning the owner's choice to pay all workers the same wage. While some may argue that this decision undermines fairness, it is important to note that it adheres to the agreed-upon terms and that the payment process is transparent. Questions may arise regarding the owner's decision to pay all workers the same wage. Some may argue that this decision violates fairness even though it aligns with the agreed terms and the payment process is transparent.

Laborers, often lacking bargaining power, traditionally expect to be compensated based on their hours worked. According to societal norms, the landowner should pay workers proportionally for their time on the job. However, he prioritizes distributive justice by ensuring all workers receive fair compensation based on their daily needs. This raises the question: Did he compromise attributive or procedural justice?

The answers to these questions depend on the reader's perspective. Some scholars view the landowner as exploitative, arguing that attributive and procedural justice are undermined because he did not pay according to the established working hours. Conversely, if we perceive the landowner as a figure who genuinely prioritizes the essential needs of all laborers, his choice to bypass established procedures may reflect a profound moral conviction. This willingness to challenge the status quo to ensure the well-being of laborers demonstrates an ethical stance that deserves recognition and respect.

In the Parable of the Father and Two Sons, the younger son receives fair treatment during the process because the primary focus is on providing him with an opportunity for repentance, restoration, and reconciliation. The emphasis is not on punishment or the expulsion of the immature son but rather on extending mercy and compassion. While procedural justice typically involves administering rewards and punishments based on behavior, this parable offers an alternative view that prioritizes restoration, with mercy playing a significant role.

In the Parable of the Unjust Steward, the manager's actions raise questions about justice, fairness, and cunning. This parable challenges conventional notions of procedural justice in a society that often emphasizes patron-client relationships, where rewards and punishments are based on perceived fairness. Although the manager violates traditional concepts of justice, he also takes risks to advocate for those who are powerless. The complexities of this parable make interpretation challenging, raising the question: fairness for what or whom?

While the aforementioned parables incorporate certain aspects of procedural justice, more direct connections can be found in the parables of the Seed Growing Secretly and the Wheat and the Weeds due to their focus on process. In the Parable of the Seed Growing Secretly, the emphasis is on the seed and the sower's observation of its growth. The sower patiently awaits the harvest without attempting to control the growth process; instead, he trusts in the natural process of growth and maturation. In the Parable of the Wheat and the Weeds, wheat and weeds grow together, illustrating that simply removing "bad" people from society is not a viable solution. This parable conveys that procedural justice requires patience, and it highlights the belief that no one can be judged too harshly, as every individual has the potential to improve if provided with the right support and care.

The Parable of the Seed Growing Secretly

Mk 4:26-29

26 He also said, "*The reign of God* is as if someone would scatter seed on the ground 27 and would sleep and rise night and day, and the seed would sprout

and grow, he does not know how. 28 The earth produces of itself first the stalk, then the head, then the full grain in the head. 29 But when the grain is ripe, at once he goes in with his sickle because the harvest has come."

Interpreting the Parable

The Parable of the Seed Growing Secretly is unique to the Gospel of Mark, while a similar story known as the Sower appears in all three Synoptic Gospels. This parable likely represents an original form of Jesus's teachings, employing vivid agricultural metaphors to illustrate the reign of God. In this context, the reign of God is compared to a sower, whose actions reveal the principles and attitudes necessary for those who embrace it.

While the main theme of this parable centers on the reign of God with the sower's actions, its focus differs significantly from that of the Sower parable. In the Parable of the Seed Growing Secretly, the sower's actions are straightforward and revolve around two primary tasks: planting and harvesting. During the time between these actions, however, the sower does little but observe the process of seed growth. Seeds fall on the ground (*gē*), symbolizing a common ground for all seeds.

In the parable of the Sower, the sower engages in numerous tasks, from sowing to harvesting. In contrast, the role of the sower in the Parable of the Seed Growing Secretly appears simpler. He scatters seeds on the ground and then returns home to rest, recognizing that while he can influence some elements, others are beyond his control. Although sowing can be tedious and challenging, it is only one aspect of a farmer's work. Despite the simplicity of the sower's actions, he must still commit to diligent effort. Furthermore, much of farming lies beyond the sower's influence. Historically, farmers have relied on the heavens to ensure their crops flourish, necessitating a mindset of trust and patience, along with prayers for a bountiful harvest.

The sower relies on various external conditions, such as weather, sunlight, water, and soil quality. The fact that the sower holds the seeds in their hand is intriguing, as they did not create them. These high-quality seeds are provided by God through nature. The sower plants the seeds in the ground (*gē*), symbolizing any parcel of land. All ground is a gift from God, suitable for growing seeds. This concept of the universality of the ground reflects Jesus's teaching of God's impartial love for all. Mark emphasizes the significance of the ground; the place where the seed falls is described as the ground, as seen in the parable of the

Mustard Seed (Mk 4:30-32). In contrast, Matthew and Luke refer to it as a "field" (*agros*, Mt. 13:31-32) and "garden" (*kēpos*, Lk. 13:18-19), respectively.

The growth process of seeds remains a mystery, and the sower does not fully understand how they develop. The sower cannot interfere with the natural progression of seed growth; instead, the results gradually become clearer over time. Until the harvest, the sower must be patient and allow nature to take its course. The earth produces growth, yielding "first the stalk, then the head, then the full grain in the head" (Mk 4:28). This growth results not solely from the seeds but from the collaboration between the seeds and the soil.

Seeds do not transform into a harvest overnight. Just as seasonal changes occur and the sun rises and sets, development occurs gradually. If humans are part of nature, they, too, must undergo a process. The focus is not on a rigid, hierarchical system like an empire, but rather on a natural procedure that respects individual potential and patiently awaits eventual achievements, whatever they may be.

Once harvest season arrives, the sower must act quickly and decisively. Additionally, harvest time is an opportunity for the sower to experience joy and humility, as it represents the fruits of his labor and the grace of God. Although his efforts may seem limited, he has done his best by scattering quality seeds across the ground, monitoring their growth, and hoping for a bountiful harvest.

Engaging Procedural Justice

In the Parable of the Seed Growing Secretly, procedural justice entails several important considerations. First and foremost, the sower understands his role and limitations. He is aware of what he can do and what he cannot do, embodying humility as he respects the natural order.

Laozi's insights are particularly relevant in this context. He posits that wisdom and enlightenment begin with recognizing one's limitations, stating, "Seeing smallness is enlightenment" (見小曰明, jiàn xiǎo yuē míng).[1] This acknowledgment aligns with the concept of "keeping weakness/softness," as he expresses, "Keeping weakness/flexibility is strength" (守柔曰強, shǒu róu yuē qiáng).[2] Together, these ideas emphasize that humanity must embrace its smallness, humility, and flexibility toward others and the world.

Laozi further elaborates, "Knowing oneself is enlightenment," suggesting that understanding one's weaknesses is a form of wisdom. He also highlights the importance of humility in the pursuit of knowledge: "Knowing not to know is the best. While not knowing, knowing is a disease" (知不知上, 不知知病, zhī bù zhī shǎng, bù zhī zhī bìng).³

The ideal sower we aspire to emulate is someone who recognizes their limitations and carries out their duties with gratitude. This person honors the potential of others and trusts the growth process. We can draw valuable lessons from the sower's example, particularly the virtues of humility and perseverance he demonstrates while nurturing the seeds. Although he may not understand how growth occurs, he appreciates the natural progression that unfolds over time and places his trust in both the power of nature and the effectiveness of the process.

While the sower's responsibility is to do his best in planting seeds, effective sowing often depends on favorable external conditions, such as high-quality seeds, fertile soil, and a suitable climate. However, real-life conditions can be inconsistent, with variations in seed quality, soil fertility, and unpredictable natural events. Without these essential environmental factors, a bountiful harvest becomes unlikely. The parable assumes a typical environment with premium seeds, fertile ground, and ideal weather. When these critical conditions are absent, it leads to struggles and poverty that must be addressed through community support or societal assistance.

We must also consider the significance of "fair processes," which require adequate time for individuals to grow and develop. Just as seeds need time to mature, individuals also need sufficient time to flourish. The duration required for growth can vary based on individual circumstances. For example, those recovering from illness need ample time to heal before resuming their professional responsibilities.

For processes to be fair, individuals must be permitted to progress through their natural growth cycles without interference. This requires trust in their potential and an understanding of their capacity for independent growth and development. In this context, individual freedom is essential for people to reach their full potential. Libertarian principles emphasize the need for a free environment that respects and supports the entire growth process, enabling individuals to cultivate their unique gifts and talents.

However, it is important to recognize that starting conditions are not always equal. As egalitarianism points out, leveling the playing field is crucial to ensure that everyone begins from similar circumstances.

In summary, the Parable of the Seed Growing Secretly offers valuable insights into trust, patience, humility, and the commitment to upholding procedural justice. By appreciating the gradual and often unseen development of fair processes, this parable encourages a focus on the integrity of actions rather than immediate outcomes. Ultimately, this fosters a more resilient and trusting community in the pursuit of justice.

Contemporary Implications

We will examine two contemporary issues: measuring student progress and addressing the educational culture for children. First, evaluating student performance raises concerns about fairness and procedural justice. While the curriculum is uniform for all students, similar to the seeds in the parable, educators must work diligently to clarify course material and enhance understanding, much like the sower in the story. The curriculum itself could be carefully designed to include high-quality content and context. Following this, educators need to consider effective delivery methods that engage students and accommodate diverse learning styles and instructional approaches.

In many seminary classes, the majority of students are middle-aged or older adults, bringing with them a wealth of diverse experiences and varied educational backgrounds. In contrast, undergraduate campuses typically feature younger students who exhibit different learning styles and ways of expressing their understanding. Given this diversity, it is crucial to employ a range of methods for delivering course content. These methods may include lectures, group discussions, guest speakers, student-led activities, and presentations. Additionally, course readings should be thoughtfully selected to include challenging texts and accessible materials, such as videos and magazines. The goal is not to overwhelm students with information but to inspire them to reimagine everything they encounter, including their self-concept.

Fairness is often understood as establishing a single deadline for all students. However, given that students have varying abilities, a uniform deadline may not be the best approach. We could consider offering flexible deadlines for those who need extra time. While some students may struggle with writing, they often demonstrate a strong understanding of course content through their participation. To accommodate this diversity, we can incorporate alternative evaluation methods, such as learning journals or oral exams.

The other issue is about educational culture, which is shaped by the interplay of children's experiences and parental guidance. Parental pressure to conform to specific career or academic paths can stifle children's potential to discover their unique talents and abilities, leading to inequities. The education system often disappoints by prioritizing standardized outcomes and recognizing only those who meet societal expectations.

In a culture that emphasizes individualism and neoliberalism, there is often pressure to choose lucrative fields that promise high salaries, fame, and other benefits. Society tends to favor specific skills and expertise, and many parents advocate for particular professions for their children. Wealthier parents may support their children's pursuits by enrolling them in extracurricular activities or hiring private tutors to ensure academic excellence. This focus often narrows children's aspirations to merely achieving wealth or fame. In a highly competitive environment, those who do not conform to preferred fields of study or professional paths may feel marginalized, resulting in a lack of recognition for the diversity of individual talents and potential.

What is truly required of children and students is not how much they know or how wealthy or famous they might become, but rather how meaningful a life they can lead and how to prepare for that. Individuals need faith in their capabilities and encouragement to cultivate self-confidence. Developing a strong sense of community identity and promoting a culture of simple well-being is crucial. By allowing children to establish roots in society, we can observe their growth over time, much like a farmer waiting for seeds to germinate. Patience is vital, as rushing the development process can stifle creativity and undermine self-assurance.

The Parable of the Wheat and Weeds

Mt. 13:24-30

24 He put before them another parable: "The kingdom of heaven may be compared to someone who sowed good seed in his field, 25 but while everybody was asleep an enemy came and sowed weeds among the wheat and then went away. 26 So when the plants came up and bore grain, then the weeds appeared as well. 27 And the slaves of the householder came and said to him, 'Master, did you not sow good seed in your field? Where, then, did these weeds come from?' 28 He answered, 'An enemy has done this.' The slaves said to him, 'Then do you want us to go and gather them?' 29 But he replied, 'No, for in gathering the weeds you would uproot the wheat along with them. 30 Let both of them grow

together until the harvest, and at harvest time I will tell the reapers, Collect the weeds first and bind them in bundles to be burned, but gather the wheat into my barn.'"

Interpreting the Parable

The Parable of the Wheat and Weeds, found only in the Gospel of Matthew, focuses on the coexistence of wheat and weeds growing together in a field. Through this story, Jesus uses various metaphors to encourage his audience to rethink the nature of God's reign, highlighting the wheat, the weeds, the enemy, and the eventual harvest that will separate them.

In contrast to the more optimistic parables of the Sower and the Seed Growing Secretly—where planting good seeds leads to positive outcomes—the Parable of the Wheat and Weeds depicts a more complex reality.[4] In this parable, the sower plants good seeds but discovers both wheat and weeds flourishing together. When his slaves inform him about the weeds, the sower explains that an enemy has sown them. He instructs his slaves not to uproot the weeds until the harvest, to prevent damage to the wheat. Ultimately, a separation between the wheat and the weeds will occur after the harvest. Until then, both will continue to grow side by side.

In this parable, Jesus likens the reign of God to the sower's attitude, which reflects his worldview, work ethic, and perspective on the harvest. The sower recognizes that the world contains both good and bad seeds. The good seeds are believed to come from God, while the weeds, representing bad seeds, are attributed to non-God sources, symbolized by "an enemy." In the main story of the parable, without delving into the extended explanation in verses 13:36-43, the enemy's specific identity is not mentioned, as identifying the source of the weeds is not the main focus.[5] Typically, weeds would be removed from wheat immediately, but the sower refrains from doing so to avoid harming the wheat. He acknowledges the complexities of reality and allows both good and bad to coexist until the harvest.

This philosophy is reflected in Jesus's ministry as portrayed in the Gospel stories. He dines with sinners and tax collectors, actively listening to and advocating for them. In doing so, he blurs the lines that separate "good" from "bad" people. This parable embodies his belief that both good and bad individuals can coexist and are equally offered opportunities for transformation, as God's grace is available to everyone.

From this perspective, the sower's work ethic is characterized by patience and a belief in the possibility of transformation. Sowing good seeds reflects his diligence in the face of harsh realities in his field. He has faith in the potential of the good seeds and the soil, regardless of the prevalence of weeds. He allows the weeds to grow alongside the wheat without removing them prematurely, even though trained workers could easily identify and remove them later. This mixed situation illustrates the tensions between good and bad people, implying that individuals must navigate difficulties within their communities.[6] This aligns with Jesus's teaching that his disciples should love their enemies, no matter how challenging that may be (Mt. 5:43-44). He also cautions that people should examine their faults before pointing out the shortcomings of others (Mt. 7:3).

The delay in removing the weeds signifies that separation occurs only at harvest time. Until then, enemies or wrongdoers should not be deprived of their place or identity; they should be given time and opportunities for change.

In summary, the parable in Mt. 13:24-30 does not focus on the origin of the weeds, as that is not the main issue; the existence of a mixed world is an unavoidable reality. The emphasis is on how both good and evil people can coexist with the potential for ultimate transformation.[7] Until the harvest, neither group is judged or condemned, as time is available for everyone.

Engaging Procedural Justice

There are several aspects of procedural justice we can explore in this parable. The sower demonstrates patience, choosing not to judge or remove the weeds. This reflects an acceptance of the complex realities in a field where wheat and weeds grow together. Such acceptance suggests that we should avoid a binary classification of people into two categories: "good" and "bad," as individuals can shift from one to the other.

In this context, everyone has their weed-like traits and faults. Given this reality, what would be the best approach? One option is to improve the conditions for those who resemble weeds by providing them with time and opportunities to change. For instance, if they are nurtured in a supportive environment through proper care and educational programs, they may transform. Conversely, those who see themselves as good (the wheat) should also engage in self-reflection, practicing grace and humility.

Laozi's wisdom is particularly relevant when reflecting on the concepts of disgrace and honor. He advises us to view both disgrace and honor as unexpected gifts, urging us to appreciate trouble and suffering as we would our bodies. This perspective encourages humility and gratitude. When things go well, we should remember to express our thanks; when they do not, we can learn valuable lessons from our failures.

Laozi points out that "both disgrace and honor can be surprisingly precious moments" (寵辱若驚, chǒng rǔ ruò jīng) because we can gain insight from both experiences, which deepens our connection with the world.[8] Similarly, Jesus teaches that disgrace and honor should not be seen as separate; both are significant moments that help us to see the world fully. The Dao De Jing (Chapter 28) reinforces this idea: "Know the glorious and keep lowly" (知其榮, 守其辱, zhī qí róng, shǒu qí rǔ). This teaching emphasizes that we cannot separate moments of disgrace from honor, as both contribute to our completeness as individuals.

Libertarianism argues against the teachings of this parable because it maintains that "problem makers" must be removed from the community to protect individual freedom and growth. From this perspective, true freedom requires the elimination of anything or anyone that interferes with one's life, envisioning an ideal world where like-minded individuals coexist. Similarly, utilitarianism also disagrees with the parable's teachings, advocating for the establishment of safe spaces that avoid engagement with perceived problem-makers in society.

In contrast, the sower's goal is to achieve a bountiful harvest, nurturing both wheat and weeds as they grow together in his field. This perspective, which focuses on the overall process aimed at the harvest, is significant for understanding procedural justice. It serves as a reminder that we may sometimes become overly focused on the events occurring along the way, losing sight of the ultimate goal of community or society: embracing the overall welfare and happiness of all individuals.

To realize this goal, the sower is careful not to remove weeds too early. Common agricultural practices often advocate for the immediate removal of weeds, which can be effective if well-trained workers can easily identify them. However, the sower chooses not to adhere to societal norms for various reasons. One reason is that completely uprooting weeds can damage the wheat. Additionally, removing weeds might disrupt the ecosystem; the presence of weeds can strengthen the wheat through the natural struggle for resources.

Ultimately, this illustrates that the reign of God operates differently from societal norms, where early removal of weeds is customary. The approach taken by the sower emphasizes a deeper understanding of patience and natural growth processes.

In the end, the sower's plan to separate the wheat from the weeds at harvest time emphasizes the importance of accountability in a fair process, which should occur at the appropriate time and under the right conditions. It is crucial to acknowledge that there is an endpoint to this process, allowing people and society to learn and progress from their experiences. A good harvest then becomes a time for celebration and a reinvigoration of our responsibilities to achieve even better results in the future.

Contemporary Implications

When considering school discipline for students' misbehavior or misconduct, it is important to approach the topic with care, as each case can vary significantly. A critical question arises regarding how to manage "difficult" students who are perceived as dangerous and noncompliant with school policies. Should these students be viewed as "weeds" to be removed or expelled from the school? Are disciplinary measures the most effective approach for them? What actions would be considered appropriate?

Alternatively, can we find ways to integrate these students into the classroom while implementing some disciplinary or restorative actions? If a student poses a threat to others, it may be necessary to separate them temporarily from their peers, but this should only follow steps taken to ensure everyone's safety. However, the objective should not be their mere removal; rather, we should assess their situations and explore ways to support their improvement in collaboration with relevant resources both inside and outside the school.

In certain situations, when a student is disruptive during class or group discussions, the instructor can intervene by engaging with that student to understand their circumstances. If the disruption is minor, a sincere and brief conversation can help the student improve his or her behavior, as he/she may respond positively to the instructor's care and attention. Often, disruptions are a cry for attention. When addressed appropriately, this approach not only benefits the individual student but also imparts valuable lessons to their peers.

This dynamic is akin to the concept of wheat and weeds growing together in a classroom. While all students can embody the qualities of "wheat," they also have the potential to exhibit "weed-like" behavior at times. Both aspects coexist within each student. By providing proper care and resources to those considered "difficult," we can facilitate their transformation. The existence of such students serves as a reminder to others about human vulnerability and the importance of love and solidarity, as everyone has weaknesses and can encounter challenging situations.

Considering the serious issue of school shootings, how can we prevent these tragedies before they occur? What steps or decisions are necessary for effective prevention? Potential shooters are often among the student population and can sometimes be difficult to identify.

In response to the school shooting that occurred in Georgia in September 2024, the Republican vice-presidential nominee addressed a journalist's question about preventing such tragic events. The nominee emphasized the need for schools to implement strong security measures but did not advocate for changes to gun laws. Instead, there was a proposal to increase funding for schools to enhance their security. In the interview, it was stated: "I don't like that this is a fact of life. But if you are a psycho and you want to make headlines, you realize that our schools are soft targets. And we have got to bolster security at our schools. We've got to bolster security so if a psycho wants to walk through the front door and kill a bunch of children, they're not able."

In contrast, the Democratic presidential nominee offered a different response. While also highlighting the importance of improving school security, this nominee asserted that stronger gun control measures are essential. The approach is more comprehensive, as the gun control suggestions aim to limit access to firearms. However, these proposals alone are not enough, as potential shooters often go unmonitored and lack adequate education and resources, both within the school curriculum and in external support systems.

To effectively prevent school shootings, we must seek fundamental solutions within educational programs and curricula supported by public resources. In summary, no single measure is sufficient; we must implement multiple strategies that encompass a range of relevant approaches. Ultimately, our core mission should be to educate, not to remove students. Achieving this goal requires fair decision-making processes that are extensive, inclusive, and thorough, involving all stakeholders: schools, families, social agencies, and community programs.

Conclusion

In this chapter, we explored procedural justice through two parables: the Seed Growing Secretly and the Wheat and Weeds. The first parable reveals aspects of

God's reign not mentioned in the Sower parable, specifically highlighting the limitations of human efforts and the sufficiency of God's grace. While humans must work diligently, they cannot control the divine mystery of life, including the power and workings of nature. This teaches us that human efforts should be accompanied by humility.

Similarly, the implications for procedural justice emphasize the importance of patience and time in human growth and development, as well as in any societal endeavor. Every individual has the potential to achieve great things and requires time to mature and ultimately reap the rewards of their efforts. Until they reach that point, it is essential to provide them with sufficient time and support to accomplish their goals.

The Parable of the Wheat and Weeds addresses different aspects of God's reign not covered in other seed parables. It highlights the reality of a mixed world where good and bad people coexist. The sower's decision to delay removing the weeds until the harvest is significant within the context of God's reign, reflecting God's impartial love toward all people, regardless of their goodness or wrongdoing. Until the end, no one can be certain of their fate, as individuals can change; good people may turn bad, and vice versa. Nothing is final until the end. Therefore, the message is not to worry about the future but rather to focus on what each person can do now to transform themselves according to God's will. Everyone is given equal opportunities and time for change until the end. While there will ultimately be judgment or accountability for their actions, we must consider whether individuals are afforded enough mercy and time to change.

Questions for Discussion

1. What do the good seeds represent in the Parable of the Seed Growing Secretly?
2. This parable presumes a good harvest at the end; however, desirable outcomes do not always materialize in the real world. Why does this happen?
3. In what ways does the sower in the Wheat and Weeds parable differ from those in the other seed parables?
4. Can we see a form of transformation in the coexistence of wheat and weeds?

Notes

1. Dao De Jing 52. This is my translation.
2. Dao De Jing 52. This is my translation.
3. Dao De Jing 71. This is my translation.
4. William Doty, "An Interpretation: Parable of the Weeds and Wheat," *Interpretation* 25, no. 2 (1971): 185–93.
5. Mt. 13:36-43 offers an allegorical interpretation of the parable, unlike Jesus's usual storytelling style. Matthew explains the parable's elements: the sower as the Son of Man, the field as the world, the good seed as the kingdom's children, the weeds as the evil one's children, the enemy as the devil, the harvest as the end times, and the reapers as angels. This simplifies the parable's deeper meaning, focusing on soteriology and Christology.
6. Neuroscience and psychotherapy suggest anxiety and uncertainty can be positive motivators, fostering creativity and resilience. Similarly, political theology sees the existence of enemies as a catalyst for community strength. See Slavoj Zizek, "Neighbors and Other Monsters: A Plea for Ethical Violence," in *The Neighbor: Three Inquiries in Political Theology*, ed. Slavoj Zizek, Eric L. Santner, and Kenneth Reinhard (Chicago, IL: The University of Chicago Press, 2005), 134–90. See also Arash Javanbakht, *Afraid: Understanding the Purpose of Fear and Harnessing the Power of Anxiety* (Lanham, MD: Rowman & Littlefield, 2023). See also Maggie Jackson, *Uncertain: The Wisdom and Wonder of Being Unsure* (Lanham, MD: Prometheus Books, 2023). In Jackson's book, Teju Cole is quoted as saying: "It is dangerous to live in a secure world" (107).
7. Yung Suk Kim, "Reading Mercy in the Parables of Jesus," 18–21. See also Robert McIver, "The Parable of the Weeds among the Wheat (Matt 13:24-30, 36-43) and the Relationship between the Kingdom and the Church as Portrayed in the Gospel of Matthew," *Journal of Biblical Literature* 114, no. 4 (1995): 643–59.
8. Yung Suk Kim, Dao De Jing 13, accessed March 18, 2025. https://drkimys.blogspot.com/p/dao-de-jing_22.html. Laozi also says, "Love wins all battles and is the strongest defense of all" (Dao De Jing 67).

6

Social Justice and Parables

Social justice aims to achieve equality and create a secure environment where individuals can live free from fears associated with poverty, racism, sexism, classism, elitism, extremist nationalism, religious extremism, xenophobia, and any other form of prejudice. While economic justice is concerned with the fair distribution of resources, social justice encompasses a broader concept, addressing various issues of justice within society. This includes themes of distributive and procedural justice, focusing on the unequal distribution of wealth or income and the unfair treatment of people. The prophet Amos powerfully addresses the affluent, stating, "Therefore because you trample on the poor and take from them levies of grain, you have built houses of hewn stone, but you shall not live in them; you have planted pleasant vineyards, but you shall not drink their wine.... you who afflict the righteous, who take a bribe, and push aside the needy in the gate" (Amos 5:11-12).

We will examine two parables related to social justice: the Pharisee and the Tax Collector (Lk. 18:9-14) and the Leaven (Mt. 13:33; Lk. 13:20-21). It is important to note that these are not the only parables addressing social justice; in fact, most of Jesus's parables touch on aspects of social justice in one way or another.

In the Parable of the Pharisee and the Tax Collector, the Pharisee is self-satisfied and dismissive of the tax collector, highlighting the issue of neglecting the less fortunate. Although the tax collector is described as a sinner, he can change his ways and become a better person. To promote social justice, people must cultivate humility and solidarity with others. Moreover, there is a need for a new vision of community where all individuals can thrive together and learn from one another.

In the parable of Leaven, a small amount of leaven plays a crucial role in breadmaking. Leaven is often viewed negatively as a symbol of corruption or decay; however, Jesus uses it in this parable to emphasize its positive function in breadmaking. This suggests that, although the leaven is typically considered insignificant or a source of trouble, it has a powerful and unavoidable impact on society. Everyone is small before God, yet each person holds potential. The parable reminds us not to overlook anyone, particularly the weak or marginalized, based on societal norms. The poor should not be viewed solely as examples of failure; instead, they deserve care and support to realize their full potential. Much like leaven that can work wonders when given the right environment, people can achieve great things with appropriate opportunities. A healthy society should embrace the diversity of people, cultures, and abilities.

The Parable of the Pharisee and the Tax Collector

Lk. 18:9-14

9 He also told this parable to some who trusted in themselves that they were righteous and regarded others with contempt: 10 "Two men went up to the temple to pray, one a Pharisee and the other a tax collector. 11 The Pharisee, standing by himself, was praying thus, 'God, I thank you that I am not like other people: thieves, rogues, adulterers, or even like this tax collector. 12 I fast twice a week; I give a tenth of all my income.' 13 But the tax collector, standing far off, would not even lift up his eyes to heaven but was beating his breast and saying, 'God, be merciful to me, a sinner!' 14 I tell you, this man went down to his home justified rather than the other, for all who exalt themselves will be humbled, but all who humble themselves will be exalted."

Interpreting the Parable

The origin of the parable is uncertain, but it reflects the characteristics typical of Jesus's parables: a succinct style that often subverts common understandings. In the parable, there is a brief story contrasting two men—one regarded as "good" and the other as "bad." Jesus juxtaposes the well-known figures of a Pharisee and a tax collector to challenge societal definitions of a good or righteous person. It is important to note that he does not generalize about all Pharisees and tax collectors; instead, he focuses on a particular Pharisee and his attitude toward the tax collector, as well as a specific tax collector who exhibits certain behaviors.

In what ways does the Pharisee fail to embody the principles of the reign of God? In what ways does he succeed? It is important to note that the tax collector is not without wrongdoing. While confession is valuable, a one-time acknowledgment does not absolve him of all his offenses. Therefore, our interpretation must take all these factors into account.

Luke employs the parable within the context of his mission to the Gentiles, wherein Judaism—particularly the Pharisees—is portrayed as inferior to the Christian Gospel championed by Jesus. Although the portrayal of the Pharisees in Luke is complex, their overall depiction is negative; they are shown to be resistant to God's compassion toward sinners and tax collectors. In this parable, Luke aims to highlight the self-righteousness shown by the Pharisee, contrasting him with the tax collector, who, despite being sinful, demonstrates genuine repentance (cf. v. 9 and 14b), which is a Lukan emphasis. Verse 9 serves as Luke's introduction to the parable, while verse 14b provides its conclusion.

We will focus our interpretation on the parable itself, specifically verses 10–14a, as our primary interest lies in Jesus's teaching. This parable features two individuals of differing social statuses who enter the Temple to pray: a Pharisee and a tax collector. Pharisees are known for their exemplary lives and are often regarded as models of good religious behavior. Jesus does not intend to label them as hypocrites; their general observance is recognized as valid and commendable. Therefore, Jesus's choice to include the Pharisee in this parable is both unexpected and shocking. Equally surprising is the tax collector's presence in the Temple to pray, which is unusual for someone in his profession.

In Jesus's time, the Temple served as a place of restoration, pilgrimage, worship, and inspiration. It was intended to embody equity, providing a space accessible to all, ensuring that everyone has equal access to these sacred spaces. In this context, the term "Temple" is not portrayed negatively. While it is customary for Pharisees to pray there, tax collectors typically avoid entering. Initially, the Pharisee's prayer seems exemplary, reflecting a dedicated religious life. His sincerity appears genuine, with no obvious hypocrisy. The tone of the prayer is admirable, devoid of apparent shortcomings. In stark contrast, the tax collector's prayer expresses remorse and a yearning for transformation, humbly seeking divine mercy to overcome his sinful past.

The Pharisee's attitude toward those unlike him raises important questions, as he states, "God, I thank you that I am not like other people: thieves, rogues, adulterers, or even like this tax collector." While gratitude is warranted and necessary, he could do more than express thanks; he could show empathy toward those he deems unrighteous. Instead of indulging in self-satisfaction, he could ponder: "Why are there so many thieves, rogues, adulterers, or tax collectors? How can I make a positive impact?" His self-complacency reveals a lack of engagement with these people.

After giving thanks, he boasts about his acts of fasting and tithing, believing these actions demonstrate the grounds for God's love. While fasting and charitable works are inherently beneficial, their value is diminished when they are not combined with genuine empathy and love. Does his self-satisfaction arise merely from that fact that he is not among the unfortunate? Where is his capacity for compassion toward those who rely on divine mercy? Despite being assured of God's favor, he fails to acknowledge the needs of others who require that same compassion.

Fasting and almsgiving are meant to foster self-awareness and humility while also demonstrating God's love for others rather than self-aggrandizement. The Pharisee's prayer, centered on self-comparison, starkly contrasts with sincere prayer, which seeks divine guidance and mercy. Even the most righteous individuals recognize their imperfections and seek God's illumination to cultivate an attitude of compassionate engagement rather than comparison toward those facing hardship.

The Pharisee's emphasis on "I"—"I thank you, . . . I am not like other people, . . . I fast twice a week; I give a tenth of all my income"—mirrors the self-centeredness of the Rich Fool (Lk. 12:13-21). While the use of "I" can signify healthy agency, thanks to divine aid, its comparative usage is problematic. The "I" language needs to shift into "we" language—the language of a community seeking the redemption of God.

In contrast, the tax collector's desperation drives him to seek God's mercy, illustrating the crucial first step of acknowledging one's deficiency or wrongdoing. Despite the temple being outside his daily routine, he chooses to enter and petition for God's compassion. Acknowledging his inadequacy to stand alongside the Pharisee, he keeps his distance, refraining from lifting his eyes to heaven as he beats his breast. He then offers a brief, heartfelt prayer, distinct from the Pharisee's verbose supplication: "God, be merciful to me, a sinner!" This sincere expression of remorse secures his place before God.

According to Jesus, "This man went down to his home justified rather than the other" (14a), indicating that justification here denotes a righteous relationship with God, similar to Gen. 15:6, where Abraham's trust is continually regarded as righteous, rather than as a singular legal verdict. However, the tax collector's brief prayer or confession alone does not ensure eternal vindication; he must also demonstrate his commitment to justice as he appreciates the mercy of God.

As the parable is open-ended, readers are invited to imagine possible endings. One viable option is a new life for the tax collector, signifying a departure from his previous profession. To illustrate his transformation, he should follow Zacchaeus' example, as seen in Lk. 19:8, by donating half of his possessions to the poor and providing fourfold restitution for any fraudulent actions. Jesus affirms this transformation in Lk. 19:9: "Today salvation has come to this house because he too is a son of Abraham." Salvation demands immediate action and fosters healthy relationships. When the tax collector shifts his focus and behavior toward God's will, his renewed identity and life will become evident to others.

Engaging Social Justice

At the root of social injustices lie judgment and discrimination against others. While the Pharisee regularly fasts and actively participates in charity by giving alms—actions that may seem exemplary—he harbors a sense of superiority over others, such as the tax collector. Healthy self-esteem is important, but the issue arises in how it is expressed and the context in which it exists. In this parable, the problem is not Pharisee's pride, but rather his uncaring and condescending attitude toward others. He assumes that God is solely on his side, distinguishing himself from those he deems "bad." His complacency prevents him from feeling any connection with them, and in a sense, he becomes hardened by his self-centeredness.

Laozi's philosophy provides valuable insights into the issue of the Pharisee in this parable. He addresses self-complacency and a hardened heart by stating, "When born, people are tender and supple. At death, they are stiff and hard. All things are tender and supple while alive. At death, they wither and dry up. Therefore, the stiff and hard are companions of death, while the tender and supple are companions of life."[1] Here, Laozi emphasizes flexibility and compassion toward others and the world. One must recognize their own vulnerability and acknowledge the needs of others. For Laozi, a core virtue to cultivate is the ability to be flexible and humble, much like water and dust. Water represents flexibility, while dust symbolizes humility. The enlightened view themselves as soft, weak, and small.[2] Strong individuals conquer themselves through flexibility, demonstrating empathy and standing in solidarity with others.

In a slightly different context, Confucius emphasizes the qualities of a noble person, stating, "The wise find joy in water and the humane find joy in mountains. The wise are active, and the humane are calm" (知者樂水, 仁者樂山, 知者動,

仁者靜, zhī zhě lè shuǐ, rén zhě lè shān, zhī zhě dòng, rén zhě jìng).[3] Here, Confucius uses water as a metaphor for change, dynamism, force, and flexibility. Just as water is never stagnant, wisdom (知, zhī) must be adaptable to ever-changing circumstances, embracing change rather than clinging too tightly to knowledge or traditions.

In contrast, humane individuals are likened to mountains, representing a big heart and a compassionate mindset toward others, synonymous with love (仁, rén). This virtue of love must be steady and unchanging, like mountains. Those who embody this love recognize and respond to the needs of those around them. Confucius's message is not about choosing between wisdom (知, zhī) and love (仁, rén); rather, both are essential. To be wise, one must embody the qualities of water, and to be humane or benevolent, one must exemplify the qualities of mountains.

The insights of the two classical philosophers illuminate the Pharisee's problem: he maintains a fixed mindset rooted in his customs and knowledge. This mindset is evident in his belief that God shows favoritism toward him and does not care for those outside the Torah. His self-centeredness and complacency hinder him from connecting with others, such as the tax collector, who are perceived as being outside of God's mercy and grace. Society deems them unworthy of God's love because of their wrongdoing.

From a utilitarian perspective, the presence of rogues and thieves is viewed as a threat that must be controlled for the benefit of the majority, often seen as incapable of transformation. Similarly, from a libertarian perspective, they are regarded as responsible for their fate and thus unworthy of mercy or the possibility of transformation.

For a society to achieve social justice, we must cultivate humility. This virtue is essential because it enables us to recognize our own biases and privileges. As Maggie Jackson observes, "Where does prejudice begin? With a glance. The instant we cast our eyes on someone, we almost immediately sort them into 'people like us' or not. From that cognitive fork in the road, all else follows."[4] In this sense, we can echo Teju Cole's assertion: "It is dangerous to live in a secure world."[5] Because we are prone to slide into "opposition and bigotry," we must confront our complacency and the frames of thought and culture we hold.[6]

We need to be vigilant, as Jackson notes: "Prejudice begins with a glance but flourishes behind the walls that we build to silence and distance one another."[7] We should also be careful to avoid "in-group bias" toward others.[8] Thus, it is important to question ourselves "as much as we ask others";[9] only then can we build "heights of understanding beyond facile assumptions."[10] By doing so, we can "look past a label and open up to the mystery of those we dismiss, seeing the other as worthy of investigation and beginning an encounter tempered by a willingness to remain open to all views."[11]

The humility of the tax collector is evident in his actions and words: "But the tax collector, standing far off, would not even lift his eyes to heaven, but was beating his breast and saying, 'God, be merciful to me, a sinner!'" (Lk. 18:13). His prayer is brief and direct, asking for God's mercy, which is available to all. These few words convey a truth we all need to hear. This sentiment is echoed in Laozi's saying: "The wise are not erudite. True words are not beautiful. Beautiful words are not truthful."[12]

To create a livable and loving society, we must speak the truth of God's mercy and tolerance to one another. We need to recognize our human frailty and our dependence on divine mercy. It is equally important that we extend mercy to one another, as this call for mercy underscores the significance of solidarity.

In summary, the parable encourages listeners to look beyond social labels and prejudices, suggesting that one's social status or perceived righteousness does not define moral worth. This perspective advocates for an inclusive view of society where justice is not based on social privilege or status. Social justice efforts should be approached with a sense of shared humanity rather than from a position of moral superiority. This viewpoint urges us to examine biases that may stigmatize certain groups, preventing them from being fully included and respected in society.

Contemporary Implications

Social justice encompasses a wide range of issues in our society today and globally. On one hand, there are various forms of discrimination, including racism, sexism, classism, and xenophobia. On the other hand, individuals often encounter inequalities and discrimination in their daily lives. Part of the problem stems from the tendency of some people to compare themselves to others, defining their identity in militaristic terms. By belittling others, they attempt to assert their superiority, which often leads supremacist groups to target minority populations. For example, following the presidential election in 2024, anonymous text messages were sent to some Black individuals, including college students, instructing them to report to a nearby plantation, implying they were slaves who must pick cotton.[13]

The pursuit of social justice requires addressing gender equality, particularly in terms of pay gaps, access to leadership, and gender-based violence. Gender inequality impacts women, LGBTQ+ individuals, and gender-nonconforming persons, who often face bias and inadequate legal protection. Fostering gender justice involves implementing policies and societal reforms that ensure equal opportunities and protection against gender-based violence and discrimination.

Economic inequality is another significant social justice issue, as the widening gap between the wealthy and lower socioeconomic groups raises concerns about fairness and equal access to opportunities. Advocates for social justice call for the universal provision of basic needs such as healthcare, housing, and education. However, persistent inequalities hinder social mobility and exacerbate cycles of poverty, ultimately undermining the ideal of equal opportunity for all.

Promoting workers' rights is also a crucial aspect of social justice, which includes fair wages, safe working conditions, and the right to form unions. Workers in low-wage sectors often face exploitation, limited benefits, and job insecurity. Implementing fair labor practices and wage justice has a significant impact on individuals' quality of life and economic stability, underscoring the necessity of strong labor laws and policies that protect workers' rights.

The Parable of the Leaven

Mt. 13:33

33 He told them another parable: "The kingdom of heaven is like leaven that a woman took and mixed in with three measures of flour until all of it was leavened."

Interpreting the Parable

The Parable of the Leaven is considered one of the most original forms of Jesus's teachings due to its subversive language, in which leaven is reimagined as a positive symbol for the reign of God. Typically, leaven is viewed negatively in society, representing something unholy or corrupt. However, in this parable, leaven takes on a positive role. These striking characteristics lead scholars to believe that this parable likely originated with Jesus himself.

In this context, leaven should not be viewed as a source of evil. Confusion arises because Jesus speaks of leaven negatively in the Gospel narratives. He warns against the leaven of the Pharisees, saying, "Watch out—beware of the yeast of the Pharisees and the yeast of Herod" (Mk 8:15; cf. Mt. 16:6; Lk. 12:1). Similarly, Paul refers to leaven negatively when discussing those who corrupt the community (1 Cor. 5:6-8; Gal 5:9).

Some scholars leverage the negative perception of leaven to critique the status quo. For example, Robert Funk observes that "the Kingdom comes as an inversion of what everyone assumes about the sacred."[14] This suggests that while leaven is typically regarded as a source of corruption, much like those marginalized in society, it embodies something radical; the inclusion of sinners and social outcasts is included in the reign of God. Similarly, Brandon Scott argues that both the woman and the leaven symbolize social outcasts and marginalized groups, emphasizing their acceptance within God's kingdom.[15] Furthermore, Audrey West suggests that "the presence of a 'contaminating' element fundamental to the reign of God might serve as an illustration of Jesus's welcome of the outcast."[16]

The interpretation of "leaven" can vary depending on the context.[17] In the Parable of the Leaven, the context is positive, reflecting a woman's preparations for a dinner or feast. Leaven is not inherently negative in Jewish tradition; in fact, it is used positively in the Old Testament. For much of the year, Jews enjoy leavened bread, which is delicious (Lev 7:13; 23:17; Amos 4:5). In contrast, unleavened bread is consumed only during Passover (Exod. 12:17-20). The first-century Jewish philosopher Philo also speaks of leaven positively, emphasizing its role in enhancing the flavor of bread.[18] Essentially, leaven is crucial for creating tasty bread.

The Parable of the Leaven stands out as one of Jesus's most compelling teachings because it transforms a common negative metaphor into a powerful, positive one.[19] Typically associated with corruption or decay, leaven is reimagined by Jesus to illustrate the transformative power of God's reign through the woman's actions in her breadmaking. Like the mustard seed, leaven is small and seemingly insignificant, yet it has the potential to create immense change. Importantly, leaven achieves its purpose when the woman places it in the appropriate context, highlighting her role in facilitating transformation.

The woman's act of hiding (*enkrypto*) the leaven within the flour needs further discussion. The typical translation of "mixing" does not fully capture the Greek nuance of hiding. The central idea is that what is hidden will eventually be revealed (see Mk 4:22).[20] The woman's efforts may often seem hidden rather than overtly displayed, yet they bring joy to others. Likewise, the leaven remains hidden within the flour for a time, but it interacts effectively with the flour through the woman's skilled hands.

The Parable of the Leaven illustrates the theme of transformation. The woman witnesses the remarkable change of flour into delicious bread, a process made possible by high-quality flour and leaven—gifts bestowed by God. The flour results from the diligent efforts of farmers who work tirelessly under the sun. The success of farming relies on favorable weather conditions; adequate rain and sunshine yield bountiful crops, while drought and adverse conditions can devastate harvests. Additionally, the woman observes the transformation when she takes the leaven in her hands and combines it with the flour.

This transformation is unlike any other, as it does not merely represent a change from one thing to another. Here, leaven humbly integrates with flour while performing its vital role in making bread tasty. This act of leaven mirrors the principle of a seed that must die to yield a rich harvest. John 12:24 encapsulates this beautifully: "Very truly, I tell you, unless a grain of wheat falls into the earth and dies, it remains just a single grain; but if it dies, it bears much fruit." Ultimately, the flour is transformed remarkably, becoming delicious bread through the power of the small leaven and the woman's leadership.

Engaging Social Justice

This parable offers profound insights into social justice in several ways. We need to reevaluate the seemingly insignificant amount of leaven. While often used negatively as a metaphor in society, when placed in the right context, it reveals its full transformative power.

Applying this idea to society and marginalized groups, we can assert that many marginalized individuals have the potential to contribute meaningfully to their communities and society through their unique identities and abilities. The issue, however, is that these contributions are frequently unrecognized and underdeveloped. Therefore, our task should be to acknowledge the potential of all individuals and ensure they are placed in suitable roles. This also involves appreciating the diverse gifts that each person brings to the table.

Each individual is akin to "the nameless uncarved wood" (無名之樸, wú míng zhī pǔ) in that such wood can be shaped for any purpose.[21] The real challenge lies in recognizing the full capacity of individuals; too often, we see only what we want to see. Anyone can make a positive impact on their community or society, provided their talents are recognized and utilized in the right context, with a trust in their potential to yield meaningful outcomes—much like the patient process of bread-making.

Social justice can begin with small steps, which include the transformative power of small actions, inclusive practices, and grassroots initiatives. The leaven's impact on an entire batch of flour illustrates how seemingly minor actions can yield substantial change. It suggests that small acts of justice, such as standing up for someone's rights, promoting inclusivity, or addressing bias within local communities, can lead to widespread effects. Social justice initiatives often begin with grassroots efforts, and this parable indicates that consistent, small actions by individuals or communities can contribute to broader societal transformation. As Laozi notes, "The tallest tree begins as a tiny sprout. A nine-story tower begins with one shovel of dirt. A journey of a thousand miles starts with a single step."[22]

Social justice requires inclusive spaces where all voices, especially those that are often overlooked, can contribute to transformative change. Anyone can serve as a "creative leaven" in their community, especially those who are excluded from public spaces and marginalized. They need platforms to engage with others, as including marginalized perspectives in social reform is crucial; diverse voices can enrich society.

The scope of social justice does not stop halfway; it must influence every area of life. Just as leaven permeates and transforms an entire batch of flour, it serves as a metaphor for the widespread impact of genuine justice on all aspects of society. Similarly, social justice aims for systemic transformation, addressing both overt issues and the deeply rooted structures of inequality and injustice. This comprehensive approach highlights that social justice extends beyond individual actions, striving to create a society where fairness and equity are inherent in all systems and institutions.

Contemporary Implications

The Parable of the Leaven powerfully illustrates how small actions can lead to extraordinary change—a concept that resonates deeply within the social justice movement. A prime example of this is Rosa Parks, whose courageous act of defiance remains a significant milestone. She is celebrated as a beacon of civic protest for her critical role in the Montgomery Bus Boycott, a turning point in the fight against racial segregation in the United States. In 1955, Parks refused to give up her seat to a white passenger on a Montgomery city bus. At the time, segregation laws mandated that African Americans sit at the back of the bus and relinquish their seats to white passengers when the bus was crowded. Her refusal to comply led to her arrest, sparking outrage and mobilizing the Black community in Montgomery to initiate a bus boycott that lasted for 381 days.

The Montgomery Bus Boycott was a pivotal event in the civil rights movement, garnering national attention and showcasing the power of organized, nonviolent protest. Parks's action serves as a reminder of the impact of individual courage in the fight for social justice. The boycott also helped elevate Martin Luther King Jr.'s leadership, as he organized the protest, marking the beginning of his prominence as a civil rights leader.

The Black Lives Matter (BLM) movement serves as a recent example of small beginnings evolving into a global movement.[23] The radical social and political initiative originated in the United States in 2013 to protest and address systemic racism, police brutality, and violence against Black individuals. The movement began in response to the case of the killing of Trayvon Martin, a Black teenager in Florida. Since then, the movement has inspired similar movements and protests worldwide, tackling issues of police violence, racism, and inequality in countries such as the United Kingdom, Canada, and Australia. Its influence has also spurred broader discussions about systemic racism and prompted changes in policies, corporate practices, and awareness campaigns.

Conclusion

While social justice encompasses a broad range of social issues, we have primarily addressed prejudices and discrimination against marginalized groups, emphasizing the importance of empathy and solidarity and the potential for social transformation through the diversity of people and their contributions. In the Parable of the Pharisee and the Tax Collector, the Pharisee's issue lies not in his religious or social work but in his attitude toward those less fortunate. He does not represent Judaism as a whole; he is a specific individual used to convey a message. In contrast, the tax collector does not symbolize all Gentiles; Jesus employs him in the story to emphasize the significance of humility. The tax collector does not achieve righteousness through a brief prayer; the focus is on his attitude toward God and himself.

In the Parable of the Leaven, the reign of God is compared to the leaven that a woman mixed into three measures of flour. This comparison is intriguing because both leaven and the woman are unconventional metaphors; leaven is often associated with corruption, and a woman's work is frequently underappreciated. However, in this parable, Jesus presents an unexpected narrative by likening the reign of God to both leaven and a woman. The message is clear: just as a small amount of leaven can affect an entire batch of dough, seemingly insignificant individuals can make significant contributions when they develop and utilize their gifts.

Questions for Discussion

1. What positive or negative aspects can be identified in the Pharisee's prayer? Does he come across as self-righteous?
2. Do you perceive the tax collector's prayer as an expression of repentance? How does he compare to another tax collector, Zacchaeus, who demonstrated true repentance by changing his behavior (Lk. 19:1-10)?
3. Why is the reign of God compared to leaven? Does this metaphor carry a positive or negative connotation?
4. What is the significance of a woman's work in this parable?

Notes

1 Dao De Jing 76, accessed March 19, 205. https://drkimys.blogspot.com/p/dao-de-jing_22.html.
2 See, for example: Dao De Jing 8, 33, 52, and 78. See also Yung Suk Kim, *Reading Jesus' Parables with Dao De Jing* (Eugene, OR: Resources, 2–19.
3 Analects of Confucius 6:23. This is my translation.
4 Maggie Jackson, *Uncertain*, 110.
5 Teju Cole, *Open City* (New York: Random House, 2011), 200.
6 Maggie Jackson, *Uncertain*, 121.
7 Maggie Jackson, *Uncertain*, 120.
8 Maggie Jackson, *Uncertain*, 110.
9 Maggie Jackson, *Uncertain*, 124.
10 Maggie Jackson, *Uncertain*, 124.
11 Maggie Jackson, *Uncertain*, 119.

12 See Yung Suk Kim, *Reading Jesus' Parables with Dao De Jing*, 64.
13 "Racist Texts About Slaves and 'Picking Cotton' Sent to Black People as State AGs, Colleges and Police Probe their Origins," accessed March 19, 2025. https://www.cnn.com/2024/11/07/us/racist-text-messages-post-election/index.html.
14 Robert Funk, "Beyond Criticism in Quest of Literacy: The Parable of the Leaven," *Interpretation* 25 (1971): 163.
15 Bernard Scott, *Re-Imagine the World*, 34.
16 Audrey West, "Preparing to Preach the Parables in Luke," *Currents in Theology and Mission* (2009): 411.
17 Amy-Jill Levine, *Short Stories by Jesus*, 117.
18 Philo, *Special Laws* 2.184-85.
19 Robert Funk, et al., *The Parables of Jesus*, 14–29.
20 Amy-Jill Levine, *Short Stories by Jesus*, 121.
21 Dao De Jing 37, accessed March 20, 2025. https://drkimys.blogspot.com/p/dao-de-jing_22.html.
22 Dao De Jing 64, accessed March 20, 2025. https://drkimys.blogspot.com/p/dao-de-jing_22.html.
23 "Black Lives Matter," accessed November 12, 2024. https://blacklivesmatter.com/.

Racial Justice and Parables

Systemic racism and discrimination continue to affect racial and ethnic minorities worldwide, creating significant barriers to education, employment, housing, and justice. The implications are profound, as racial inequities contribute to social stratification, limit access to resources, and foster mistrust. Efforts to promote racial justice call for anti-discrimination policies, fair policing practices, and more inclusive institutions to dismantle these long-standing barriers and create a fairer society.

In political philosophy, racial justice refers to the principles, practices, and policies required to establish a society where racial equality and fairness are realized. It examines how systemic inequalities are perpetuated and offers strategies to dismantle them through political and philosophical frameworks. This often intersects with discussions about identity, structural power, and the historical legacies of oppression.

Key questions in the pursuit of racial justice include: How can societies address the legacies of historical injustices, such as slavery and colonialism? What role should reparations play in achieving racial equity? How do policies aimed at advancing racial justice intersect with universal principles of equality? To what extent should cultural differences be recognized or accommodated in the pursuit of justice?

Core concepts in racial justice focus on addressing systemic inequality, ensuring recognition and respect, and redistributing resources within restructured transformative systems. This involves exploring how institutions—such as legal, educational, and economic systems—perpetuate racial disparities, as well as examining historical injustices like colonialism, slavery, and segregation, and their continuing effects. It is crucial to acknowledge the unique experiences and histories of marginalized racial groups and to advocate for the inclusion of diverse voices in political, cultural, and academic spaces. To implement racial justice in society, we must consider measures such as reparations, affirmative action, or wealth redistribution to effectively address both historical and current inequalities.

Different schools of thought offer various approaches to racial justice. Liberal egalitarianism emphasizes equal rights and opportunities for all, advocating for policies such as affirmative action to level the playing field. In contrast, Critical Race Theory explores how racism is embedded within laws, institutions, and social practices, calling for a critical interrogation of these systems. Other perspectives take intersectionality into account, highlighting how racial justice intersects with other forms of justice, including gender, class, and disability, thereby revealing the need for nuanced solutions to overlapping forms of oppression. Additionally, some scholars approach race issues from postcolonial perspectives, challenging Eurocentric frameworks and addressing global racial injustices that stem from colonialism.

Racial justice is intrinsically linked to other forms of justice. It is a subset of social justice, which seeks fairness across all dimensions of social life by addressing intersecting issues such as economic inequality, education, and healthcare. Racial justice also ensures equal political representation and eliminates voter suppression—key aspects of racial justice. Furthermore, racial justice must be examined at a global level, considering disparities such as the exploitation of the Global South, migration policies, and international human rights. As seen here, racial justice is deeply intertwined with other forms of justice, reflecting the interconnectedness of identity, power, and opportunity. Achieving racial justice often requires addressing multiple layers of inequity simultaneously.

In this chapter, we will analyze the parables of the Good Samaritan and the Mustard Seed, highlighting their profound relevance to themes of racial justice through the lenses of inclusion, bias challenge, and transformative action. The Samaritan, a marginalized and despised figure, emerges as the unexpected hero in Jesus's narrative, disrupting conventional notions of who can embody goodness or moral authority.[1] The Samaritan's response is characterized by active, comprehensive, and costly engagement. Consequently, the lawyer is prompted to consider not, "Who is my neighbor?" but rather, "How can I be a neighbor?" As Levine interprets, the parable serves as a Jewish story with a universal message: true neighborliness necessitates overcoming prejudices, embracing risks, and providing radical, boundary-crossing care to those in need.[2] Conversely, the parable of the Mustard Seed presents the notion of small beginnings leading to significant transformations. The mustard seed symbolizes small yet transformative initiations and aligns well with contemporary movements for racial justice.

The Parable of the Good Samaritan

Lk. 10:25-37

25 Just then a lawyer stood up to test Jesus. "Teacher," he said, "what must I do to inherit eternal life?" 26 He said to him, "What is written in the law? What do you read there?" 27 He answered, "You shall love the Lord your God with all your heart, and with all your soul, and with all your strength, and with all your mind; and your neighbor as yourself." 28 And he said to him, "You have given the right answer; do this, and you will live." 29 But wanting to justify himself, he asked Jesus, "And who is my neighbor?" 30 Jesus replied, "A man was going down from Jerusalem to Jericho, and fell into the hands of robbers, who stripped him, beat him, and went away, leaving him half dead. 31 Now by chance a priest was going down that road; and when he saw him, he passed by on the other side. 32 So likewise a Levite, when he came to the place and saw him, passed by on the other side. 33 But a Samaritan while traveling came near him; and when he saw him, he was moved with pity. 34 He went to him and bandaged his wounds, having poured oil and wine on them. Then he put him on his animal, brought him to an inn, and took care of him. 35 The next day he took out two denarii, gave them to the innkeeper, and said, 'Take care of him; and when I come back, I will repay you whatever more you spend.' 36 Which of these three, do you think, was a neighbor to the man who fell into the hands of the robbers?" 37 He said, "The one who showed him mercy." Jesus said to him, "Go and do likewise."

Interpreting the Parable

This parable is unique to Luke and is frequently interpreted allegorically.[3] In this allegorical reading of the Good Samaritan, key figures are identified as follows: the man represents Adam, Jerusalem symbolizes paradise, Jericho reflects the world, robbers signify hostile powers, the priest and Levite correspond to the Law and prophets, respectively, and the Samaritan equated with Christ. Furthermore, the inn represents the church, its manager symbolizes the head of the church, and the Samaritan's promise to return serves as a metaphor for Christ's second coming.

While the Samaritan is often associated with Jesus in allegorical interpretation, it is crucial to recognize that this narrative functions primarily as a parable that challenges conventional understandings of neighborliness.[4] It is not merely a Christological story; instead, it offers a provocative redefinition of the term "neighbor." In the parable, a lawyer poses a question to Jesus in an attempt to test him: "Who is my neighbor?" Rather than providing a direct answer, Jesus narrates the story of a Jewish man who is attacked by robbers and left half-dead. Following the parable, Jesus poses a reflective question to the lawyer: "Which of these three, do you think, was a neighbor to the man who fell into the hands of the robbers?" Ironically, the lawyer ends up proving the answer to his own initial query: "The one who showed him mercy." In response, Jesus instructs him, "Go and do likewise."

In the narrative, the initial focus is on the alarming news of a daylight robbery and the violence inflicted upon an ordinary Jew traveling to Jericho. This harrowing incident serves as a reminder that such occurrences can happen to anyone, at any time. The victim is left abandoned, barely clinging to life, rendering him powerless and in urgent need of assistance to prevent his death. His survival hinges on the intervention of others, as religious affiliation holds little significance if it does not translate into tangible acts of salvation.[5]

Religious individuals pass by the scene, one after another. A priest walks by, seemingly oblivious to the plight of the victim, followed by a Levite who behaves similarly. Neither intervenes to help, illustrating a profound failure of religious obligation and personal ethics. Impurity was not a concern for either individual, even if the victim had been lifeless, given that they were en route to Jericho, where the Temple was not located. According to Jewish tradition, however, the obligation to care for an abandoned corpse falls upon a priest. The Mishna (*Nazir* 7.1) states, "A high priest or a Nazirite may not contract uncleanness because of their dead, but they may contract uncleanness because of a neglected corpse." Furthermore, the Babylonian Talmud stipulates the responsibility for proper burial in exceptional circumstances: "As long as there are no other people to look after the burial of a corpse, the duty is incumbent on the first Jew that passes by, without exception, to perform the burial" (*Nazir* 43b).

A wealthy Samaritan traveler encountered a victim of violence and *was moved with compassion* (*esplanchnisthē*), a response that transcends religious and ideological boundaries.[6] The root verb *splanchnizomai* implies a stirring of the innermost being or inward parts (*splanchna*). Ruben Zimmerman elucidates this concept by stating, "Having pity is not a cognitive decision but a holistic feeling. . . . It is like feeling the pain of the suffering person as if it were one's own."[7]

Martin Luther King Jr. poignantly interprets this parable, noting, "And so the first question that the priest [and] the Levite asked was, 'If I stop to help this man, what will happen to me?' But then the Good Samaritan came by, and he reversed the question: 'If I do not stop to help this man, what will happen to him?'"[8] Similarly, Marshall notes, "The concept of neighborly love illustrated by the Samaritan is characterized not by a detached concern for the victim's needs but by a deep empathic engagement with his suffering and isolation. Love for God mirrors this complexity; it encompasses not just actions but also empathetic feelings and motivations."[9]

Compassion prominently appears in the Synoptic Gospels, particularly in instances where Jesus assists the crowd out of pity for them. His actions are driven not by thought or ideology but by a profound emotional response akin to a stirring of the inward parts. For example, Mk 1:41 states, "Moved with pity, Jesus stretched out his hand and touched him, and said to him, 'I do choose. Be made clean!'" (see also: Mk 6:34; 8:2; Lk. 7:13; 10:33; Mt. 9:36; 14:14; 15:32).

Similarly, in the parable of the Unmerciful Slave, the master exhibits the same verb in expressing compassion toward the slave he forgives (Mt. 18:27). In the Parable of the Father and Two Sons, the father is *filled with compassion* (*esplanchnisthē*) upon seeing his younger son return home. He then "ran and put his arms around him and kissed him" (Lk. 15:20).

In the parable of the Good Samaritan, the Samaritan's deep compassion compelled him to stop and assist the victim without regard for the man's identity—be it Jew or Samaritan. He focused on tending the injured man's wounds, bandaging them and applying oil and wine. Subsequently, he placed the victim on his animal and took him to an inn, where he remained to care for him overnight. When departing the inn, the Samaritan paid the innkeeper two denarii and instructed him to continue looking after the man, stating, "Take care of him; and when I come back, I will repay you whatever more you spend."

It is significant to note that restoration is not achieved through a single act or moment; rather, it is a lengthy process that involves ongoing care and a commitment to responsibility. The Samaritan's compassionate response evokes "emotion, imagination, and motivation" in the readers, highlighting the depth of his engagement with the victim's plight.[10]

The recognition of a long-term restoration process serves as a poignant reminder for society to take deliberate steps in rehabilitating individuals across various contexts. This involves carefully assessing situations and implementing gradual, step-by-step actions. After initially providing emergency care by bandaging the wounds and applying oil, the Samaritan alters his journey to ensure the victim is transported to an inn. He remains there until the following day, covering the expenses and promising to pay additional costs if they arise. Through the Samaritan's actions, we gain insight into the true meaning of being deeply invested in the restoration process, which demands significant financial resources, time, and emotional commitment.[11]

As noted earlier, the central theme of Jesus's story is the restoration following tragedy. In such a dire circumstance, the lawyer's question about the identity of his neighbor becomes a rather trivial concern. After hearing the parable, he understands that the true neighbor is the one who shows compassion toward the victim. However, this realization is not enough; Jesus asks, "Go and do likewise."

This directive echoes the teachings of Rabbi Hillel, a contemporary of Jesus, who succinctly summarizes the Torah with the phrase: "What is hateful to you, do not do to others." All actions are to be evaluated through the lens of neighborly love. A neighbor must be an active agent of assistance, not merely a passive recipient of charity. Being a neighbor extends beyond needing help; it involves actively reaching out to those in need. The Samaritan is identified not by his racial or cultural background but by his compassionate actions.[12]

Engaging Racial Justice

In the story, Jesus answers a lawyer's question, "Who is my neighbor?" by telling the parable of a Samaritan who tends a wounded Jewish man. This act subverts the prevailing animosity between Jews and Samaritans and challenges assumptions rooted in race and social division. Through this narrative, we gain valuable insights regarding our moral obligations toward all individuals, especially those marginalized or labeled as "other" by society.

The Samaritan does not categorize the victim by ethnicity or social status; instead, he is driven by genuine wisdom and authentic love. Confucius emphasizes that true wisdom must adapt to changing circumstances, akin to the flow of water, as he notes with the phrase 知者動 (zhī zhě dòng), which means that the wise person must be flexible.[13] He notes that the most humane and wise person is humble enough to recognize their own limitations, stating:

"Shall I teach you about knowledge? What you know, you know, what you don't know, you don't know. This is knowledge" (知之爲知之, 不知爲不知, 是知也, zhī zhī wéi zhī zhī, bù zhī wéi bù zhī, shì zhī yě).[14] The Samaritan embodies this flexibility, as he transcends traditional racial and cultural boundaries in his understanding of the situation. Meanwhile, authentic love remains steadfast and calm, like mountains, as Confucius notes with the phrase 仁者靜 (rén zhě jìng), which means that the humane person is the one who is steadfast and calm.[15] Likewise, the Samaritan's compassion does not waver, regardless of the circumstances. Ultimately, his actions reflect a harmony of adaptability, like water, and unwavering love, like mountains.

Jesus reframes the concept of "neighbor" and highlights that our moral responsibilities extend to anyone in need, transcending race, class, or creed.[16] This redefinition emphasizes the imperative for society to be inclusive and to recognize the dignity and worth of all people. The parable urges us to embrace all-encompassing love, illustrating that the boundaries separating people into hostile groups can be dismantled by our shared humanity and compassion. Addressing racial injustices requires us to "cross the road" and engage, even when it is inconvenient or challenging. The true love we must embrace is not rooted in cultural codes or norms but in God's love, which transcends such boundaries and influences every aspect of life.[17]

This story has powerful implications for racial justice today, as it insists that care and justice are due to everyone, especially those facing systemic exclusion or harm. It encourages readers to acknowledge the dignity and worth of all people, challenging systems of racial discrimination and segregation. As Marshall notes, "The story of the Good Samaritan demonstrates how the boundaries that separate people into hostile groups are destabilized by two fundamental experiences: the experience of profound need and the experience of profound love."[18] Ultimately, the story reinforces the importance of all-embracing love, regardless of one's identity.

Similarly, the parable "shifts the focus from 'neighbor' as a fixed identity defined by the law to 'neighboring' as an ongoing task applicable in all interpersonal relationships. The important issue is not the definition of 'neighbor', as assumed by the lawyer, but rather the essence of 'love'. Neighbors are not merely defined by legal terms; they are revealed through acts of love, which precede any legal categorization."[19]

Marshall also notes, "The law commands such all-embracing love not by equating love to mere external actions or by suggesting it can be invoked at will, but because it views love as an intentional commitment that precedes emotion and action. However, this commitment inevitably yields both emotional and active expressions."[20] He goes on to say, "Love is integral to the law's structure. . . . . Love is, in essence, a free and voluntary response that cannot be legislated for in any detailed way."[21] In this sense, as Paul notes, "love fulfills the law" (Rom. 13:8-10; cf. Gal 5:14).

The parable of the Good Samaritan presents a vision of racial justice rooted in radical empathy, active solidarity, and a redefinition of community boundaries. It encourages us to view the pursuit of racial justice as not just a moral duty but also a shared social responsibility. Helping others enhances the overall well-being of society, emphasizing our interconnected existence and the importance of being a good neighbor.

While the moral mandate to assist those in need resonates with Kant's categorical imperative and resonates with Jesus's teaching to love our enemies (Mt. 5:44), it is also crucial for fostering a healthy society where everyone feels safe. This perspective aligns with communitarian views that assert individuals are not separate from society but rather embedded within it. This understanding engenders a collective responsibility toward one another, reinforcing our interdependence. When one person's welfare is neglected, it can create ripple effects that threaten the overall harmony and safety of the community.

This perspective sharply contrasts with the libertarian view, which posits that individuals are solely responsible for their own lives and are not obligated to help others. Such a stance can foster excessive individualism, leading one to become insensitive to the tragedies or social injustices faced by others. However, the parable of the Good Samaritan serves as a powerful reminder that true neighborly love involves recognizing and responding to the needs of others.

Ultimately, the parable invites us to reflect deeply on our role in promoting justice and compassion. It challenges us to confront our complacency and actively engage with our communities, pursuing justice not only for ourselves but for those who are marginalized or wronged. By embodying the principles illustrated in this story, we can cultivate a more inclusive and just society where the values of empathy and support extend to all individuals, regardless of their circumstances.

In conclusion, the parable of the Good Samaritan offers a timeless lesson on the essence of justice and the accompanying responsibilities. It underscores the need for a radical rethinking of how we define our obligations to one another, moving beyond mere legal definitions to embrace a broader understanding of compassion and community. As we strive for racial justice and equity, we need to remember that being a neighbor transcends boundaries and requires active participation in the pursuit of a fair and just world for everyone. Embracing this vision not only nurtures individual lives but also strengthens the foundation of our communities.

Contemporary Implications

In the parable of the Good Samaritan, the Samaritan serves as a beacon of light, transcending social, cultural, religious, and ethnic boundaries by sharing a common humanity and demonstrating deep empathy for the victim. This example must be applied to our world, where rampant racism harms many marginalized people.

Racial justice encompasses a range of issues, each with significant implications for individuals, communities, and systems. We often witness horrendous acts of racist violence, police brutality, and misconduct against Black people, such as in the case of George Floyd, illustrating that racial justice in America has a long way to go. Many societal institutions—from criminal justice to education to healthcare—have entrenched systems that disadvantage racial minorities. These systemic inequalities stem from historical and ongoing policies and practices that uphold white privilege while creating barriers for marginalized communities. Addressing these issues requires not only individual awareness but comprehensive policy changes and institutional reform.

We must recognize racism in all its forms. The underrepresentation and stereotypical portrayal of racial minorities in media and popular culture contribute to public misperceptions and perpetuate biases. The lack of diversity in leadership roles in industries like film, publishing, and advertising reinforces this issue, not to mention academia. Achieving racial justice in the media and culture involves promoting diverse voices, challenging stereotypes, and ensuring accurate, respectful representation of all racial groups.

Racism must also be viewed through the lens of intersectionality, recognizing that individuals' experiences of racism intersect with other forms of discrimination, such as gender, class, or sexual orientation. Racial justice must address these intersecting identities to understand the diverse challenges and create more inclusive and effective solutions.

Furthermore, experiencing or witnessing racial discrimination can have long-lasting psychological effects, including trauma, anxiety, and a sense of alienation. These effects can affect mental health and community well-being across generations. Addressing racial justice involves recognizing these psychological consequences and providing culturally sensitive and accessible support services, such as counseling.

The Parable of the Mustard Seed

Mk 4:30-32

30 He also said, "With what can we compare the kingdom of God, or what parable will we use for it? 31 It is like a mustard seed, which, when sown upon the ground, is the smallest of all the seeds on earth; 32 yet when it is sown it grows up and becomes the greatest of all shrubs, and puts forth large branches, so that the birds of the air can make nests in its shade."

Mt. 13:31-32

31 He put before them another parable: "The kingdom of heaven is like a mustard seed that someone took and sowed in his field; 32 it is the smallest of all the seeds, but when it has grown it is the greatest of shrubs and becomes a tree, so that the birds of the air come and make nests in its branches."

Lk. 13:18-19

18 He said therefore, "What is the kingdom of God like? And to what should I compare it? 19 It is like a mustard seed that someone took and sowed in the garden; it grew and became a tree, and the birds of the air made nests in its branches."

Interpreting the Parable

According to Markan Priority, Mark serves as a literary source for both Matthew and Luke. We can observe how Matthew and Luke utilized Mark's text in their own writings. For instance, in Mark, the seed is sown on the "ground" (*ge*), while in Matthew it is described as being sown in the "field" (*agros*), and in Luke, in the "garden" (*kepos*).[22]

In Mark, the "ground" symbolizes an indiscriminate place where the rule or reign of God spreads impartially to all. Matthew, however, modifies this concept by referring to the "field," which signifies the community (*ekklesia*) specific to Matthew, highlighting a more cultivated and defined space—"his field." The Matthean Jesus says, "I will build my church/community (*ekklesia*)." In this context, the Matthean Jesus states, "I will build my church/community (ekklesia)" (Mt. 16:18), emphasizing the collective and nurtured nature of the community.

Conversely, Luke opts for the term "garden," reflecting the urban environment of the Lukan community. This choice underscores a setting perhaps more familiar or relevant to a city-dwelling audience. Although it is not entirely clear why Luke favored the "garden," it suggests an intentional adaptation to resonate with specific community characteristics.

While Mark states that the mustard seed is "the smallest of all the seeds on earth," Matthew removes the phrase "on earth," likely because the mustard seed is not the smallest seed on earth. Furthermore, Luke omits any mention of the seed's size altogether, which may indicate that the size is not significant to the parable's message or that, similar to Matthew's reasoning, the mustard seed does not hold the title of the smallest seed on earth.

Mark describes the mustard seed becoming "the greatest of all shrubs," which presents a realistic description. In contrast, both Matthew and Luke, expanding on the mustard seed's growth, state that it becomes a tree—a hyperbolic assertion. However, as it grows, the mustard plant can resemble a tree, developing shrubs and soft branches. Ironically, while Matthew and Luke exaggerate the mustard plant's transformation into a tree, they are careful to address the seed's actual size. Their concern is not to convey a scientific truth about the mustard seed or plant, but rather to illustrate God's miraculous work in transforming a small seed into something remarkable. Similarly, the birth of Jesus is portrayed in both Matthew and Luke as a miraculous virgin birth, emphasizing the uniqueness of the Son of God.

While there are other differences among the accounts of Mark, Matthew, and Luke, the details mentioned above indicate that the Markan version serves as a source for Matthew and Luke. The essential point is not that the mustard seed becomes a tree, but rather that a small mustard seed grows into a beneficial plant commonly found in nearby villages, providing value for the people.

The parable of the Mustard Seed has been interpreted in various ways. The seed's small size growing into a tree has often been understood as a metaphor for the immense growth of the kingdom of God, universal redemption, or the expansion of the church.²³ Some interpretations emphasize "the transgressive aspect of the kingdom," viewing the mustard seed as a "despised and rejected weed" that invades the garden, challenges the empire, and disrupts the status quo.²⁴

However, this parable may primarily focus on the transformation of a small mustard seed into a plant. The emphasis is not on the idea that anyone can achieve greatness or make a significant impact, but rather on the notion of smallness as the essential starting point for all beginnings. This perspective implies that no individual should be overlooked or dismissed because of their current circumstances.

A small mustard seed symbolizes a potential or possibility that is inherent rather than created by humans. Each person is endowed with unique gifts that can grow and serve others. However, the mustard seed does not transform into a majestic cedar tree, which represents glory in the Old Testament. Instead, its growth into a shrub, rather than a towering cedar, contrasts sharply with biblical depictions of great trees that symbolize empires or divine power (e.g., Ezek 17:22-24, Dan 4:10-12).

Cedar trees are tall and thrive in deep, mountainous regions, while the mustard plant reaches only a few feet high. Nonetheless, the mustard plant is widespread near villages or small hills and serves practical purposes in everyday life. It can be used for medicinal purposes and provides shade for birds in need of rest.

Engaging Racial Justice

A small seed reflects our human nature. Our beginnings can be seen as insignificant, as no one chooses to enter the world through their own decision or efforts. Even parents do not fully understand how life begins and creates a child. Life remains an ineffable mystery, and we often feel small or inconsequential. While scientists trace our origins to the Big Bang, Christians attribute our existence to God. Regardless of the perspective, we are not indestructible; we come from dust, echoing the creation story in the Bible and the origins described by science. Ultimately, life begins with something small, whether dust or something else.

We must accept our smallness. A recurring theme in Jesus's parables is the significance of being small, as seen in the parables of the Sower, the Seed Growing

Secretly, the Wheat and Weeds, and the Mustard Seed.²⁵ First, smallness indicates that anyone can accomplish great things—not by worldly standards of fame or success but through meaningful contributions to the common good. Thus, a person's potential, no matter how small, should be cherished and developed to become "the greatest of all shrubs" with expansive branches. Second, smallness embodies an attitude of humility; we are all small from birth, and no one can claim superiority over others. Every seed, regardless of its size, possesses potential. Therefore, the appropriate attitude toward others must be humility, allowing us to recognize their potential. Third, this humility fosters mutual solidarity, grounded in the shared understanding that we are all formed from dust. When we embrace our common humanity through humility and solidarity, we become more aware of the misfortunes of others and are compelled to share their burdens.

Those who recognize their smallness and act with humility and love are truly blessed, as they nurture both self-love and love for others. They do not seek extravagant possessions or flaunt what they have; instead, they find contentment in their surroundings and the culture where useful mustard plants grow abundantly.

From the mustard seed and its plants, we learn that while we are small, we can be grateful for the many blessings that exist both within and around us. The parable highlights growth from modest beginnings, but a deeper interpretation emphasizes the mustard seed's potential for abundance and universal benefit.²⁶ Unlike a weed, the mustard plant is a natural and readily available resource, providing a curative harvest that is shared freely with all.²⁷

The parable of the mustard seed has significant implications for racial justice, emphasizing the unexpected and transformative growth of God's kingdom from humble beginnings. While it does not directly address racial issues, its themes of small origins, inclusivity, and transformation resonate strongly when considered in the context of racial justice.

Racial justice begins in a society where individuals acknowledge their humility and respect others for their inherent potential. Laozi highlights the importance of recognizing our smallness and embracing humility. In this philosophy, the highest virtue is self-knowledge; understanding one's smallness is the foundation of wisdom. As stated in Dao De Jing, "Seeing smallness is enlightenment" (見小曰明, jiàn xiǎo yuē míng).²⁸ Similarly, it observes, "Those who know others are clever. Those who know themselves are enlightened. Those who conquer others are forceful. Those who conquer themselves are strong."²⁹

The term "small" about the mustard seed does not imply that it is trivial or insignificant. Instead, it signifies that God's gifts may initially appear modest. In the realm of divine love and justice, every individual is endowed with dignity and potential. Laozi similarly emphasizes the unique power of diversity by comparing individuals to "the nameless uncarved wood" (無名之樸, wú míng zhī pǔ).[30] This metaphor highlights the idea that each person possesses distinct gifts that must be acknowledged and cherished.

Although the mustard seed is one of the tiniest seeds, its growth into a large tree symbolizes how seemingly insignificant efforts can lead to profound transformations within society. This indicates that initiatives aimed at promoting racial justice, regardless of how minor they may seem, have the potential to catalyze widespread change. Small, collective actions can create ripples throughout communities, resulting in a lasting impact.

When the mustard seed flourishes into a tree that provides shelter for birds, this imagery reflects a vision of God's kingdom that is inclusive and celebrates diversity. In the context of racial justice, it emphasizes the creation of communities where individuals of all races are welcomed and protected. This notion reaffirms that God's desire for flourishing encompasses everyone, especially those facing marginalization and exclusion.

In the agricultural landscape of the ancient Near East, mustard plants were often regarded as weeds, unwanted and invasive. However, in Jesus's parable, this "weed" transforms into a powerful symbol of the kingdom's growth, encouraging us to reconsider our perceptions of marginalized racial and ethnic groups. It invites us to acknowledge that those society often deems "insignificant" or "unwanted" can play crucial roles within God's kingdom, underscoring the importance of valuing all individuals.

Moreover, the mustard seed's resilience serves as a metaphor for the steadfastness of justice movements. The transformation from seed to tree illustrates that, despite challenges, the pursuit of justice is destined to flourish. This idea offers hope to advocates for racial justice, affirming that their efforts contribute to an unwavering journey toward equity and inclusion.

The humble origins and unexpected growth of the mustard seed highlight the potential of marginalized individuals to act as catalysts for change. By elevating those who have been overlooked, this parable encourages historically silenced voices to recognize the transformative power of their actions. Racial justice movements often arise from grassroots efforts, reinforcing the significant influence local initiatives can have on societal progress.

In summary, the parable of the mustard seed encapsulates the transformative potential of small, consistent efforts in the quest for racial justice. It emphasizes the need to foster inclusive communities and uplift those whom society may neglect. Ultimately, this parable calls for a commitment to racial justice rooted in hope, resilience, and a belief in the inherent dignity and capabilities of every individual. By reflecting on the lessons of the mustard seed, we are invited to engage in actions that promote equity and solidarity, cultivating a just society where everyone can thrive.

Contemporary Implications

In today's culture, one of the pervasive evils we confront is racism, rooted in the belief that those who are racially different are inferior. This mindset reduces others to objects of control or exclusion, ignoring their potential as equals. However, if we perceive ourselves as small as a mustard seed, we can recognize the beauty and capabilities within others, acknowledging their unique gifts from God that deserve development. By doing so, we can help others achieve their potential, though we cannot control their growth.

Conversely, Christian nationalists often read the Bible without an understanding of small beginnings or humility. Their perspective lacks self-criticism, emphasizing a sense of oneness or the melting pot theory centered on whiteness. They view the United States as a new biblical Israel, seeing themselves as God's chosen warriors to establish his kingdom, similar to the earlier European settlers who considered America a promised land.

At the heart of this ideology is American exceptionalism, which they use to build a narrative of superiority while neglecting the inclusive biblical mandate to love one's neighbor, including one's enemies. Their interpretation of scripture is rigid, framing current events, such as natural disasters and social changes, as warnings or blessings in alignment with their beliefs. They often employ apocalyptic interpretations, viewing modern occurrences as fulfillments of biblical prophecy, which can influence their foreign policy, particularly regarding Israel and the Middle East. Ultimately, Christian nationalists manipulate the Bible to serve their own interests of superiority and power, distorting the faith to align with their vision of God.

Affirmative action in college admissions is a policy adopted by certain institutions to promote diversity and provide opportunities for minority students who have historically faced systemic barriers in education.[31] This initiative aims to address past injustices and foster a more equitable environment within higher education. However, it has generated considerable debate from various philosophical perspectives, each offering distinct arguments for and against the policy.

Libertarians criticize affirmative action mainly because they champion a system that prioritizes free competition. They argue that all applicants should be assessed solely on merit and qualifications, without any preferential treatment based on race or ethnicity. According to this perspective, applying uniform criteria ensures a level playing field where only the most qualified candidates succeed.

From a utilitarian standpoint, there are concerns that affirmative action may not produce the greatest overall benefit to society. Utilitarians focus on outcomes that maximize happiness and well-being for the largest number of people. They might contend that an admissions policy based solely on academic merit would select highly qualified students capable of making significant contributions to society, ultimately enhancing overall societal well-being. In their view, an admissions process emphasizing abilities rather than demographics could lead to better outcomes for the community.

Kantian deontological ethics presents significant challenges to the framework of affirmative action. According to Kant's principle of universality, moral actions must adhere to a single universal rule applicable to all individuals, regardless of race or ethnicity. Proponents of this ethical approach argue that favoring applicants based on identity rather than merit undermines the principle of treating individuals as equal ends in themselves. They emphasize fairness and contend that justice requires a neutral admissions process that neither discriminates in favor of nor against any group.

Conversely, supporters of affirmative action assert that the policy is crucial for promoting diversity, equity, and inclusion within academic institutions. They argue that affirmative action benefits not only minority students but also enriches the educational experience for all by fostering a diverse environment where multiple perspectives can thrive. By leveling the playing field, often dominated by the majority, primarily white students, affirmative action aims to rectify historical disparities and create opportunities for those who have been marginalized.

Advocates further contend that affirmative action plays a vital role in dismantling systemic inequalities that persist in society. They believe that providing access to education for minority students helps break cycles of poverty

19 Christopher Marshall, *Compassionate Justice*, 78.
20 Christopher Marshall, *Compassionate Justice*, 74.
21 Christopher Marshall, *Compassionate Justice*, 74.
22 Yung Suk Kim, *Jesus's Truth*, 24–8.
23 Amy-Jill Levine, *Short Stories by Jesus*, 152–3.
24 Amy-Jill Levine, *Short Stories by Jesus*, 153. See also Bernard Scott, *Re-Imagine the World*, 39–40.
25 Seed parables are the basis of all other parables because they are from agriculture. See Klyne Snodgrass, *Stories with Intent: A Comprehensive Guide to the Parables of Jesus* (Grand Rapids, MI: Eerdmans, 2008), 145. See also John Heil, "Reader-Response and the Narrative Context of the Parables about Growing Seed in Mark 4:1-34," *Catholic Biblical Quarterly* 54, no. 2 (1992): 278.
26 Amy-Jill Levine, *Short Stories by Jesus*, 166.
27 Amy-Jill Levine, *Short Stories by Jesus*, 166.
28 Dao De Jing 52. This is my translation.
29 Dao De Jing 33.
30 Dao De Jing 37.
31 Michael Sandel, *Justice*, 167–83.

8

Restorative Justice and Parables

Restorative justice is an approach that prioritizes repairing the harm caused by criminal behavior through inclusive processes involving victims, offenders, and the community.[1] By placing the needs of those affected by crime at the forefront, this model moves beyond mere punishment or retribution, fostering healing, establishing accountability, and promoting reconciliation.[2]

Restorative justice contrasts with retributive (criminal) justice in several significant ways. First, while retributive justice emphasizes the broken laws and the corresponding punishment, restorative justice focuses on the harm inflicted upon individuals and relationships. Second, in many criminal justice systems, the state or government is viewed as the primary "victim," treating crimes as violations of law. Conversely, restorative justice centers on the victims, allowing them to participate actively by sharing their needs and feelings, often supported by their community.

Third, accountability in retributive justice is typically associated with punishment or incarceration. In contrast, restorative justice defines accountability as the acknowledgment of harm, taking responsibility for one's actions, and actively working to repair the damage done. This approach cultivates an environment where offenders can comprehend the impact of their actions.

Lastly, while retributive justice underscores punishment as a deterrent, often neglecting the long-term well-being of victims, offenders, and the community, restorative justice emphasizes healing and resolution. Its goal is to achieve outcomes that restore relationships, reduce recidivism, and address the root causes of criminal behavior, thus fostering a more holistic approach to justice.

Restorative justice differs significantly from compensatory justice. While restorative justice emphasizes addressing harm and rebuilding relationships through dialogue and active participation from all affected parties, compensatory justice is primarily concerned with providing compensation for loss or damage.

This compensation typically takes the form of financial or material restitution, aiming to restore the victim's situation to its pre-harm state.

Compensatory justice tends to be more straightforward and generally does not involve direct interaction between the parties. The determination of compensation can occur through legal proceedings or mutual agreements, often without fostering dialogue or reconciliation.

Restorative justice is increasingly applied in various contexts, including schools, communities, and criminal justice systems, where it serves as an alternative to conventional punitive measures. However, this does not imply that restorative justice disregards punitive or retributive justice. In some situations, it is essential to consider multiple aspects of justice simultaneously.

A poignant example of this is the tragic crowd crush that occurred in South Korea on October 29, 2022, during Halloween celebrations in the Itaewon neighborhood. This horrific event resulted in the deaths of 159 people, predominantly young adults, and left approximately 200 others injured due to the surge of the crowd. The police's failure to implement effective crowd control measures that night underscores the need for a multifaceted approach to justice.

In this case, retributive justice addresses the shortcomings in crowd surge management, while restorative justice focuses on providing support for the victims and their families. Additionally, compensatory justice involves offering financial restitution to those affected. This combination of justice approaches ensures a comprehensive response to the tragedy, addressing accountability, healing, and relief for those impacted.

Some of Jesus's parables effectively illustrate concepts of restorative justice. For instance, in the parable of the Lost Sheep, the good shepherd goes in search of the lost sheep and brings it back to the fold, emphasizing the importance of the lost sheep rather than focusing on the offenders. Similarly, the parable of the Good Samaritan centers on the Samaritan's compassionate care for the victim, leading to the latter's restoration to a state of normalcy.

While these parables underscore themes of restoration, this chapter will explore two additional parables that highlight the complexities of relationships within families and society: the Parable of the Father and Two Sons (Lk. 15:11-34) and the Parable of the Unmerciful Slave (Mt. 18:21-35).

The Parable of the Father and Two Sons tells the story of a young son who recklessly squanders his share of the family inheritance. In this narrative, the younger son serves as both an offender and a victim, damaging his father's property and ultimately losing everything he possesses. While the parable does not present a typical criminal case, it raises an important moral question: Why is the younger son not punished upon his return home? Instead of facing retribution, he is forgiven and reinstated within the family. Is the father's act of forgiveness a form of justice? The answer is yes. This act embodies the principles of restorative justice, which we will explore further in this chapter.

The Parable of the Unmerciful Slave highlights a crucial aspect of restorative justice, particularly within economic relationships in society. In this story, a slave whose substantial debt is forgiven fails to extend the same mercy to a fellow slave who owes him a much smaller sum. Rather than forgiving this minor debt, he punishes his fellow slave by imprisoning him, exacerbating the latter's suffering and resulting in irreversible consequences. In this context, restorative justice encompasses the offender, the victims, and the community. In this chapter, we will examine these aspects of restorative justice in detail.

The Parable of the Father and Two Sons

Lk. 15:11-32

11 Then Jesus said, "There was a man who had two sons. 12 The younger of them said to his father, 'Father, give me the share of the wealth that will belong to me.' So he divided his assets between them. 13 A few days later the younger son gathered all he had and traveled to a distant region, and there he squandered his wealth in dissolute living. 14 When he had spent everything, a severe famine took place throughout that region, and he began to be in need. 15 So he went and hired himself out to one of the citizens of that region, who sent him to his fields to feed the pigs. 16 He would gladly have filled his stomach with the pods that the pigs were eating, and no one gave him anything. 17 But when he came to his senses he said, 'How many of my father's hired hands have bread enough and to spare, but here I am dying of hunger! 18 I will get up and go to my father, and I will say to him, "Father, I have sinned against heaven and before you; 19 I am no longer worthy to be called your son; treat me like one of your hired hands."' 20 So he set off and went to his father. But while he was still far off, his father saw him and was filled with compassion; he ran and put his arms around him and kissed him. 21 Then the son said to him, 'Father, I have sinned against heaven and before you; I am no longer worthy to be called your son.' 22 But the father said to his slaves, 'Quickly, bring out a robe—the best one—and put

it on him; put a ring on his finger and sandals on his feet. 23 And get the fatted calf and kill it, and let us eat and celebrate, 24 for this son of mine was dead and is alive again; he was lost and is found!' And they began to celebrate. 25 "Now his elder son was in the field, and as he came and approached the house, he heard music and dancing. 26 He called one of the slaves and asked what was going on. 27 He replied, 'Your brother has come, and your father has killed the fatted calf because he has got him back safe and sound.' 28 Then he became angry and refused to go in. His father came out and began to plead with him. 29 But he answered his father, 'Listen! For all these years I have been working like a slave for you, and I have never disobeyed your command, yet you have never given me even a young goat so that I might celebrate with my friends. 30 But when this son of yours came back, who has devoured your assets with prostitutes, you killed the fatted calf for him!' 31 Then the father said to him, 'Son, you are always with me, and all that is mine is yours. 32 But we had to celebrate and rejoice, because this brother of yours was dead and has come to life; he was lost and has been found.'"

Interpreting the Parable

Traditionally, this parable has been interpreted allegorically, with the older son representing Pharisees or Jews and the younger son symbolizing sinners or Gentile Christians. However, it is rather a story about a dysfunctional family.[3] The central issue is the family's disunion due to the younger son's immature and rash actions.[4] Although the conflict between the two brothers echoes the rivalry between Jacob and Esau in Gen. 25:19-34, this parable subverts the motif of sibling preference, as the father does not favor the younger. He explicitly states he loves both the older and younger sons. The father welcomes the younger son solely because he returns home safely, reaffirming that his lost son is still his son.

Therefore, interpretations that demonize the older son or brother miss the crucial point that the father loves both of his sons. His primary concern is to restore the broken family to a state of reconciliation. Consequently, the immediate priority is to welcome his younger son back home. Within this family, all three members are important, and their shared goal should be to create a union characterized by love and justice. Thus, the primary focus is not on punishment but on fostering understanding among each other and living with mercy, justice, and peace.[5]

The cause of the family's disunion is the younger son, who was disloyal to his father and left for a distant region to spend his inherited property. In contrast, the older son remained loyal and worked diligently in the fields.[6] After spending all he had, the younger son faced hunger and desperation, leaving him no option but to return home, driven by memories of better days. He decided to go back to survive and practiced a remorseful speech for his father, though he did not consider his brother at all. His return was motivated not by genuine repentance but by a need to survive.[7] His words echo those of Pharaoh, who sought to avoid further plagues: "I have sinned against the Lord your God, and against you" (Exod. 10:16). When he met his father, he did not recite his rehearsed speech verbatim; instead, he said: "Father, I have sinned against heaven and before you; I am no longer worthy to be called your son" (Lk. 15:21), omitting, "Treat me like one of your hired hands." Regardless of what the younger son said or did, the big difference between this parable and the other two "lost" parables (the lost sheep and the lost coin) is that the younger son returned home on his own. He was not found by anyone but chose to walk home to survive.

The younger son did not realize that his father was waiting outside for him, ready to accept him unconditionally. The father welcomed him not because his son truly repented, but because he had returned home seeking survival and the possibility of restoration. What the son urgently needed was a safe home and food. The father understood that his son had made mistakes and recognized that the family required additional time to address unresolved issues. It would take time for his son to be fully restored to the family through genuine repentance and hard work. The father could have approached the situation differently, perhaps with a more disciplinary method rather than offering such an easygoing welcome. However, he chose not to do so because there is a priority in family matters.

While the younger son ruined the family union and squandered the property, the older son diligently served his father. Yet, he felt unappreciated because he had never been celebrated with a party. The father took for granted his older son's loyalty and failed to express his appreciation through grand gestures such as a big party or big praise.

The older son demanded justice for his family, believing that his younger brother not only wasted their inheritance but also neglected his responsibilities as a family member. The younger brother did not contribute to the work in the fields, and in this context, the father's intervention was necessary to discipline the immature son and prevent him from repeating his mistakes. However, there was no system in place to restrain his behavior within the family. The younger son exhibited a "laissez-faire" attitude; if he chose to live life by his own rules, he should also take responsibility for his actions. Therefore, if he returned home after squandering everything, he should have faced reprimands and consequences from both his father and brother.

The father's response, however, was different. He unconditionally welcomed his immature son and threw a welcome party in his honor. Meanwhile, he took the time to explain the situation to his older son, who was upset and refused to join the celebration. The older son's complaint echoed like a thunderstorm, ringing true in its call for justice: "Listen! For all these years I have been working like a slave for you, and I have never disobeyed your command; yet you have never given me even a young goat so that I might celebrate with my friends. But when this son of yours came back, who has devoured your property with prostitutes, you killed the fatted calf for him!" (Lk. 15:29-30).

His complaint was so valid that even the father could not deny its truth. It seemed unjust for a father to treat his sons this way, showing apparent indifference to his older son while hosting an extravagant welcome for the younger. In that moment, the father likely felt both remorse and responsibility, recognizing the accuracy of his older son's words. Consequently, he replied gently: "Son, you are always with me, and all that is mine is yours. But we had to celebrate and rejoice, because this brother of yours was dead and has come to life; he was lost and has been found" (Lk. 15:31-32).

The father explains to his older son why he gives the grand welcome party for his younger brother: his lost son has returned home alive. Indeed, nothing is more important than life itself. However, this party is not the concluding chapter of the story; all family members must work together to achieve true peace and restoration.

Since the parable is open-ended, readers are invited to engage with it, exploring the ongoing work and dialogue within the family. Each member has a role in addressing their shortcomings, and we can identify an ideal framework for achieving reconciliation. First, it is essential to recognize that a family or community is incomplete without every member. Even if one member, such as a younger sibling, is immature, they remain an integral part of the family. A family without one member is not truly whole. The goal of restorative justice is to facilitate the recovery of the lost member, allowing for healing and growth. Throughout this process of restoration, other aspects of justice can also be addressed. For instance, the younger son must learn the importance of hard work and take responsibility for his actions, which falls under attributive justice. Additionally, the older son needs to understand that his younger brother is still his sibling and should engage with him over time.

Second, love and mercy should come before justice in a family. A father's unconditional love for his immature son may appear weak or misguided in a culture that prioritizes strict rules and discipline more than kindness. Society often operates under a merciless hierarchical order, making the father's loving approach seem unusual, as he is not strict with his son. However, from the father's perspective, what his son truly needs is acceptance and love. He believes that issues of justice can be addressed over time through love.

Third, one must choose to return on his own. Regardless of the younger son's intentions, one thing is clear: there is hope in his father's home. He remembered the good memories associated with his father and his home, which inspired him to embark on his journey back, fostering a sense of hope along the way. Thus, his return holds greater significance than his other motives. Whether he truly repented is not the primary concern at this moment; that question will be addressed later when he demonstrates his good intentions through his actions with his father and brother.

Fourth, the concept of justice, or the understanding of right and wrong, will be addressed alongside the notion that all family members should engage with love. Justice can feel hollow without love. Each member has areas for growth, as no one is perfect. The father must strike a balance between love and justice when interacting with his sons. The older son needs to develop a greater sense of justice while also embracing love and patience. Meanwhile, the younger son must learn the importance of hard work and taking responsibility for his actions.

Ultimately, the family's goal is reconciliation and restoration, which requires love, justice, and patience. The father aims to rebuild a home filled with love and peace. To achieve this, all members must work diligently, listen to one another, and show mutual respect. Restorative justice involves both individuals and the family as a whole. Initially, the younger son felt lost due to his mistakes, and as a result, the older brother also experienced feelings of confusion or loss regarding his own place within the family. The absence of female members leaves the father feeling empty and lost. With two very different sons, he often feels uncertain about how to guide them, which contributes to his sense of being lost. All family members require restoration to find their way.

Engaging Restorative Justice

The Parable of the Father and Two Sons exemplifies the concept of restorative justice while emphasizing themes such as forgiveness, reconciliation, and the restoration of relationships. However, this does not imply that accountability is overlooked within the family dynamics. Instead, it underscores the importance of prioritizing how restorative justice is implemented. With this understanding, we will explore the elements of restorative justice present in the parable.

Restorative justice seeks to heal relationships rather than pursue retribution. The father's response to his younger son exemplifies this principle. Instead of offering judgment or punishment, the father defies the common expectation that fathers should be strict. He welcomes his son back without holding his past actions against him, radiating compassion (*esplanchnisthē*, 15:20). The root verb used here, *splanchnizomai*, conveys "a deep, visceral feeling of compassion or pity."[8] The noun *splanchna* refers to the inward parts. The same verb appears in the story of the Good Samaritan, where the Samaritan is moved with compassion upon seeing a victim nearly dying in a ditch (Lk. 10:30), as well as in the parable of the unmerciful slave, where the king is filled with compassion (Mt. 18:27). Together, these references illuminate the father's feelings in the parable of the Father and His Two Sons, demonstrating how his inner being is stirred by compassion for his son. The father embodies a soft, merciful heart, reminiscent of water in Laozi's philosophy: "Keeping softness is strength" (守柔曰強, shǒu róu yuē qiáng);[9] "Water is the best thing in the world" (上善若水, shàng shàn ruò shuǐ).[10]

For restorative justice to be effective, we must cultivate an environment that fosters healing and transformation rather than one of judgment or condemnation. This emphasizes the importance of community, as Confucius points out the need for harmony within that community, where individuals can aspire to a higher ideal: flourishing together while embracing diverse perspectives, lifestyles, and cultures. In pursuing this goal, it is crucial not to simply follow the crowd. As Confucius states, "The wise seek harmony but do not follow the crowd; the inferior follow the crowd but do not seek harmony" (君子和而不同,小人同而不和, jūn zǐ hé ér bù tóng, xiǎo rén tóng ér bù hé).[11]

While the father's forgiveness is unconditional, the younger son undergoes a significant moment of self-reflection and accountability. He recognizes his mistakes and decides to return home, illustrating how restorative justice helps individuals understand the consequences of their actions and promotes personal responsibility. Although his father welcomes him unconditionally, the son still has a moral obligation to fulfill upon his return. From this perspective, the father's acceptance does not absolve his son of moral responsibility for his actions. Classical liberalism reinforces the idea that ethical responsibility is a core element of individual freedom; thus, the younger son remains accountable for his choices.

The parable contrasts sharply with the older brother's reaction, which reflects a mindset rooted in retributive justice. His concerns are not entirely unfounded because the younger brother's actions have undeniably disrupted this sense of justice. From the older brother's perspective, punishment seems essential for his sibling, as he firmly believes that his brother's misdeeds merit appropriate consequences. However, his initial step should be to extend mercy to his brother, just as their father did. Ultimately, the greater goal of a family is to seek reconciliation, which requires prioritizing welcome and then engaging in a healing process that includes demonstrating proper conduct.

The older brother needs to reflect on Laozi's wisdom: "Reversion is the movement of the Way. Weakness is the function of the Way" (反者道之動, 弱者道之用, fǎn zhě dào zhī dòng, ruò zhě dào zhī yòng).[12] Reversion signifies a return to what is most important, often veering from traditional expectations. This concept aligns closely with the biblical notion of repentance—*metanoia* in Greek, meaning "a change of mind"—or *shuv* in Hebrew, which means "turning back." Weakness denotes a mindset of flexibility and compassion. Therefore, the older brother's first response should be a return to the ideal goals of family and a loving heart. As Laozi also notes, "Love wins all battles."[13]

Contemporary Implications

Restorative justice has significant implications for modern society as it emphasizes the damage and suffering experienced by victims. It recognizes the importance of their healing and involves both offenders and the broader community. A tragic example is the crowd crush that resulted in the deaths of hundreds of young people in South Korea, underscoring the necessity of restorative justice for the victims' families. This incident occurred in the Itaewon neighborhood of Seoul during Halloween festivities on October 29, 2022, revealing the government's role and responsibility in the tragedy. The aftermath left lingering social trauma and stress throughout South Korea, highlighting that healing and restoration will not happen without transparent investigations and accountability for those responsible.

The crowd crush claimed 159 lives, igniting calls for accountability and justice. The families of the victims continue to endure tremendous hardships, haunted by the loss of their loved ones and the image of victims collapsed on the streets. They are still in search of justice—an issue of life and death—while the government has yet to fully confront its failures in managing the event.

Similar calls for restorative justice are critically important in America and globally, particularly in cases of school violence, racially motivated shootings, police misconduct, domestic violence, and issues affecting incarcerated individuals. True justice cannot exist without proper care for the victims and their families.

The Parable of the Unmerciful Slave

Mt. 18:21-35

21 Then Peter came and said to him, "Lord, if my brother or sister sins against me, how often should I forgive? As many as seven times?" 22 Jesus said to him, "Not seven times, but, I tell you, seventy-seven times. 23 "For this reason the kingdom of heaven may be compared to a king who wished to settle accounts with his slaves. 24 When he began the reckoning, one who owed him ten thousand talents was brought to him, 25 and, as he could not pay, the Lord ordered him to be sold, together with his wife and children and all his possessions and payment to be made. 26 So the slave fell on his knees before him, saying, 'Have patience with me, and I will pay you everything.' 27 And out of pity for him, the Lord of that slave released him and forgave him the debt. 28 But that same slave, as he went out, came upon one of his fellow slaves who owed him a hundred denarii, and seizing him by the throat he said, 'Pay what you owe.' 29 Then his fellow slave fell down and pleaded with him, 'Have patience with me, and I will pay you.' 30 But he refused; then he went and threw him into prison until he would pay the debt. 31 When his fellow slaves saw what had happened, they were greatly distressed, and they went and reported to their Lord all that had taken place. 32 Then his Lord summoned him and said to him, 'You wicked slave! I forgave you all that debt because you pleaded with me. 33 Should you not have had mercy on your fellow slave, as I had mercy on you?' 34 And in anger his Lord handed him over to be tortured until he would pay his entire debt. 35 So my heavenly Father will also do to every one of you, if you do not forgive your brother or sister from your heart."

Interpreting the Parable

This parable is situated within the community discourse found in Chapter 18 of Matthew, which also includes the parable of the Lost Sheep. When Peter asks Jesus how many times he should forgive someone, Jesus responds by saying seventy-seven times. Following this, he shares the parable of the Unmerciful Slave. In the parable, a slave owes his king ten thousand talents—an impossibly large sum of money to repay. To put this into perspective, one talent is equivalent to 6,000 denarii. Therefore, ten thousand talents amount to 60 million denarii—roughly the wage for 164,000 years of work. We are not told why such an enormous amount of money was borrowed; it is an exaggeration to demonstrate that no one in society could feasibly handle a debt of this magnitude. For context, according to Josephus, the entire annual tax revenue for Judea to Rome was between 600 and 800 talents.[14]

The slave who owed the king ten thousand talents was brought before him, but he could not pay his debt. Perhaps he had already wasted much of his money while still having some left. As a result of his debt, his family faced the possibility of lifelong slavery. In his desperation, he pleaded for mercy. Falling to his knees before the king, he said, "Have patience with me, and I will pay you everything" (Mt. 18:26). However, he should not claim that he would pay everything, as his debt was far too large to settle in full. If he were sincere about repaying his debt, he would have offered to make installment or partial payments, possibly with an initial payment upfront. It seems he may simply be attempting to evade the ongoing consequences facing his family.

Upon hearing this, the king felt pity for him (*esplanchnisthē*). As we saw before, this verb conveys a deep emotional response like gut feelings of the inner parts (cf. Lk. 10:33; 15:20). Moved by compassion, the king decided to release him and forgive his debt. In a way, the king was somewhat naive, as he believed the slave too easily. However, the real issue lies not with the merciful king but with the slave, who later failed to forgive his fellow slave for a debt of only a hundred denarii.

The forgiven slave was happy, but he did not truly understand the meaning of forgiveness beyond a sense of complacency, thinking he had outsmarted the king. Forgiveness involves showing mercy, and he was expected to extend the same kindness to others that he received from the king. Although his own debt had put him and his family at risk of dire consequences, he failed to show the same mercy to his friend, who owed him only a hundred denarii, equivalent to three months' wages.

The man who owed a hundred denarii could not realistically claim he would repay the entire amount, as even repaying a hundred denarii would be challenging soon. He was beaten and imprisoned without hope, underscoring his complete devastation. This highlights his need for external assistance, such as more time to repay the debt or financial support. He may be a victim of oppression or economic exploitation by the elite. Ultimately, he is the one who requires mercy and restoration to recover from the hardships affecting his life and family.[15]

Engaging Restorative Justice

The Parable of the Unmerciful Slave provides a profound perspective on restorative justice, particularly regarding forgiveness, accountability, and the risks of double standards in justice. The king's initial act of forgiving the slave's tremendous debt exemplifies radical forgiveness, as he cancels the debt out of mercy. This highlights restorative justice's emphasis on repairing and transforming relationships rather than imposing penalties. However, the king ultimately resorts to punitive measures when the slave's actions demonstrate a lack of commitment to compassion and restoration of others.

In restorative justice, forgiveness is paramount, as it facilitates healing and reconciliation rather than perpetuating cycles of punishment and retribution. This principle is emphasized in the parable, which illustrates that true justice in the reign of God begins with mercy and a willingness to forgive.

The parable also highlights the importance of reciprocity in restorative justice. The forgiven slave, upon encountering someone who owes him a much smaller amount, fails to extend the same mercy he received. Within a restorative framework, accountability is shared; when forgiveness is granted, recipients are expected to reflect that grace in their interactions with others. This illustrates that true justice involves both receiving and giving grace, fostering a cycle of restorative forgiveness.

The slave's refusal to forgive his debtor, though having been forgiven himself, indicates a breakdown in communal justice. Restorative justice is rooted in a community ethic; when one member fails to uphold values like mercy and forgiveness, it undermines the integrity of the community. From a communitarian perspective, his callous actions disrupt the sense of solidarity within the community. He must recognize how small he is, like dust—a metaphor for human frailty and transience.

The imagery of dust as a symbol of human frailty is deeply rooted in the Hebrew Bible. In Gen. 2:7, we are formed from the dust of the ground, emphasizing our humble beginnings. Psalm 103:14 states, "For he knows our frame; he remembers that we are dust," while Ecclesiastes 3:20 echoes this sentiment regarding humanity's destiny: "All go to the same place; all come from dust, and to dust all return." Together, these verses underscore the themes of human frailty and the transient nature of life, illustrating that humans, made from such humble origins, are ultimately mortal. Therefore, we must embody humility. Laozi takes this concept further by using dust as a positive metaphor for humility, stating that we must "become one with dust" (同其塵, tóng qí chén)[16] and see ourselves as small (見小曰明, jiàn xiǎo yuē míng).[17]

As noted above, restorative justice requires a sustained commitment to mercy, compassion, and community well-being, extending beyond a singular act of forgiveness. It cautions against hypocrisy and emphasizes the reciprocal nature of forgiveness and accountability, demanding transformative change both personally and relationally.

In our complex society, it is essential to cultivate an attitude of forgiveness and mercy toward others, including ourselves. Though we have received immense gifts from God, akin to ten thousand talents, we have not fully utilized these gifts. Nonetheless, God forgives our debts and restores us to our community. Likewise, God extends love to those who are different from us, as they too possess valuable gifts. When others struggle or make mistakes, they require adequate time and resources to recover. If conflicts arise, we should strive to understand their perspectives and work toward resolving issues collaboratively.

Whatever it takes to achieve reconciliation, we can approach others with mercy and love, just as God has forgiven us our overwhelming debt. There is no separation between the love of God and the love of our neighbors, as emphasized in Jesus's Sermon on the Mount: "So when you are offering your gift at the altar, if you remember that your brother or sister has something against you, leave your gift there before the altar and go; first, be reconciled to your brother or sister, and then come and offer your gift" (Mt. 5:23-24).

Our lives are interconnected. Just as we are generous to ourselves, we must extend the same generosity to others, which is the essence of restorative justice. Rabbi Hillel summarizes Judaism succinctly: "What is hateful to you, do not do to others. That is the whole Torah, and the rest is commentary. Go and learn it."[18] Similarly, Jesus teaches, "In everything, do to others as you would have them do to you; for this is the law and the prophets" (Mt. 7:12).

Confucius offers a similar teaching in the Analects 15:24: "Zi Gong asked: 'Is there a single concept that we can take as a guide for the actions of our whole life?' Confucius says, 'What about reciprocity? What you don't like done to yourself, don't do to others.'"[19] Laozi's words also emphasize the importance of mutual care, especially in times of economic hardship and exploitation. He states: "After settling a massive resentment, there is always an aftermath of negative feelings. How can this be deemed worthwhile? Therefore, the wise consider the position of a debtor in a business contract and do not blame the other party. Virtuous people empathize with debtors, while those without virtue impose obligations on others. The Way of Heaven is impartial; it always aligns with the good."[20]

The insights from the Parable of the Unmerciful Slave underscore the vital importance of forgiveness and accountability in restorative justice. They remind us that true justice transcends mere retribution; it involves a committed effort to foster healing, empathy, and communal integrity. By embracing the principles of mercy and reciprocity, we can work toward a society where justice is not solely about punishment but about restoring relationships and uplifting individuals. As we navigate our interconnected lives, we can extend to others the same grace we have received, cultivating a spirit of restorative justice in our communities and beyond.

Contemporary Implications

Restorative justice actively engages communities in addressing harm, fostering collective accountability, and strengthening community bonds. When implemented in schools, workplaces, or neighborhoods, it cultivates a culture of empathy, open communication, and shared responsibility for maintaining peace. In educational settings, restorative justice offers alternatives to suspension and expulsion by focusing on constructively resolving behavioral issues rather than resorting to punitive measures. This approach has the potential to improve school climates, reduce disciplinary disparities, and ensure that students remain actively involved in their education.

Successful implementation of restorative justice in schools requires a cultural shift among educators, comprehensive training in conflict resolution, and ongoing support for all staff. This approach not only promotes a positive school environment but also addresses issues of accountability and personal growth. While some administrators or parents may initially resist these practices, viewing them as too lenient for serious behavioral challenges, it is important to recognize that restorative justice can effectively reduce misconduct and build stronger relationships within the school community.

In the context of criminal justice, restorative practices can reduce recidivism by addressing the root causes of criminal behavior while encouraging accountability and personal growth. By allowing offenders to understand the impact of their actions and actively work toward making amends, this approach fosters genuine rehabilitation and community reintegration.

For restorative justice efforts to succeed, society must shift its perception of offenders. While they are accountable for their actions, they should not be viewed as irredeemable. Offenders must have the opportunity to lead new lives after genuinely repenting, regardless of whether they are incarcerated or reintegrating into society. Strengthening prison ministry and social support networks is crucial in this context.

It is important to clarify that this approach does not mean offenders go unpunished; they remain responsible for their crimes. The key distinction is that they are given a chance to change their lives, acknowledge their mistakes, and make amends to their victims.

While restorative justice offers numerous benefits, it also faces practical challenges in implementation. Resistance to adopting restorative practices can be encountered, particularly for violent crimes. Additionally, effective reintegration requires significant support, such as social services and community acceptance, which are often lacking.

Restorative justice offers promising pathways toward a more humane and community-centered approach to justice. However, to realize its full potential, we must overcome cultural, institutional, and practical obstacles. This requires a societal commitment to addressing the underlying issues of harm, inequity, and disconnection. Many communities lack the resources, training, and infrastructure needed to support restorative programs, and there may be reluctance to take responsibility for crime prevention and resolution, especially in areas where trust in the justice system is low and community ties are weak.

In summary, restorative justice promotes a morally grounded approach that emphasizes human dignity, respect, and the potential for change. It aligns with ethical theories that prioritize relationships, community health, and the long-term well-being of society.

Conclusion

We have examined the parables of the Father and Two Sons and the Unmerciful Slave through the lens of restorative justice. In the first parable, the primary focus is on restoring the family to either its original or ideal state. The desire for restoration within a family context is often deeper than in the broader society. When the younger son decides to return home, the father welcomes him unconditionally; however, this should not be interpreted as absolving the son of moral responsibility. He must demonstrate his sincerity following the celebration by engaging in meaningful communication with both his father and older brother.

As the parable is open-ended, we are left to wonder what actions are necessary for the complete restoration of the family. The priority is not retribution but mercy. While the younger son must take responsibility for his actions and show genuine effort during the restoration process, the initial step toward healing is the act of welcoming him with compassion rather than punishment.

In the parable of the Unmerciful Slave, the central message emphasizes the importance of caring for those who are socially vulnerable and unable to repay even small debts. The slave who was forgiven an astronomical debt of 10,000 talents fails to show mercy to his fellow slave, who owes him only a modest sum of 100 denarii. This underscores that true restoration involves social responsibility. We are interconnected; we have a moral obligation to care for and extend compassion to those who are less fortunate. It is crucial to shift our perspective and recognize that our blessings, whatever they may be, are not solely ours but have been bestowed upon us. Therefore, when we encounter others in difficult situations, we must extend mercy and offer our resources to assist them.

Questions for Discussion

1. In the Parable of the Father and Two Sons, the father welcomes his younger son unconditionally. Does this suggest he is unconcerned about his son's wrongdoings?
2. Envision the restoration process following the welcome party. What steps might be necessary to achieve complete restoration?
3. Is the king naive for forgiving the slave such an enormous debt without hesitation, to the extent that the slave fails to appreciate the value of forgiveness that should be extended to others?
4. Considering the other slave's situation, where he cannot repay a small debt soon, what kind of support does he need, given his social and economic circumstances? How does the concept of restorative justice apply to him, and what role does society play in addressing this situation?

Notes

1 Howard Zehr, *The Little Book of Restorative Justice* (New York: Good Books, 2002), 21.
2 "About Restorative Justice," accessed Nov 15, 2024. https://law.wisc.edu/fjr/rjp/justice.html.
3 Yung Suk Kim, *Jesus's Truth*, 88–91.
4 Yung Suk Kim, "Reading Mercy in the Parables of Jesus," 18–21.
5 Yung Suk Kim, *Jesus's Truth*, 91–4. See also Alicia Batten, "Dishonor, Gender and the Parable of the Prodigal Son," *Toronto Journal of Theology* 13 (1997): 187–200.
6 The older son's perspective is not to be seen negatively. See Carol Schersten LaHurd, "Re-viewing Luke 15 with Arab Christian Women," in *A Feminist Companion to Luke*, ed. Amy-Jill Levine (London; New York: Sheffield Academic, 2002), 264). For the positive aspects of the older son/brother are seen in the following, as cited in Yung Suk Kim, *Jesus's Truth*, 91: Donald Juel, "The Strange Silence of the Bible," *Interpretation* 51 (1997): 5–19; Nancy Duff, "Luke 15:11-32," *Interpretation* 49 (1995): 66–9; Heikki Räisänen, "The Prodigal Gentile and His Jewish Christian Brother, Luke 15:11-32," in *The Four Gospels*, ed. F. Van Segbroeck et al. (Leuven: Leuven University Press, 1992), 1617–36; Charles Carlston, "Reminiscence and Redaction in Luke 15:11-32," *Journal of Biblical Literature* 94 (1975): 368–90. See also O'Rourke, "Some Notes on Luke 15:11-32," *NTS* 18 (1972): 431–3.
7 Amy-Jill Levine, *Short Stories by Jesus*, 53–9.
8 "Strong's Greek: 4698. σπλαγχνίζομαι," accessed March 21, 2025. https://biblehub.com/greek/4697.htm.
9 Dao De Jing 52. The translation is mine.
10 Dao De Jing 8. The translation is mine.
11 Analects of Confucius 13:23. The translation is mine.
12 Dao De Jing 40. The translation is mine.
13 Dao De Jing 67. The translation is mine.
14 Josephus, *Antiquities of the Jews* 14.78; 17.319-20.
15 Yung Suk Kim, *Jesus's Truth*, 64–7.
16 Dao De Jing 4, 56.
17 Dao De Jing 52.
18 Babylonian Talmud, *Shabbat* 31a.
19 Analects of Confucius, accessed March 21, 2025. http://www.acmuller.net/con-dao/analects.html#div-16.
20 Dao De Jing 79. The translation is mine.

9

Compensatory Justice and Parables

Compensatory justice focuses on restoring victims by compensating them for losses caused by others, typically through monetary payments or the return of property.[1] Unlike retributive and distributive justice, which have broader aims, compensatory justice is solely concerned with reparation for victims. It is distinct from restorative justice, which emphasizes healing relationships and emotional restoration; instead, compensatory justice focuses on material compensation for individual harm.

In this framework, accountability is transactional, centering on compensation rather than addressing the root causes of harm or preventing future incidents. While outcomes may provide tangible benefits, they often fall short of addressing emotional or systemic issues. In contrast, restorative justice seeks reconciliation and emotional healing through dialogue and understanding, aiming to prevent future harm. Both forms of justice can complement each other, tailored to the context, to more effectively address harm and promote justice.

It is important to note that Jesus's parables often explore various forms of justice simultaneously. For instance, the Parable of the Father and Two Sons illustrates restorative justice alongside an underlying notion of retributive justice. This parable also touches on compensatory justice due to the loss of the father's property. Similarly, the Parable of the Unmerciful Slave presents multiple aspects of justice, including restorative, retributive, and distributive justice. Lastly, the parable of the Unjust Judge and the Widow emphasizes retributive justice while potentially incorporating compensatory justice if the widow seeks to recover her property.

In this chapter, we will examine the Parable of the Unjust Steward (Lk. 16:1-13) and its reflection of compensatory justice within ancient economies characterized by inequality. The steward's actions, often interpreted as attempts to rectify his past mismanagement, create a complex scenario that invites multiple interpretations. If seen as a challenge to societal economic norms by redistributing wealth, the parable may also embody elements of distributive justice. Alternatively, if the emphasis shifts to repairing relationships and fostering reconciliation among the parties involved, it can be viewed through the lens of restorative justice.

However, this chapter will focus on compensatory justice, as it addresses critical issues in everyday economic transactions and provides a framework for understanding accountability and reparation. We will explore how the steward's actions, despite being deemed "unjust," may represent a strategic effort to balance economic and relational factors, offering insights into the complexities of justice within economic contexts.

The Parable of the Unjust Steward

Lk. 16:1-13

1 Then Jesus said to the disciples, "There was a rich man who had a manager, and charges were brought to him that this man was squandering his property. 2 So he summoned him and said to him, 'What is this that I hear about you? Give me an accounting of your management because you cannot be my manager any longer.' 3 Then the manager said to himself, 'What will I do, now that my master is taking the position away from me? I am not strong enough to dig, and I am ashamed to beg. 4 I have decided what to do so that, when I am dismissed as manager, people may welcome me into their homes.' 5 So, summoning his master's debtors one by one, he asked the first, 'How much do you owe my master?' 6 He answered, 'A hundred jugs of olive oil.' He said to him, 'Take your bill, sit down quickly, and make it fifty.' 7 Then he asked another, 'And how much do you owe?' He replied, 'A hundred containers of wheat.' He said to him, 'Take your bill and make it eighty.' 8 And his master commended the dishonest manager because he had acted shrewdly, for the children of this age are more shrewd in dealing with their own generation than are the children of light. 9 And I tell you, make friends for yourselves by means of dishonest wealth so that when it is gone, they may welcome you into the eternal homes.

10 "Whoever is faithful in a very little is faithful also in much, and whoever is dishonest in a very little is dishonest also in much. 11 If, then, you have not been faithful with the dishonest wealth, who will entrust to you the true riches? 12 And if you have not been faithful with what belongs to another, who will give

you what is your own? 13 No slave can serve two masters, for a slave will either hate the one and love the other or be devoted to the one and despise the other. You cannot serve God and wealth."

Interpreting the Parable

The Parable of the Unjust Steward is intricately complex, addressing themes of patronage, lending, and the moral dilemmas of honesty and dishonesty about wealth, as well as the choice between serving God or wealth. There are competing interpretations, primarily divided into two distinct perspectives. The first, a liberation-oriented, socially critical reading, views the steward's actions as a subversion of economic norms aimed at redistributing wealth within exploitative systems.[2] Esler places the parable in the sociopolitical context of first-century Palestine, emphasizing how the steward's actions critique the exploitative practices of wealthy landowners and suggesting a connection to notions of compensatory justice.[3]

In contrast, Herzog adopts a more critical perspective, focusing on the liberation of the oppressed within unjust economic systems.[4] He interprets the parable as a critique of systemic injustice and a model for creative resistance against oppressive structures. In his view, the steward embodies resistance, situated within the exploitative economic landscape of first-century Palestine, where wealthy landowners frequently oppressed tenant farmers and debtors. Faced with dismissal, the steward reduces the debts owed by the tenant farmers, likely by canceling interest and excessive surcharges that he had originally imposed to benefit himself or his master. This action not only secures his future but also challenges the unjust system by alleviating the burden on the debtors.

Herzog contends that Jesus's parables often employ veiled language to critique the status quo without directly challenging the ruling powers.[5] By reducing the debts, the steward not only cultivates goodwill with the debtors but also compels the master into a position of reluctant approval. If the master were to reverse the reductions, he would risk losing honor in the community. In this way, the steward deftly manipulates the honor-shame dynamics of his society to achieve a just outcome.[6]

Within this context, the steward exemplifies resourcefulness for those living under oppression. The parable encourages the oppressed to act shrewdly and courageously within unjust systems, creating opportunities for justice and survival. Ultimately, Herzog's interpretation frames the parable as a critique of economic exploitation and a call to resist through ingenuity and compassion. Though flawed, the steward emerges as a symbol of how even small, pragmatic actions can disrupt oppressive systems and foster justice.

The other distinctive interpretation emphasizes the economic and social context of the parable. It can be understood within the framework of first-century Jewish practices related to debt, reciprocity, and honor.[7] The steward's reduction of debts highlights the pervasive issue of economic exploitation in the ancient world. However, rather than viewing the steward's actions as purely altruistic or morally justifiable, we can interpret them as a pragmatic strategy to secure his own future. While the steward acts out of self-interest, his decisions also benefit others, complicating our understanding of justice and generosity. Although his motivations may be selfish, his actions inadvertently align with compensatory justice. By reducing debts, he alleviates economic inequalities and fosters goodwill among the debtors, potentially redistributing wealth in the process.

In a similar vein, Snodgrass offers a comprehensive analysis of the parable of the dishonest steward, emphasizing its complexity and its focus on wisdom, resourcefulness, and wealth within the context of discipleship.[8] He argues that the parable is not primarily concerned with morality or justice, but rather with the prudent use of resources. The steward's actions are praised not for their ethical purity, but for their shrewdness in planning for the future—a form of wisdom that Jesus highlights for his disciples. While the steward's main motive is self-preservation, his actions inadvertently benefit the debtors. Snodgrass views this as a secondary effect rather than the parable's primary focus. The debt reductions indicate a redistribution of resources but stem from pragmatic concerns rather than a conscious pursuit of justice. He interprets the master's commendation of the steward as an acknowledgment of his cleverness, not his dishonesty. This distinction is crucial for understanding the parable's message: it emphasizes the steward's resourceful use of wealth to build relationships. Snodgrass recognizes the parable's moral ambiguity, but he argues that its core lesson lies in the call to act decisively and creatively within flawed systems. While the steward's actions may not be entirely just, they exemplify the kind of resourcefulness that disciples should emulate. In summary, Snodgrass interprets the parable as a call for wisdom in resource utilization, rather than a direct critique of economic injustice. The steward's shrewdness serves as a model for Christians to approach wealth with intentionality, creativity, and a focus on eternal values.

As we see above, the parable is an enigmatic narrative that encompasses multiple layers of human experience—personal, communal, and societal—touching on various issues within an ancient, unequal society. The steward's actions can symbolize several elements, including social challenge and resistance to an exploitative system, advocacy for the oppressed, efforts to maintain his job or protect his relationships, and the pursuit of his own honor. Additionally, he represents a skillful and wise individual navigating a complex environment.

While the Parable of the Unjust Steward is often viewed as morally problematic, given that a rich man appears to commend his dishonest manager (16:8), the emphasis is less on the manager's dishonesty and more on understanding his actions in context. In the parable, the manager squanders the master's money and faces imminent dismissal. Although the specifics of his mismanagement are unclear, one possibility is that he imposed excessively high interest rates (usury) on the master's customers.[9] In this scenario, the impoverished borrowers are already struggling and are unlikely to survive under such burdensome debts. Many of these individuals may eventually go bankrupt, which means the master will not recover his property, as they cannot repay what they owe.

In this narrative, there are no winners. The borrowers suffer from high interest rates and are driven to bankruptcy, while the manager faces job loss due to his selfish usury practices. The master also loses out, as he will see his property diminish, along with his reputation.[10]

Upon realizing his impending dismissal, the manager devised a plan to reduce the debts of the borrowers, hoping to gain their goodwill once he was fired. In response, the master unexpectedly commended his manager: "And his master commended the unjust steward because he had acted shrewdly; for the children of this age are shrewder in dealing with their generation than are the children of light. And I tell you, make friends for yourselves using dishonest wealth so that when it is gone, they may welcome you into the eternal homes" (Lk. 16:8-9).

Although dishonesty is integral to his actions—having deceived his master—the crux of his wrongdoing lies in his exploitation of the poor. The master's praise stems from the fact that the manager "acted shrewdly," suggesting that he took steps to correct the excessive charges he had imposed on the borrowers.

As a result, the borrowers are relieved and better able to manage their lives, while the master will regain his property as they are now in a position to fulfill their obligations. The manager, too, secures his future. Ultimately, all parties emerge as winners. The parable's implication, seen in verses 16:10-13, is clear: one should not succumb to the temptation of possessions or wealth. The most important aspect of life is to serve God, which entails serving his people through various means.

The manager's failure in this parable stems from the destruction of customary lending practices, which leads to the suffering of the borrowers. His shrewd actions address the issue of usury, representing a form of reparations for those in debt. He demonstrates an understanding of how to wield his power and authority by reducing the borrowers' debts.

In sum, as the parable's meaning is inherently complex, simplistic moral conclusions should be avoided. It resists neat resolutions, inviting readers to engage deeply with questions of ethics, resourcefulness, and justice. The parable incorporates humor and irony, exemplified by the steward's cunning behavior and the master's surprising commendation. This playful tone encourages readers to reconsider traditional notions of morality and justice in favor of a more nuanced, context-specific understanding. Ultimately, the parable calls for practical wisdom and active engagement with complex economic realities, challenging listeners to think creatively about justice, generosity, and survival in the face of systemic oppression, all without providing easy answers.

Engaging Compensatory Justice

This parable has positive implications for compensatory justice. The steward's decision to reduce the debts of his master's debtors can be seen as a form of compensatory justice. By alleviating their financial burdens, he provides immediate economic relief to those in debt. This aligns with the principle of compensatory justice, which focuses on making reparations for past hardships or imbalances—an especially vital consideration in societies marked by significant economic disparities.

Furthermore, the steward's debt reductions imply a subtle shift in economic power, redistributing wealth by easing the burden on the debtors. Addressing inequities often requires providing relief to those disproportionately affected by the economic system. This act of redistribution quietly challenges the concentration of wealth and power, resonating with the broader goals of compensatory justice to rectify structural inequities.

The steward's clever, yet dishonest, approach to reducing debt emphasizes a crucial lesson about using resources to support one's community in times of crisis. Compensatory justice often necessitates innovative strategies to address economic inequalities and assist marginalized communities. The parable serves as a call to utilize resources wisely to create opportunities for those who lack access or power, even if the steward's actions raise ethical concerns. The master praises the steward not for his dishonesty but for his cleverness, prompting important questions about accountability and responsibility in the pursuit of justice.

In the context of compensatory justice, those in positions of power (like the master) have a responsibility to engage in fair dealings with those who are less fortunate. The master's acceptance of the steward's actions may reflect an understanding of the need for leniency or compensation for individuals burdened by debt, even though this relief was not achieved through ideal means.

There are limitations to this parable in the context of compensatory justice. While the steward's debt reductions provide temporary financial relief, they fail to address the underlying issues of the debtors' hardships or the power imbalance with the master. Compensatory justice necessitates true redress, but the parable implies that financial compensation alone cannot resolve deeper systemic inequalities. Such compensatory justice would require not only temporary economic relief but also a sustainable restructuring of the conditions that lead to economic dependence and hardship.

The steward's actions also raise ethical questions. Although his actions benefit the debtors, they are motivated by self-interest, as he manipulates the debts to secure his own future after being dismissed. This tension highlights a common challenge in compensatory justice: whether the end—relief from economic burdens—justifies the means, particularly when those means involve deception or questionable ethics. This suggests that authentic compensatory justice requires transparency and integrity in addressing inequalities.

In summary, the Parable of the Unjust Steward illustrates the complexities of compensatory justice, especially in the context of economic inequality. It emphasizes both the potential and limitations of financial relief as a means of achieving justice, along with the importance of shrewdness, accountability, and the moral ambiguities that can arise in efforts to address systemic imbalances. Ultimately, the parable advocates for a pragmatic approach to justice—one that seeks to redistribute resources and support those in need, even when the ethical path to doing so is complicated.

Contemporary Implications

In our study of the Parable of the Unjust Steward, we focused on economic life and the issues related to debt within ancient exploitative systems. We encountered a limited view of compensatory justice, primarily addressing reparations for borrowers, who are often vulnerable victims of economic exploitation. Debtors frequently feel weak and overwhelmed by the heavy burdens of debt, leading to significant emotional and psychological distress.

Expanding the concept of compensatory justice to address contemporary issues in our society will open a broader discussion focused on providing restitution, reparation, or compensation for past wrongs. This framework aims to rectify historical injustices, particularly those inflicted on marginalized groups through colonization, slavery, and discriminatory policies. Initiatives such as reparations for the descendants of enslaved individuals and restitution for Indigenous lands seek to acknowledge and address the lasting harm caused by these injustices.

In particular, compensatory justice regarding African slavery in America focuses on the historical, legal, and moral arguments for reparations. Scholars analyze the legacy of slavery, which includes economic disparities, systemic racism, and social inequities, while proposing methods to address these injustices. They examine how the institution of slavery generated immense wealth for America, all the while systematically depriving enslaved individuals of their rights, freedom, and economic opportunities. These scholars argue that reparations serve as a form of compensatory justice for centuries of unpaid labor and oppression.[11]

Determining who is entitled to compensation, what form of restitution is appropriate, and how to implement it fairly can be quite complex. There are political and social tensions surrounding these issues. Some people question whether the present generations should be held responsible for past actions, while others argue that historical injustices continue to affect descendants today. Libertarians contend they should not be held accountable for the past because they consider themselves free individuals, independent of historical circumstances.

Economic redistribution faces significant resistance, particularly from those who argue that wealth redistribution through taxation or government programs is unfair to those who have earned their wealth. Egalitarian and communitarian approaches, on the other hand, support reparations for past wrongs in various ways. While the arguments from these different perspectives may seem valid within their contexts, we must address "present" wrongs rooted in the past. Divine justice prioritizes the needs of people in today's world.

We cannot overstate the importance of compensatory justice in the context of exploitation and historical wrongdoings, as individuals cannot find peace without a substantial material foundation. Mencius's insights regarding property and the mind are particularly relevant in this context. He states 無恒産無恒心 (wú héng chǎn wú héng xīn), which translates to "If there is no property, there is no mind."[12] This highlights the profound impact that property has on the human psyche and underscores the interconnectedness between material security and moral development. For individuals to live peacefully and cultivate their virtues, they require access to basic provisions and resources.

Mencius argues that a strong foundation of material stability—consisting of land, resources, and a sufficient livelihood—is essential for fostering ethical behavior. When individuals have secure property, they are more likely to be reflective, open-minded, and capable of altruistic actions. Conversely, without this security, people often react to life's challenges with desperation and survival instincts, leading to unethical behavior and societal discord.

Moreover, Mencius suggests that material stability is not merely an individual concern but a communal one. When a society ensures that its members have met their basic needs, it promotes a sense of responsibility and care for one another, which ultimately contributes to social harmony. He posits that the well-being of individuals is intrinsically linked to the collective well-being of society; thus, when people feel secure, they are more inclined to invest in their communities, engage in virtuous deeds, and participate in the betterment of society.

In this light, Mencius emphasizes that achieving material stability is a fundamental step toward creating a just and harmonious society. By acknowledging the relationship between property ownership and the cultivation of moral character, we can better understand the role of economic justice in promoting ethical behavior and social cohesion.

Conclusion

The Parable of the Unjust Steward is complex and can be challenging to interpret due to the ambiguity surrounding the steward's actions. It invites readers to look beyond his perceived dishonesty and examine his interactions with the debtors. While his initial actions may be questionable, he ultimately engages in reparative measures that benefit those who owe money. This focus on restitution highlights an essential aspect of justice: acknowledging harm done and the need to address it.

The steward's actions can be seen as a strategic response to his precarious situation. Faced with the impending loss of his position, he chose to build relationships with the debtors by reducing their debts, alleviating their burdens while ensuring his own relevance and utility. The master's commendation of the steward stems not from an endorsement of dishonesty, but from recognition of the "tactful" measures he employed. This response reflects a nuanced understanding of the situation, emphasizing that sometimes unconventional actions in the pursuit of justice can yield beneficial outcomes for multiple parties.

Furthermore, the parable illustrates a unique social dynamic where everyone stands to gain: debtors receive relief, the steward preserves his job, and the master avoids scandal. This scenario raises essential questions about the nature of justice and the motivations behind ethical behavior. Is it enough for actions to produce positive outcomes, or must they also stem from pure intentions? The parable encourages reflection on the multifaceted nature of morality and how varied motivations can converge to create favorable results.

This exploration of reparation resonates deeply with contemporary discussions surrounding social justice. As we navigate modern issues of inequality and injustice, the parable serves as a timely reminder of the importance of making amends for those who suffer. Whether addressing economic disparity, racial injustice, or environmental degradation, the idea of repairing harm inflicted upon victims remains critical. Just as the steward took steps to mitigate the harm faced by his debtors, we too must seek ways to address grievances caused by systemic injustices in our societies.

In conclusion, while the Parable of the Unjust Steward invites diverse interpretations, its central message underscores the importance of reparations and the interconnectedness of our actions. By focusing on making amends for victims, we can foster a culture of accountability and empathy, paving the way for more equitable outcomes for all. This perspective encourages us to consider how we can implement measures that acknowledge and rectify past harms, ultimately contributing to a more just and harmonious society.

Questions for Discussion

1. What is the primary motive behind the steward's decision to reduce debt? Are his actions aimed at social change or resistance, or are they primarily a survival strategy?

2. Is the end more important than the means in this context? Specifically, is the reduction of debt or making reparations for debtors more significant, even if the steward's motivations are selfish?
3. Why does the master commend his manager's actions?
4. What other types of justice might be relevant to this parable? Consider concepts such as procedural justice, social justice, or retributive justice.

Notes

1 Elizabeth Mullen and Tyler G. Okimoto, "Compensatory Justice," in *The Oxford Handbook of Justice in the Workplace*, ed. Russell Cropanzano and Maureen L. Ambrose (New York: Oxford University Press, 2015), 477–96. H. Khatchadourian, "Compensation and Reparation as Forms of Compensatory Justice," *Metaphilosophy* 37 (2006): 429–48.
2 Richard Hays, *The Moral Vision of the New Testament: Community, Cross, New Creation, A Contemporary Introduction to New Testament Ethics* (New York: Harper, 1996).
3 See Philip F. Esler, *Community and Gospel in Luke-Acts: The Social and Political Motivations of Lucan Theology* (New York: Cambridge University Press, 1989).
4 William Herzog, *Parables as Subversive Speech*, 79–97.
5 William Herzog, *Parables as Subversive Speech*, 79–97.
6 David Landry and Ben May, "Honor Restored: New Light on the Parable of the Prudent Steward (Luke 16:1-8a)," *Journal of Biblical Literature* 119, no. 2 (2000): 287–309.
7 Brad Young, *The Parables*, 237–44.
8 See Klyne Snodgrass, *Stories with Intent: A Comprehensive Guide to the Parables of Jesus* (Grand Rapids, MI: Eerdmans, 2008).
9 Yung Suk Kim, *Jesus's Truth*, 97–9.
10 David Landry and Ben May, "Honor Restored," 287–309.
11 Ta-Nehisi Coates, "The Case for Reparations," in *The Atlantic* (2014), accessed Nov 20, 2024. https://www.theatlantic.com/magazine/archive/2014/06/the-case-for-reparations/361631/. See also Eric Williams, *Capitalism and Slavery* (Chapel Hill, NC: The University of North Carolina, 1994).
12 This is my translation. *Mencius*, Book 1.A.7.

10

Retributive Justice and Parables

Retributive justice concentrates on the criminal justice system to prevent wrongdoing and punish offenders. It is important to distinguish this framework from revenge; retributive justice emphasizes fair punishment that is proportional to the offense committed. The primary objective is to establish a system where individuals who engage in harmful behavior face appropriate consequences, serving as both a deterrent to potential offenders and a means of promoting accountability within society.

This approach is predicated on the belief that crimes violate the social contract binding individuals to their communities. Thus, it is essential to address these violations through legal mechanisms that ensure offenders are held accountable for their actions. By doing so, the system reinforces societal norms and values, making it clear that harmful behavior will not be tolerated. Significantly, retributive justice seeks to restore order and safety, allowing victims and the community to feel that justice has been served.

Furthermore, legal justice requires that offenders face the consequences of their actions in a formal setting, such as a court of law. This process involves not only determining guilt but also establishing penalties that appropriately reflect the severity of the crime committed. Transparency in legal proceedings is crucial for maintaining public trust in the justice system, as it ensures that no one is above the law and that all individuals are held to the same standards of accountability.

It is essential to recognize that forgiveness within the framework of retributive justice does not imply absolution for wrongdoers. While victims may personally choose to forgive their offenders, this choice does not lessen the need for legal consequences. Forgiveness can be a powerful tool for the victim's healing; however, it must coexist with a commitment to justice that holds individuals accountable for their actions. In essence, forgiving does not condone offenders' behavior or exempt them from facing consequences. Instead, it complements the legal framework by enabling victims to move forward while still acknowledging the need for a just society.

Moreover, retributive justice plays a vital role in shaping the moral fabric of a community. By ensuring that offenders are punished, it conveys a clear message about the values society upholds. This understanding fosters a collective sense of security among community members, reassuring them that systems are in place to address and rectify wrongdoing. In this way, retributive justice contributes to social cohesion and order, emphasizing that justice is not solely about punishment but also about promoting a safe and respectful environment for all.

While retributive justice has its merits, it also faces criticism for potentially perpetuating cycles of violence and failing to address the root causes of criminal behavior. Critics argue that this emphasis on punishment may overlook opportunities for rehabilitation and restorative approaches that could foster deeper societal healing. Consequently, there is ongoing discourse about how to balance retributive justice with restorative practices, prompting broader discussions on achieving effective justice in a complex world. Ultimately, retributive justice remains a vital component of the overall justice system, aiming not only to punish offenders but also to reinforce societal values and protect the community as a whole.

In the parable of the Unjust Judge and the Widow, the widow pleads with the judge to vindicate her by avenging her against her adversaries (Lk. 18:3). The Greek verb she employs, "ekdikeo," expresses a strong desire for justice and the reclamation of her rights from those who have wronged her. This plea emphasizes the deep human longing for fairness and acknowledgment, as well as the expectation that justice should prevail, particularly for the vulnerable. The widow's relentless appeals to the judge not only highlight her resilience but also reveal the inherent injustices within society that demand an authoritative response.

Similarly, in the Parable of the Tenants (Mk 12:1-12), wrongdoing is evident on the part of both the tenants and the master, depending on one's interpretation of the narrative. The tenants exploit the resources entrusted to them, disregarding the landowner's rights, while the master's treatment of the tenants can also be scrutinized. This duality raises critical questions about accountability and retribution, underscoring the complexities of justice in both individual and societal contexts. Regardless of the interpretive perspective, the need to address these wrongdoings resonates strongly with the principles of retributive justice, which seeks to ensure accountability for actions that violate moral and legal standards.

However, it is important to recognize that the parables do not exist in isolation; they encompass broader themes related to various forms of justice. In addition to retributive justice, concepts such as restorative justice, social justice, and distributive justice are intricately woven into the narratives. For instance, restorative justice focuses on healing relationships and restoring balance between the parties involved. The widow's plea for vindication can be viewed as a call to restore her dignity and social standing, which may have been diminished by the injustice she has experienced.

Social justice is also a crucial theme in these parables, particularly concerning the protection of the rights of marginalized individuals like the widow. It encourages reflection on societal structures that permit exploitation and injustice while advocating for an ethical framework that prioritizes equity and fairness. In the case of the Tenants, the story prompts an examination of the larger systems that allow those in power to exploit those at the bottom of the hierarchy, urging a reevaluation of responsibilities across social classes.

Distributive justice is also relevant, especially regarding the equitable allocation of resources and opportunities. The master's expectations of the tenants and the resulting punitive measures raise questions about fairness in resource distribution and the ethical use of power. These themes compel the audience to consider that justice should not only focus on punishment but also address the underlying inequalities present in society.

While our primary focus here is on retributive justice due to its prominence and clarity in these narratives, it is essential to recognize that the interplay of various forms of justice enhances the meaning and implications of the parables. Each type of justice offers unique insights into the moral dilemmas and societal issues addressed in these stories. Furthermore, exploring these intricate layers of justice encourages a deeper understanding of the complexities involved in achieving true justice, prompting discussions that extend beyond punitive measures to include healing, equity, and social responsibility. This holistic perspective fosters a more comprehensive approach to justice, emphasizing that the pursuit of fairness and dignity often requires navigating the intersections of various justice frameworks in our efforts to create a just world.

The Parable of the Unjust Judge and Widow

Lk. 18:1-8

Then Jesus told them a parable about their need to pray always and not to lose heart. 2 He said, "In a certain city there was a judge who neither feared God nor had respect for people. 3 In that city there was a widow who kept coming to him and saying, 'Grant me justice against my opponent.' 4 For a while he refused; but later he said to himself, 'Though I have no fear of God and no respect for anyone, 5 yet because this widow keeps bothering me, I will grant her justice, so that she may not wear me out by continually coming.'" 6 And the Lord said, "Listen to what the unjust judge says. 7 And will not God grant justice to his chosen ones who cry to him day and night? Will he delay long in helping them? 8 I tell you, he will quickly grant justice to them. And yet, when the Son of Man comes, will he find faith on earth?"

Interpreting the Parable

Luke uses the parable of the Unjust Judge and the Widow to emphasize the importance of prayer. In 18:1, he conveys the parable's message: "Pray always and do not lose heart." However, the parable itself is not about prayer but about justice because the parable proper might be 18:2-5 only, with Luke's comments (18:1, 6-8).[1]

In ancient Israel, widows were among the most marginalized individuals, often lacking male advocates. The widow's persistence reflects the struggles of the powerless in their pursuit of justice. Despite her marginal status, she is portrayed as an active and determined figure confronting systemic injustice. She embodies agency and faith in divine justice. Rather than merely symbolizing persistent prayer, the widow represents active resistance, showcasing courage, resourcefulness, and determination as she refuses to accept injustice.[2]

Rather than depicting her as a helpless victim, Levine emphasizes the widow as a proactive agent in securing justice, inspiring others to take action against systemic wrongs.[3] While widows often symbolize vulnerability, they also embody moral authority. The widow's demand for justice resonates with the biblical tradition of advocating for the oppressed, specifically widows, orphans, and strangers, as highlighted in passages like Isa. 1:17 and Deut. 10:18. Levine encourages readers to move beyond simply identifying with the widow or critiquing the unjust judge's actions.[4] Instead, she challenges them to reflect on how they might mirror the unjust judge, who often resists addressing others' needs, and to consider how they can become agents of justice like the widow.[5]

Herzog aligns with Levine but focuses on systemic change in an oppressive world.[6] He interprets the widow as an agent of change, with her persistence symbolizing the ongoing struggle of the poor and marginalized against entrenched systems of oppression. The unjust judge represents the systemic corruption within the judicial system of Jesus's time, which often favored the wealthy and powerful while neglecting the needs of the poor. His admission of neither fearing God nor respecting people underscores his moral bankruptcy and the broader societal injustice. In Herzog's view, the parable emphasizes human ingenuity and courage in confronting systemic injustice rather than divine intervention.[7]

The main point of the parable is that the widow sought justice in response to issues with her opponent. Although the specifics of her case remain unknown, her determination in requesting justice is clear. The widow continually approached the judge, insisting, "Grant me justice against my opponent" (Lk. 18:6). The verb "ekdikeo," used here, means to avenge. Nothing deterred her from pursuing justice; she persisted in her appeals to the unjust judge until she was finally heard. This persistence highlights her urgent need for retributive justice. Rather than remaining passive at home, she defied societal expectations of silence and passivity among women. For her, justice is paramount; without it, she feels diminished. Justice serves as her lifeblood, compelling her to step outside her traditional role to seek it. Although the judge initially refused to listen, he ultimately granted her justice simply to rid himself of her. His decision stemmed from selfish motives, but the essential takeaway is that she did receive the retributive justice she sought.

Engaging Retributive Justice

The parable of the Unjust Judge and the Widow offers valuable insights into the nature of retributive justice. It underscores the challenges inherent in a justice system dependent on individuals in power who may lack integrity. Retributive justice, which seeks to rectify wrongs and hold offenders accountable, faces significant obstacles in the circumstances depicted in this parable, highlighting the difficulties of achieving true justice amid power imbalances and indifference. Several key implications for retributive justice emerge from this narrative.

Justice requires more than mere legal obligation; it demands moral commitment. The unjust judge is described as someone who "neither feared God nor cared about people." This lack of a moral compass is central to understanding his reluctance to assist the widow, despite his authoritative position. Retributive justice heavily relies on the integrity of those responsible for enforcing the law. Without a genuine commitment to fairness, legal authority alone may fail to deliver justice, particularly for vulnerable individuals. This scenario emphasizes the need to anchor justice in ethical principles rather than relying solely on legal mandates.

The parable illustrates how power dynamics can distort retributive justice. The judge possesses unchecked authority and initially refuses to act on the widow's behalf, demonstrating how those in power can prioritize cases based on self-interest rather than fairness. This imbalance suggests that retributive justice is vulnerable to bias, with its application being inconsistent, particularly when judges or authorities lack accountable mechanisms.

The widow's repeated pleas highlight the challenges marginalized individuals face in securing justice within the system. Those without power or influence often must exert significant effort to be heard, reflecting a systemic issue: retributive justice can be applied unevenly, with disadvantaged individuals encountering more obstacles. This underscores the necessity for accessible and equitable systems designed to prevent vulnerable individuals from having to "wear down" authorities to achieve justice.

The saying "justice delayed is justice denied" is a crucial takeaway from this parable. The judge grants justice to the widow only because of her persistence, not out of a genuine commitment to justice. In the context of retributive justice, delays can cause further harm, frustration, and a lingering feeling of futility for victims seeking redress. This parable suggests that when justice relies solely on the persistence of individuals rather than prompt action, it risks failing those who need it the most.

The dynamics presented in the parable emphasize the need for accountability and integrity within the justice system. For retributive justice to be effective and fair, those in positions of authority must be held accountable for their actions and decisions. This accountability can create a system where justice is not only enforced more uniformly but also perceived as legitimate by the community it serves.

In summary, the parable of the Unjust Judge and the Widow highlights the complexities of retributive justice and serves as a powerful reminder of its limitations when integrity and compassion are lacking. By emphasizing moral commitment, the significance of equitable power dynamics, and the persistence required by marginalized individuals, this parable calls for reforms that promote justice through transparency, accountability, and a sincere dedication to fairness. A just society must work toward ensuring that all individuals, regardless of their social standing, can access and receive timely and equitable justice.

Contemporary Implications

The concept of retributive justice is inextricably linked with restorative justice, as illustrated by the devastating maritime disaster in South Korea on April 16, 2014. A total of 304 lives were lost among the 476 passengers and crew, including approximately 250 students from Danwon High School in Ansan City, Korea. This tragedy was precipitated by systemic failures, culminating in a profound failure of justice. In response, the public clamored for retributive justice, recognizing its indispensable role in facilitating restoration. The victims' families were consumed by grief, while the captain and crew's betrayal led to the senseless loss of numerous young lives.

The sinking ferry was visible to the public for several days, courtesy of extensive media coverage. The public watched live footage from the scene, including faint images of passengers clinging to windows in hopes of being rescued. Unfortunately, all rescue efforts were in vain. The ferry eventually sank, with 99 percent of it disappearing beneath the surface. Families of the victims, as well as thousands of bystanders, assembled to await news of survivor rescues. In addition, the recovery of the victims' bodies was extremely difficult due to strong sea currents, which blocked divers' access to the submerged ferry.

Some survivors committed suicide due to stress. Some teachers who survived felt guilty for not saving their students. The ferry tragedy prompted the formation of a formal investigation team, which released a report that failed to provide satisfactory explanations for the incident. A formal apology was not extended by either the ferry company or government officials. Moreover, those involved in the government's rescue efforts were not held accountable. While the captain and some crew members faced partial charges, their sentences were deemed insufficient by the public. In response, families of the victims organized protests against the government, demanding a full and transparent investigation. To date, a clear and acceptable report has yet to be released, and survivors and families of the victims continue to seek justice.

In this context, forgiveness is an unaffordable luxury and illogical, given the absence of clear charges and a comprehensive report implicating all parties involved. Who is capable of forgiving whom? The victims have been overlooked, and without retributive justice, they cannot rest in peace. Consequently, their families remain unable to find solace. Forgiveness can only be considered after the administration of retributive justice by both the victims' families and the public. Moreover, the notion of loving one's enemies is inapplicable here, as retributive justice operates independently of personal emotions or will.

In this response, it is essential to clearly outline the specifics of the situation: namely, what transpired incorrectly, who faced charges, and the applicable sentences. Not even the families of the victims possess the authority to waive criminal charges against offenders, as retributive justice is a matter of public interest. We often discuss forgiveness and reconciliation too lightly. In the absence of appropriate retributive justice, forgiveness becomes an uninformed notion, and reconciliation remains an empty concept.

To maintain a safe society, fair systems of criminal justice are essential. This entails ensuring fair trials and proportionate sentencing. A Korean idiom, "money buys innocence, poverty invites guilt," highlights the unfair practices among prosecutors and defense lawyers. This is exemplified by wealthy CEOs receiving lenient sentences for serious crimes while impoverished individuals face harsher penalties for lesser offenses.

The Parable of the Tenants

Mk 12:1-12

12 Then he began to speak to them in parables. "A man planted a vineyard, put a fence around it, dug a pit for the winepress, and built a watchtower; then he leased it to tenants and went to another country. 2 When the season came, he sent a slave to the tenants to collect from them his share of the produce of the vineyard. 3 But they seized him, beat him, and sent him away empty-handed. 4 And again he sent another slave to them; this one they beat over the head and insulted. 5 Then he sent another, and that one they killed. And so it was with many others; some they beat, and others they killed. 6 He had still one other, a beloved son. Finally, he sent him to them, saying, 'They will respect my son.' 7 But those tenants said to one another, 'This is the heir; come, let us kill him, and the inheritance will be ours.' 8 So they seized him, killed him, and threw him out of the vineyard. 9 What then will the owner of the vineyard do? He will come and destroy the tenants and give the vineyard to others. 10 Have you not read this scripture: 'The stone that the builders rejected has become the cornerstone; 11 this was the Lord's doing, and it is amazing in our eyes'?" 12 When they realized that he had told this parable against them, they wanted to arrest him, but they feared the crowd. So they left him and went away. (NRSV)

Interpreting the Parable

The Parable of the Tenants (Mk 12:1-12; Mt. 21:33-46; Lk. 20:9-19) is a widely analyzed parable within the New Testament, with scholars offering various interpretive perspectives. A common allegorical interpretation views the parable as a reflection of the tensions between Jesus and the Jewish leadership, where the vineyard symbolizes Israel, the tenants represent the religious leaders, and the son embodies Jesus.[8] Additionally, the killing of the son is seen as a prefiguration of the crucifixion. Scholars note strong allusions to Isa. 5:1-7, which portrays Israel as an unfruitful vineyard, reinforcing the judgment of its leaders.

As a result, traditional Christian theology often interprets the parable as an illustration of God's patience and ultimate judgment. The rejected son becomes the cornerstone, signifying Jesus's resurrection and vindication, while the rejection of the tenants represents the leadership's failure, resulting in the vineyard being entrusted to a new community, commonly understood as the church.

Similarly, France interprets the parable as an allegory of Israel's history, with the tenants symbolizing the Jewish leaders and the vineyard representing God's covenantal relationship with Israel.[9] The parable depicts the tenants' violent actions as deserving of severe punishment. France highlights that the judgment imposed by the landowner foreshadows the eschatological retributive justice that God will exact upon those who reject his Son.

An alternative reading emphasizes agrarian economics in first-century Palestine, where conflicts frequently arose between absentee landowners and tenant farmers.[10] Through this lens, scholars examine themes of justice, exploitation, and resistance, perceiving the parable as resonating with the experiences of oppressed peasants. The tenants' violent actions symbolize resistance against unjust power structures, providing a critique of exploitative systems. This interpretation redirects the focus to the tenants' actions as responses to systemic injustice. These readings underscore how the parable has been used in colonial and postcolonial contexts, analyzing its implications for power and resistance.

As noted, the Parable of the Tenants is challenging to understand, not only due to its violent elements but also because it is presented allegorically. Since Jesus rarely delivers parables in this manner, one might wonder whether the parable in Mk 12:1-12 originated with him or if only part of it came from his teachings. Some scholars argue that the parable concludes at 12:9a ("What then will the owner of the vineyard do?"), while others believe it ends at 12:9b ("He will come and destroy the tenants and give the vineyard to others"). The subsequent verses (12:10-12) are seen as comments by Mark, who contextualizes the parable by referring to the tenants as Jews.

In the parable (Mk 12:1-9), a vineyard owner leases his land to tenants and leaves the country. The terms of the agreement are unspecified, but the tenants appear to work under unfavorable conditions with minimal compensation. Without organizational support like a labor union, they are powerless against a potentially exploitative owner.

In time, the owner sends servants to collect his share of the harvest (12:2). The exact portion owed is not defined, leaving the reader to infer the tenants' potential dissatisfaction. The tenants respond violently, beating the servants and sending them away empty-handed.

The situation escalates as the tenants kill subsequent messengers, including the owner's beloved son, hoping to seize the vineyard. This act is a naive provocation, as the owner still holds considerable power. The parable concludes with the storyteller's question (12:9a): "What then will the owner of the vineyard do?" The narrative allows for two possible outcomes. One possibility is that the owner will kill the tenants or warn them. Alternatively, if the story ends at 12:9b, a violent response is certain: "He will come and destroy the tenants and give the vineyard to others."

Engaging Retributive Justice

The story of the Tenants leaves us pondering various issues of justice. This parable raises important questions about fairness, retribution, and the ethical implications of the characters' actions. If there is an unfair contract between the owner and the tenants, it undermines both distributive and attributive justice. The benefits of the harvest should adequately meet the basic needs of the tenants and should not disproportionately advantage the owner beyond reasonable costs and any exceptional effort he may have contributed. Distributive justice demands equitable resource distribution, ensuring that all parties involved receive their fair share based on their contributions and needs. When attributive justice is properly applied, diligent workers can expect to be compensated slightly more than those who exert less effort, reflecting their contributions to the vineyard's success.

However, even in the presence of an unfair contract, we must question whether the tenants have the right to retaliate against the owner by harming or killing his innocent slaves and beloved son. This raises a critical distinction between revenge and retributive justice. Retributive justice is grounded in established legal principles and guided by an accepted moral framework that dictates appropriate responses to wrongdoing. It emphasizes accountability within a structured legal context, ensuring that punishment aligns with the common good and serves a constructive purpose.

What the tenants intended was not to seek justice through legitimate means but to execute a revolutionary act involving violence and extreme measures to seize the vineyard from the owner. This action raises profound ethical questions: Is such behavior ever justifiable? While the tenants may feel their grievances are warranted due to an exploitative relationship, resorting to violence complicates the moral landscape.

If the tenants have issues of injustice, they will need to defend themselves in a court of law. Failing to do so could result in facing the consequences of retributive justice, which is intended to hold individuals accountable for their unlawful actions.

Furthermore, if the owner is portrayed as an abusive and exploitative figure—an implication not explicitly stated in the story—then he must indeed face the rigors of retributive justice for failing to treat the tenants fairly. However, the application of justice must never be arbitrary. Allegations of injustice should be addressed through fair trials within a legal system that allows for thorough examination of evidence and context.

Such processes are vital for ensuring that justice is delivered appropriately and that accountability is established for all involved. The principle of retributive justice reaffirms that wrongful actions necessitate responses that hold individuals legally accountable for their misconduct.

On another note, we might consider Laozi's perspective, as he states: "If people do not fear death, how can anybody control them by the threat of death?"[11] This statement encourages a deeper understanding of the motivations behind violence and conflict. If people are starving, for example, it is often due to excessive taxation and exploitation by those in power. In Laozi's view, the root causes of conflict and resentment must be examined before simply resorting to retaliation.

Laozi suggests that the injustices faced by the tenants, which can lead to their desperate actions, are symptomatic of a larger systemic failure.[12] People tend to take life lightly when they find no value in it due to the oppressive conditions imposed by those in authority.[13] This context calls for a more compassionate approach to understanding the drivers of human behavior.

In the broader context of Jesus's teachings, the parable serves as a profound warning to religious leaders and communities who reject God's messengers and ultimately turn away from divine truth, as represented by Jesus himself. The narrative implies that dismissing divine authority and refusing correction have serious consequences—not only for individuals but for society at large.

This serves as a reminder that retributive justice extends beyond mere punishment for wrongdoing; it acts as a critical warning to others who might be tempted to behave similarly. It encourages respect for authority and accountability while reinforcing the understanding that actions have consequences.

Ultimately, this parable invites us to reflect on the nature of justice, the moral implications of our choices, and the foundational principles that govern fair treatment in society. As we unravel the complexities presented in the story, we are reminded of our collective responsibility to seek justice not only for ourselves but also for those who are marginalized or wronged.

Justice must be pursued through rightful channels, ensuring that accountability is upheld and that individuals are treated with integrity and respect. In this way, we cultivate a just society that honors both the rights of individuals and the authority of the systems established to maintain order and fairness.

Contemporary Implications

The Emmanuel African Methodist Episcopal Church in Charleston, South Carolina, was the site of a tragic event on June 17, 2015, when a young white supremacist entered the church and murdered nine African American church members during a Bible study session.[14] The victims included prominent community leaders and dedicated church members. This horrific act, fueled by racism and hatred, sent shockwaves throughout the nation and sparked a much-needed racial dialogue within communities across America.

In the days and weeks that followed the massacre, media coverage highlighted the extraordinary responses of the victims' families and community members. During the bond hearing for Roof, family members of the victims expressed their willingness to forgive him, stating that they did not harbor hatred despite the immense pain he had caused. For example, one family member said, "I forgive you, and my family forgives you." This profound capacity for forgiveness was widely covered and left many, including myself, shocked by the apparent ability to look beyond the immediate need for retributive justice.

However, this act of forgiveness raises important questions about the relationship between forgiveness and justice. Forgiveness, in many ways, has been portrayed as a noble response, but it often relies on the offender showing genuine remorse and taking responsibility for their actions. In this situation, Roof's subsequent reactions in court—exhibiting indifference and failing to express any true contrition—further complicate the notion of whether forgiveness should come readily or if it should be contingent upon sincere accountability.

While the expression of forgiveness was profoundly moving, it is crucial to recognize that retributive justice must still be pursued through the courts. The legal system plays an essential role in holding individuals accountable for their actions, especially in heinous crimes such as this one. Dylann Roof was ultimately convicted and sentenced to death for his actions, which reflects the necessity of formal justice processes that go beyond individual feelings of forgiveness.

Additionally, the pursuit of restorative justice must be considered. Restorative justice is a process that seeks to repair the harm done to victims and communities, fostering healing conversations and rebuilding trust. However, it requires time and active participation from all involved parties and cannot be achieved merely through a single act of forgiveness—it demands ongoing dialogue and a commitment to reconciliation that might take years to cultivate.

Moreover, other forms of justice, such as social justice, racial justice, and compensatory justice, also need to be addressed in the wake of this tragedy. Social justice seeks to tackle the broader systemic issues that enable racism and violence to persist in society, promoting equality and fairness across different racial and socioeconomic groups. Racial justice specifically focuses on dismantling the structures of oppression that disproportionately affect African American communities and ensuring equitable treatment and opportunities for all. Compensatory justice may involve addressing the needs of the victims' families and the affected community, recognizing that financial reparations or support can be an important part of their healing process.

Moreover, while divine love is often presented as an essential aspect of forgiveness and moral frameworks, it is critical to clarify that this should not be misconstrued as a simplistic or naive approach to justice. True justice requires grappling with the complexities of human behavior, systemic inequalities, and the need for accountability. It acknowledges that divine love can coexist with the pursuit of fairness and the establishment of systems that protect the vulnerable and serve the collective good.

In summary, the tragic events at the Emmanuel African Methodist Episcopal Church illustrate the complex interplay between forgiveness and justice. While the victims' families' willingness to forgive was inspiring, it should not eclipse the necessity of pursuing justice through legal channels and addressing the broader societal issues rooted in racism and inequality. Ultimately, achieving true justice encompasses a multifaceted approach that honors the victims, supports healing, and advances societal change.

A further concern regarding retributive justice is when or how to utilize this concept in our society, given its importance in acknowledging that retributive justice, while necessary, must be balanced with other types of justice. Retributive justice focuses on punishing wrongdoing, upholding accountability, and reinforcing that harmful actions will result in punishment—a core principle of many justice systems. This approach seeks to deter crime by establishing clear consequences, thus maintaining order and protecting society.

It is also important to note that punishment can have widespread consequences for offenders' families, including economic hardship, social stigma, and emotional trauma. Communities with high incarceration rates may face long-term social and economic disadvantages, underscoring how retributive justice can inadvertently perpetuate intergenerational harm.

The incarceration system can have a disproportionate impact on marginalized communities, exacerbating social inequalities and perpetuating systemic injustice. Discrepancies in sentencing, which are often influenced by factors such as race, socioeconomic status, and implicit biases, raise concerns about the fairness of retributive justice. Research has shown that minority groups frequently receive more severe sentences for similar offenses, prompting questions about the equitable application of retributive justice.

Retributive justice alone may not sufficiently address the underlying social issues driving criminal behavior, such as poverty and lack of education. While retributive justice serves an essential role in holding individuals accountable for their actions, it often operates in isolation from the broader socioeconomic factors that contribute to crime. This narrow focus can lead to cyclical patterns of offense and punishment without addressing the root causes that compel individuals to engage in wrongdoing. Therefore, we must employ a range of concepts of justice in conjunction with retributive justice to create a more effective and meaningful justice system.

God's justice in society is holistic, encompassing retributive justice, restorative justice, social justice, and other forms. Each of these approaches offers unique insights and tools for addressing justice-related issues. Restorative justice, for instance, emphasizes healing and reconciliation among victims, offenders, and the community. By facilitating dialogue and understanding, restorative justice can foster personal accountability while repairing relationships and rebuilding trust. This approach can be particularly effective in communities that have been deeply fractured by crime, as it encourages collective healing rather than mere punishment.

Social justice, on the other hand, focuses on creating equitable conditions that can prevent injustice from occurring in the first place. It addresses systemic inequalities by advocating for fair access to resources such as education, healthcare, employment, and housing. By tackling these fundamental issues, social justice aims to cultivate an environment where individuals can thrive, thereby reducing the likelihood of criminal behavior stemming from desperation and hopelessness.

Incorporating these various forms of justice into our understanding equips us with a comprehensive framework for approaching societal issues. It emphasizes that justice is not solely about retribution but rather about creating a balanced system where individuals are held accountable while also being given opportunities for growth and rehabilitation.

To fulfill divine justice, we must recognize it as an all-encompassing principle that guides our lives, urging us to act with compassion and empathy toward others. This involves not only promoting justice within formal institutions but also embodying the values of love, respect, and dignity in our daily interactions. By loving our neighbors as ourselves, we actively oppose evil and wrongdoing, contributing to a society where justice is actionable and experienced by all.

Ultimately, a holistic vision of justice requires us to engage with one another as active participants in dismantling systems of oppression and inequality. It calls for collective effort, where community members, policymakers, and advocates work together to create inclusive environments that prioritize both accountability and support. In doing so, we honor the essence of justice as envisioned in God's design, fostering a world where everyone can realize their potential free from the shackles of injustice. By integrating and harmonizing these various aspects of justice, we pave the way toward a more equitable and just society, ultimately contributing to the common good and flourishing of all individuals.

Conclusion

In this chapter, we have analyzed the parables of the Unjust Judge and the Widow, as well as the Tenants, which engage the concept of retributive justice. The widow in the former serves as an example of an activist advocating for justice, remaining relentless in her pursuit until her voice is heard. Conversely, the unjust judge exemplifies a counterexample, demonstrating a callous disregard for justice. Although the specifics of the widow's legal case remain unknown, the parable suggests that while retributive justice may ultimately prevail, other forms of justice are also at play.

The Parable of the Tenants offers two contrasting interpretations: one centered on theological exegesis emphasizing divine judgment, and the other on the systemic evil perpetuated by the landowners who drive exploitative systems. While the narrative's conclusion is ambiguous, leaving the reader to wonder whether the story culminates in violent retribution by the master or a moral challenge to the unfaithful, the emphasis lies on the tenants' actions, deemed unfaithful and deserving of consequences.

Relying solely on retributive justice to interpret these parables is inadequate, as they may also illustrate restorative or social justice. We must recognize and distinguish the intertwined aspects of justice within these stories. When applying these principles to contemporary contexts, it is essential to exercise caution with the concept of retributive justice.

Questions for Discussion

1. If the parable centers on justice, what type of justice is being addressed, and what challenges might the widow encounter?
2. Is the unjust judge's behavior unique to him, or does it reflect a broader systemic issue?
3. If retributive justice is a theme in the parable of the tenants, where do you see it illustrated?
4. How can the concept of retributive justice be applied to contemporary society?

Notes

1 Yung Suk Kim, *Jesus's Truth*, 104–6.
2 Amy-Jill Levine, *Short Stories by Jesus*, 221–31.
3 Amy-Jill Levine, *Short Stories by Jesus*, 221–31.

4   Amy-Jill Levine, *Short Stories by Jesus*, 221–31.
5   Amy-Jill Levine, *Short Stories by Jesus*, 221–31.
6   William Herzog, *Parables as Subversive Speech*, 89–90.
7   William Herzog, *Parables as Subversive Speech*, 89–90.
8   Joachim Jeremias, *The Parables of Jesus*. See also Robert H. Stein, *The Method and Message of Jesus' Teachings* (Louisville, KY: Westminster John Knox, 1993).
9   R.T. France, *The Gospel of Matthew* (NICNT); on the contrary, Bailey sees cultural aspects of the story where the issue is repeated violence against the landowner, who demands justice. See Kenneth E. Bailey, *Jesus Through Middle Eastern Eyes: Cultural Studies in the Gospels* (Lisle, IL: IVP, 2008).
10 William Herzog, *Parables as Subversive Speech*, 98–113.
11 Dao De Jing 74. Translation is mine.
12 Dao De Jing 75. Translation is mine.
13 Dao De Jing 75. Translation is mine. The full text is here: "If people do not fear death, how can anybody control them by the threat of death? Suppose they are afraid of death, and we capture and kill those who are lawbreakers; who would dare to do so? There is always an official executioner to deal with this. If you play the role of the official executioner, it is like cutting wood instead of the master carpenter, and nobody can save their hands from being wounded."
14 "White gunman caught in killing of 9 in historic black church," accessed Nov 22, 2024. https://apnews.com/article/politics-south-carolina-religion-charleston-arrests-8747b77ae03a426e864f042454cab603.

11

Global Justice and Parables

Global justice in political philosophy explores the principles and practices governing fairness, equity, and morality in international relations and the global order. It addresses the distribution of resources, rights, and responsibilities among individuals, nations, and entities on a global scale. Key questions in this field include: Should principles of justice apply universally to all human beings, or are they restricted to specific nations, communities, or cultures? What obligations, if any, do wealthy nations or individuals have to alleviate global poverty? How should resources and opportunities be allocated to address disparities in wealth, healthcare, and education? What universal rights should be granted to everyone, including freedom, equality, and access to resources? Who is responsible for addressing global environmental crises, such as climate change?

While cosmopolitanism emphasizes moral obligations to all individuals globally, regardless of nationality or citizenship, statism prioritizes justice within the boundaries of sovereign states. John Rawls extends his theory of justice on a global scale, focusing on "well-ordered" societies cooperating under principles of fairness.[1] Thomas Pogge argues that global institutions and practices perpetuate poverty and that affluent nations have a moral duty to reform unjust systems that contribute to global inequality.[2] He critiques the existing global order and discusses how it fails to respect the human rights of the poor. His work highlights the responsibilities of the wealthy to address the structural causes of global poverty.

In contrast, Amartya Sen underscores the importance of individual capabilities and freedoms as fundamental components of development.[3] He argues that genuine development should focus on expanding individual freedoms rather than merely increasing economic wealth. Sen's approach addresses global inequities by emphasizing the need for social arrangements that empower individuals to pursue their own goals and enhance their circumstances. Similarly, Martha

Nussbaum advocates for a capabilities approach, highlighting what individuals can achieve and become.[4] She calls for a global framework that ensures everyone has the opportunity to pursue a life they value. Her work integrates ethical considerations with practical policies, aiming to inform how societies can be structured to enhance well-being and justice for all individuals.

Together, these thinkers enrich the discourse on global justice by exploring the complexities of justice, rights, and ethical obligations in our interconnected world. Their ideas advocate for an approach to justice that incorporates moral philosophy, economic policy, and social reform. By examining the interactions between nations and individuals, they offer deeper insights into what it means to pursue justice on a global scale and the responsibilities that accompany that pursuit.

This chapter primarily focuses on global poverty and international solidarity, taking cosmopolitanism seriously while adhering to the parables' mandate to care for all people. The concept of a single God of love and justice demands a commitment to global justice for all individuals, transcending national borders and cultural divides. It is vital to recognize that the ethical implications of this belief compel us to pursue tangible solutions to alleviate poverty and promote equity on a global scale. Among the parables that illuminate these themes are the Parable of the Rich Fool (Lk. 12:13-31) and the Parable of the Lost Sheep (Mt. 18:12-14; Lk. 15:3-7).

In the parable of the Rich Fool, we encounter a wealthy man whose abundance leads him to prioritize his own security and comfort over the needs of those around him. The question arises: Why does the rich man not consider sharing his surplus with others? This parable serves as a crucial critique of materialism and self-centeredness, challenging us to reflect on our responsibilities to the broader community. It highlights the moral imperative to use one's resources not merely for personal gain but to promote the well-being of others, particularly the marginalized and impoverished. By asking this question, we are invited to consider our own excesses and how these may impact those less fortunate.

On the other hand, the Parable of the Lost Sheep presents a powerful image of care and concern for the vulnerable. In this story, the shepherd leaves the ninety-nine sheep behind to search for the one that has gone astray. This illustrates the idea that every individual has inherent value and that efforts must be made to seek out and support those who are lost or in distress, particularly in impoverished regions. The challenge of finding lost sheep in poor countries reminds us of the systemic issues contributing to global inequality, where individuals often slip through the cracks of society due to a lack of access to resources, education, and support networks. It also emphasizes the urgent need for compassion and solidarity in addressing the suffering experienced by marginalized communities.

Incorporating these parables into conversations about global poverty inspires us to take action and consider how we can actively contribute to promoting justice. By acknowledging our interconnectedness, we can cultivate a sense of global citizenship that motivates us to advocate for policies aimed at eradicating poverty, supporting sustainable development, and addressing social injustices that impact the most vulnerable populations.

This chapter advocates for a holistic approach to global justice that recognizes the responsibilities of individuals, communities, and nations in addressing the needs of the poor. It challenges readers to engage with the complexities of global poverty and the various contributing factors, such as economic exploitation, political instability, and social inequities.

Ultimately, the teachings of these parables remind us that our faith and ethical beliefs extend beyond the personal to encompass the communal and global. By committing ourselves to care for and support all people, especially those in dire circumstances, we embody the divine principles of love and justice. In doing so, we take meaningful steps toward fostering international solidarity and realizing the vision of a just world where everyone can thrive. Thus, this chapter serves as a call to action, urging readers to reflect on their roles within the broader narrative of global justice and to seek ways to positively impact the lives of those who are suffering.

The Parable of the Rich Fool

Lk. 12:13-21

13 Someone in the crowd said to him, "Teacher, tell my brother to divide the family inheritance with me." 14 But he said to him, "Friend, who appointed me to be a judge or arbitrator over you?" 15 And he said to them, "Take care! Be on your guard against all kinds of greed; for one's life does not consist in an abundance of possessions." 16 Then he told them a parable: "The place of a rich man produced abundantly. 17 And he thought to himself, 'What should I do, for I have no place to store my crops?' 18 Then he said, 'I will do this: I will tear down my barns and build larger ones, and there I will store all my grain and my

goods. 19 And I will say to my soul, Soul, you have plenty of goods stored up for many years. Relax, eat, drink, be merry.' 20 But God said to him, 'You fool! This very night your life is being demanded of you. And the things you have prepared, whose will they be?' 21 So it is with those who store up treasures for themselves, but are not rich toward God."

Interpreting the Parable

This parable warns against "all kinds of greed; for one's life does not consist in the abundance of possessions" (12:15). The parable is set in the agricultural setting in which "the land of a rich man produced abundantly" (12:16). In Luke, there are complex images of the rich. On the one hand, the rich and the powerful are condemned, as in Mary's song: "He has shown strength with his arm; he has scattered the proud in the thoughts of their hearts. He has brought down the powerful from their thrones, and lifted up the lowly; he has filled the hungry with good things and sent the rich away empty" (Lk. 1:51-53). On the other hand, the rich are also saved if they repent and share what they have with others. Zacchaeus was a tax collector and rich (Lk. 19:2). But he was saved when he decided to give to the poor: "Look, half of my possessions, Lord, I will give to the poor; and if I have defrauded anyone of anything, I will pay back four times as much" (Lk. 19:8).

The rich man's wealth itself is not condemned; rather, it is his failure to consider the needs of others that is problematic. He does not share his abundance or express gratitude to God or his community. His self-centered monologue, in which he refers to himself multiple times, highlights his isolation and lack of relationships. His focus on building bigger barns instead of helping those in need reveals a flawed understanding of security and success.

In the parable, the land contributes to an abundant harvest, yet the rich man worries about his inadequate warehouse for storing his crops. This worry is ironic, as he would not need such a large warehouse if he chose to share part of his abundance with his neighbors. He should expand his heart, embracing the reign of God within his land and community. He needs to realize that God is behind every abundant harvest; the land is not solely his creation. Weather and community support contribute to his success.

The rich man neither thanks God nor acknowledges the efforts of others who worked in the fields. Instead, he focuses solely on himself, using self-referential language in verses 17-19: "What should I do, for I have no place to store my crops? I will do this: I will pull down my barns and build larger ones, and there I will store all my grain and my goods. And I will say to my soul, 'Soul, you have ample goods laid up for many years; relax, eat, drink, be merry.'" This self-centered attitude is mirrored in the Pharisee's prayer in the Parable of the Pharisee and the Tax Collector. Lk. 18:11-12 states: "God, I thank you that I am not like other people: thieves, rogues, adulterers, or even like this tax collector. I fast twice a week; I give a tenth of all my income." Whenever there is an excessive focus on "I," there is little room for God or others. The "I" becomes a shadowy deity, eclipsing true worship and community connection.

The rich man's preoccupation with hoarding for the future prevents him from living meaningfully in the present. His greed and desire for self-sufficiency distract him from fostering relationships and contributing to the well-being of others. The parable is a critique of an individualistic view of wealth. In a first-century agrarian society, surplus grain would have been seen as an opportunity to support the community, not as private property to be stored selfishly. The man's refusal to think communally makes him "foolish." In this view, the parable is not a warning about eternal punishment but a challenge to live a fulfilling and ethical life now. The man's sudden death underscores the urgency of making wise choices about wealth and relationships.

The rich man plans to spend the rest of his life with many good things.[5] But God says that he is foolish since his life may be taken away at any time. What is wrong with this rich man is his selfish mind and greed that do not consider others in the community.[6] Indeed, all he has in the large warehouse is not by his effort. Moreover, he did not create the land. Workers helped to produce a lot on the land. Then, why should he take all provisions for himself without sharing them equally or proportionally, for example, based on the workers' needs?

The attitude of this wealthy man toward his success reflects the laissez-faire ideology, which suggests that one's achievements are solely because of one's efforts. He believes that his life would be fulfilling and content even if he did not share his wealth with others. However, if the rich man's life is taken away, his dream of living a full and happy life without sharing the harvest with others will never come true. This is because his success is not solely based on his effort but also the contributions of his community. If he fails to acknowledge this and continues to believe that he can achieve success on his own, he will not be respected by the people of his village and will not experience the real joy of human life that comes from rich relationships in the community. In addition, a lack of social relationships and community involvement can lead to negative health outcomes, such as increased stress, depression, and anxiety. For example, Cohen discusses how social relationships impact health outcomes, emphasizing that social support can buffer stress and promote health benefits, while a lack of social ties can lead to increased morbidity and mental health issues.[7] Therefore, individuals need to prioritize building and maintaining meaningful relationships with others in their community to promote overall well-being.

While the laissez-faire camp argues that the rich are not responsible for the poor, the fairness camp addresses social and economic inequalities in society. The former thinks that one is free and not responsible for the poor. The latter tries to remedy social maladies by fixing wrongs and redistributing wealth via taxes or the welfare system. The communitarian or common good approach emphasizes the well-being of all in society. Individuals and society are inseparable, and all are bound by moral responsibilities to help one another.

The debate between the laissez-faire and fairness camps centers around the question of whether the wealthy bear any responsibility for the plight of the poor. The laissez-faire camp argues that individuals are free to pursue their interests without any moral obligations toward the less fortunate. In contrast, the fairness camp contends that social and economic inequalities are inherently unjust and require active intervention to address them. This may involve redistributing wealth through progressive taxation or welfare programs or providing universal access to necessities such as healthcare and education. Another approach, advocated by the communitarian or common good camp, emphasizes the interconnectedness of individuals in society and the moral responsibility to promote the well-being of all. This view holds that all members of society must help one another and work toward the greater good.

Engaging Global Justice

The Parable of the Rich Fool offers valuable insights into global justice issues, particularly regarding wealth inequality, resource distribution, and the ethical responsibilities of those with power and resources. In this narrative, a wealthy man hoards an abundance of grain, believing he can live in comfort for many years, only to die that very night. Through this story, Jesus highlights the futility of hoarding wealth without regard for others.

The rich fool's decision to store wealth for himself reflects a broader issue of economic inequality. Today, a small percentage of the world's population controls most of its resources, while billions live in poverty. This stark imbalance raises important ethical questions about the responsibilities of the wealthy toward those in need. The parable critiques the selfish accumulation of resources, suggesting that wealth should be directed to support broader community needs rather than being used solely for individual security.

The rich man's focus on his own comfort and security exemplifies the pitfalls of self-centeredness in resource management. In a global context, this perspective speaks to issues of international responsibility and solidarity. Wealthy nations and individuals possess the power to address critical global challenges such as poverty, hunger, and access to clean water. However, a lack of action or the prioritization of self-interest can perpetuate these injustices, leaving vulnerable populations without support.

In accumulating wealth without consideration for the future or the impact on others, the rich fool's actions mirror the overconsumption of resources frequently observed in affluent nations today. This unchecked accumulation often leads to environmental degradation, disproportionately affecting poorer countries that lack the resources to adapt. The parable advocates for mindful stewardship, calling for sustainable and equitable resource use instead of exploiting resources for personal gain.

By storing his grain without acknowledging those who may be hungry, the rich fool neglects the wider community. This behavior reflects how certain countries or corporations amass vast resources while others struggle to meet basic needs. A call for global justice emphasizes the need for fair distribution systems, where wealth and resources are allocated to alleviate poverty and create opportunities for all, rather than remaining concentrated among a select few.

The rich fool had the potential to utilize his resources to benefit others, yet his self-centered mindset prevented him from recognizing this possibility. This scenario speaks to the moral responsibilities of individuals and nations with wealth and power to actively engage in solutions for global issues, ranging from climate change to healthcare access. The parable implies that wealth should serve as a tool for good, promoting global justice and addressing crises that affect marginalized populations.

The rich fool's isolated thinking illustrates a lack of solidarity with others. Global justice emphasizes the inherent dignity of all people and the necessity of a shared sense of responsibility across nations and communities. The parable highlights the folly of focusing solely on personal wealth without considering the broader needs of humanity, urging a perspective that values compassion, generosity, and community well-being.

In conclusion, the Parable of the Rich Fool serves as a powerful reminder of the ethical implications of wealth accumulation and resource management. By urging individuals and nations to acknowledge their obligations to others, it challenges us to consider the interconnectedness of our actions within the global community. The narrative calls for a more equitable society—one that prioritizes justice, compassion, and shared responsibility, paving the way for a world where resources are used to uplift rather than isolate.

Contemporary Implications

Moltmann reflects on the parable in the context of ecological and economic ethics, emphasizing the consequences of greed on a global scale.[8] The parable's critique of the rich man's disregard for others is extended to global systems that exploit natural and human resources, urging sustainable practices and equitable distribution. Similarly, Myers interprets the parable through the lens of "Sabbath economics," which critiques economic practices that hoard wealth and ignore community needs.[9] He draws parallels between the rich fool and modern global capitalism, advocating for practices that prioritize communal well-being and environmental stewardship. Johnson also sees the parable as a critique of isolationist wealth and the failure to build relationships with others.[10] He extends this critique to global structures, suggesting that nations and individuals must prioritize interdependence and communal well-being over individual wealth.

Global justice encompasses the idea of fairness and equity across nations and populations, aiming to address disparities and improve well-being on a global scale. We will see a few areas that need attention to improve. First, there is a massive wealth gap between wealthy and poorer nations, as well as within nations. This disparity affects access to basic necessities like food, healthcare, education, and housing, especially in developing regions. Addressing global poverty requires policies that support fair trade, debt relief, and equitable access to resources and initiatives that empower economically disadvantaged communities.

Second, climate change disproportionately impacts poorer countries that have contributed the least to greenhouse gas emissions but bear the greatest consequences, such as extreme weather events, droughts, and sea-level rise. Climate justice calls for wealthy, industrialized nations to reduce their emissions and contribute to mitigation and adaptation efforts, ensuring that vulnerable nations have the resources needed to cope with climate impacts.

Third, multinational corporations often extract resources from poorer nations, leading to environmental damage and depletion of natural resources. This often happens without adequate compensation from local communities, leaving them with pollution and degraded land. Global justice involves holding corporations accountable, promoting sustainable practices, and ensuring that local communities benefit from their resources.

In summary, global justice touches on nearly every aspect of life, from environmental and economic equality to health. Achieving it requires a collective commitment to fair policies, responsible use of resources, and a focus on lifting those who are marginalized. This means creating systems that not only address immediate needs but also tackle the underlying causes of injustice, working toward a world where everyone can thrive.

The Parable of the Lost Sheep

Mt. 18:10-14

10 "Take care that you do not despise one of these little ones, for I tell you, in heaven their angels continually see the face of my Father in heaven. 12 What do you think? If a shepherd has a hundred sheep and one of them has gone astray, does he not leave the ninety-nine on the mountains and go in search of the one that went astray? 13 And if he finds it, truly I tell you, he rejoices over it more than over the ninety-nine that never went astray. 14 So it is not the will of your Father in heaven that one of these little ones should be lost.

Lk. 15:3-7

3 So he told them this parable: 4 "Which one of you, having a hundred sheep and losing one of them, does not leave the ninety-nine in the wilderness and go after the one that is lost until he finds it? 5 When he has found it, he lays it on his shoulders and rejoices. 6 And when he comes home, he calls together his friends and neighbors, saying to them, 'Rejoice with me, for I have found my sheep that was lost.' 7 Just so, I tell you, there will be more joy in heaven over one sinner who repents than over ninety-nine righteous persons who need no repentance.

Interpreting the Parable

The Parable of the Lost Sheep appears in Matthew and Luke. Yet, the two versions of the parable are not the same. The differences may be explained by the evangelists' theology.[11] In Matthew, this parable appears within the community discourse in chapter 18 along with the parable of the Unmerciful Slave. The focus of the Parable of the Lost Sheep in Matthew is how to take care of the ones that went astray from the community, who are among the marginalized ("one of these little ones"). While the reason for their going astray is unknown ("going astray" is mentioned three times in verses 18:12-13), they are among the most vulnerable like children whom Jesus alludes to as "one of these little ones" (18:6 and 10), including those who are among the least—those who are poor and oppressed, as indicated in the eschatological discourse in Mt. 25:31-46. Jesus explains why some are on the right side of the sheep and others are on the left side of the goats. The criterion is whether they took care of the hungry and the thirsty, who are called "one of the least of these" (Mt. 25:40, 45).

In Luke, the Parable of the Lost Sheep appears with other "lost" parables in chapter 15: the parable of the lost coin (Lk. 15:8-10) and the parable of the lost son (Lk. 15:11-32, "Father and Two Sons"). The focus of the lost sheep is the missing sheep; that is, what is lost is the greatest theme in Luke, as Lk. 19:10 says: "The Son of Man came to seek out and to save the lost," who are sinners and Gentiles. In the parable of the Lost Sheep, one lost sheep is compared to a sinner who repents (Lk. 15:7), which poses an irony because the lost sheep cannot return and repent.[12] The lost sheep was found by the shepherd. Nevertheless, Luke's allegory seems clear in that a lost sheep represents a Gentile sinner who returns and repents. In the end, the sinner's repentance brings the utmost joy to God and the community. This motif of "lost and found" also applies to the parable of the lost coin (Lk. 15:8-10) and the parable of the lost son (Lk. 15:11-32).

But our concern is not to explore the evangelist's theology in Matthew or Luke but to investigate the parable in context and explore aspects of global justice. The kernel of the original parable may be simple; once we remove possible redaction layers from Matthew and Luke, it may go like this: "Once upon a time, a shepherd had a hundred sheep but lost one of them. Then he left the ninety-nine in the wilderness and made every effort to find it. Once he finds it, his joy would be overflowing and he will rejoice with other friends."[13]

In the story, the point is that even one sheep in a hundred cannot be lost or ignored because it is precious and cannot be sacrificed. This parable shows what the good shepherd looks like in the community. Shepherds in first-century Judea were responsible for the financial well-being of the sheep's owners. The shepherd's determination to recover the lost sheep demonstrates his accountability and commitment to his duty. The parable resonates with themes of God as the shepherd who cares for the flock (e.g., Psalm 23, Ezekiel 34), but it also challenges the audience to consider their role in ensuring communal well-being.

The good shepherd noticed immediately that one sheep was lost. This is a very surprising moment, and it will not be easy to notice one lost sheep immediately. He cannot give it up because the lost sheep will be killed by predators. He leaves the ninety-nine to someone else's care, which means he does not put them in danger. If he were the good shepherd, he would not give up his ninety-nine sheep just for one lost sheep. Rather, the point is that he did not continue on his way with one sheep lost. Common sense suggests that he must find someone who will take care of his ninety-nine while he looks for the lost one.[14] His shepherd march stopped for a while, and his sheep were under the care of someone else.

Finding his lost sheep is risky and costly because there is no guarantee of finding it. But he cannot give it up without making any effort. He must believe in himself first. He searched for it, and after some pain, he found it. Then, the joy is overflowing not simply because one has recovered from death but because his fold is complete. The whole without one is not whole.

Engaging Global Justice

The Parable of the Lost Sheep tells the story of a shepherd who leaves ninety-nine sheep to search for one that has gone astray, joyfully celebrating its return. While this parable is often interpreted as a lesson on divine compassion and care for the marginalized, it also provides significant insights relevant to the broader context of global justice.

The shepherd's decision to leave the ninety-nine sheep to find the one lost sheep demonstrates a profound commitment to those who are most vulnerable. In the realm of global justice, this signifies a focus on marginalized populations, such as refugees, impoverished communities, and victims of human rights abuses. The parable suggests that true justice involves prioritizing the needs of those at risk rather than solely concentrating on the majority of the comfortable.

Furthermore, the shepherd's special attention to the lost sheep, rather than treating all sheep equally, illuminates the vital distinction between equality and equity in global justice. True justice requires additional effort and resources to assist those who are behind or in need, rather than merely distributing resources evenly across the board. The parable implies that justice entails giving particular attention to those who require the most assistance and acknowledging their unique circumstances.

The active search of the shepherd for the lost sheep emphasizes a proactive approach to justice. Instead of passively waiting for the lost sheep to return, the shepherd takes the initiative to find it, demonstrating a commitment to action. In terms of global justice, this implies that those in positions of power should actively work to address poverty, inequality, and systemic injustices, rather than remaining inactive and hoping for change.

Moreover, the shepherd's choice not to punish the lost sheep for straying but instead to rejoice upon its return signifies an attitude of restoration. In the context of global justice, this calls for strategies that focus on restoring dignity and opportunity for those who have been marginalized, rather than punitive measures. Examples include rehabilitation for displaced communities and economic development initiatives aimed at impoverished nations, all reflecting a commitment to healing and reintegration.

The shepherd's joy when finding the lost sheep illustrates that true justice brings happiness not only to those who are found but also to the entire community. In a global context, ensuring justice for marginalized groups enhances the well-being of all, contributing to a more inclusive, fair, and compassionate world. This collective joy emphasizes the positive impact justice can have on the global community.

Furthermore, the shepherd's care for the lost sheep reflects a holistic view of the flock's well-being, affirming that every individual is important to the community. In the notion of global justice, this perspective necessitates acknowledgment that systemic issues, such as poverty, inequality, and climate change, affect both individuals and communities as interconnected parts of a global ecosystem. The parable stresses the need for justice approaches that address root causes and systemic problems to ensure the flourishing of all.

The shepherd's celebration upon the sheep's return reiterates that justice is fundamentally about restoration rather than punishment. In the realm of global justice, this translates into approaches that celebrate the empowerment and recovery of marginalized groups, whether this involves welcoming refugees, supporting the economic development of under-resourced areas, or creating pathways for disenfranchised individuals to reclaim their rights and opportunities.

In conclusion, the Parable of the Lost Sheep invites reflection on the importance of valuing every individual, particularly the marginalized and vulnerable. It challenges us to prioritize proactive measures in addressing systemic inequalities and stresses that justice should focus on restoration and community well-being, embracing refugees, supporting economic development in under-resourced areas, or creating pathways for disenfranchised people to regain their rights and opportunities.

Contemporary Implications

The Parable of the Lost Sheep emphasizes the well-being of the whole community or global society, where each member, community, culture, and country matters. A healthy global society is one that thrives together with the cultural diversity and autonomy of all communities. Indigenous communities, for example, often face cultural erasure and land dispossession. A just global society recognizes and respects the unique cultural contributions of all groups, supporting their rights to self-determination and cultural preservation.

On November 19, 2024, over 40,000 Māori people in New Zealand protested against legislation aimed at erasing their special rights as Indigenous peoples.[15] This protest highlighted concerns over a treaty made between the Māori and the British Crown, which new legislation proposed to undermine by limiting Indigenous rights related to culture and language. As always, a significant challenge remains in how to coexist while honoring differences in culture, religion, and identity.

With the spirit of global justice, we can deal with the crises of refugees and migration differently. They are lost in their countries due to war or other reasons and seek a new life elsewhere beyond the country's borders. Refugees and migrants often face discrimination, limited rights, and poor living conditions. Global justice involves supporting refugees with humane policies, legal protections, and resources that recognize their rights and dignity.

If we expand the community to a global stage, we must see people who struggle due to a lack of justice. For example, women and girls face systemic discrimination in many parts of the world, limiting their rights and access to opportunities. Issues like gender-based violence, limited economic opportunities, and lack of access to education disproportionately impact women. Achieving gender justice requires global efforts to ensure equal rights, protect women's health, and provide economic and educational opportunities. Another example is found in exploitative labor practices, including low wages, unsafe working conditions, and child labor, which are common in the production of goods for wealthier markets. Workers in developing countries often lack protection, fair wages, and benefits. Global justice advocates for fair trade practices, responsible corporate behavior, and international labor standards to ensure dignity and rights for all workers.

Conclusion

In this chapter, we have thoroughly examined the parables of the Rich Fool and the Lost Sheep, uncovering valuable insights relevant to the concept of global justice. While these parables are often interpreted through the lens of local community dynamics, it is crucial to extend their lessons to encompass a global perspective, particularly given the global nature of God's care. The God who oversees all of humanity is deeply concerned with the well-being of every individual, transcending national boundaries and cultural divides. This understanding compels us to acknowledge that our responsibilities extend beyond our immediate communities to include a commitment to justice and compassion for all people around the world. Recognizing God's inclusive love challenges us to reflect on how our actions can contribute to a more equitable global society where the needs of the marginalized are prioritized and addressed. By interpreting these parables in a broader context, we not only enrich our understanding of their meanings but also affirm our shared obligation to work toward a more just and compassionate world for everyone.

Questions for Discussion

1. What prevents the rich fool from considering sharing his surplus with others?
2. Engage in a debate between libertarian and communitarian perspectives on the rich man's behavior. The libertarian viewpoint may argue that the rich man exclusively owns his wealth and has no obligation to share,

while the communitarian perspective emphasizes the importance of sharing with others.
3. Is the shepherd's decision to leave ninety-nine sheep in the wilderness justifiable, or is it an exaggeration intended to underscore the significance of one lost sheep?
4. What qualities are essential for a good shepherd in the parable of the Lost Sheep?

Notes

1 John Rawls, *The Law of Peoples: With "The Idea of Public Reason Revisited"* (Cambridge, MA: Harvard University Press, 2001).
2 Thomas W. Pogge, *World Poverty and Human Rights* (Cambridge: Polity, 2008).
3 Amartya Sen, *Development as Freedom* (New York: Anchor Books, 2000).
4 Martha Nussbaum, *Creating Capabilities: The Human Development Approach* (Cambridge, MA: Belknap, 2013).
5 Barbara Reid, *Parables for Preachers, Year C*, 137–8.
6 Yung Suk Kim, *Jesus's Truth*, 80–1.
7 Sheldon Cohen, "Social Relationships and Health," *The American Psychologist* 59, no. 8 (2004): 676–84.
8 Jürgen Moltmann, *Ethics of Hope* (Minneapolis, MN: Fortress, 2012).
9 Ched Myers, *The Biblical Vision of Sabbath Economics* (LAB/ORA Press, 2023).
10 Luke Timothy Johnson, *The Gospel of Luke* (Collegeville, MN: Liturgical, 2018).
11 Yung Suk Kim, *Jesus's Truth*, 36–9.
12 Amy-Jill Levine, *Short Stories by Jesus*, 37.
13 Yung Suk Kim, *Jesus's Truth*, 37–8.
14 Eric F. Fox, "The Parable of the Lost or Wandering Sheep: Matthew 18:10-14; Luke 15:3-7," *Anglican Theological Review* 44, no. 1 (1962): 50.
15 "Why Māori are Protesting in New Zealand," https://theweek.com/world-news/why-maori-are-protesting-in-new-zealand; See also "NPR," accessed Nov 23, 2024. https://www.npr.org/2024/11/19/nx-s1-5196056/new-zealand-maori-Indigenous.

12

Environmental Justice and Parables

Environmental justice addresses the disproportionate impact of environmental harm, such as pollution, climate change, and resource depletion, on marginalized communities. It aims to ensure fair treatment and meaningful participation in environmental decision-making for all individuals.

Environmental justice strives to provide equal access to clean air, clean water, green spaces, and healthy environments, working to prevent marginalized communities from shouldering the undue burdens of pollution, hazardous waste, and environmental degradation. It supports the inclusion of diverse voices, particularly those from underrepresented or directly impacted groups, in environmental policy-making. This approach highlights the significance of cultural and Indigenous knowledge in shaping effective and inclusive environmental policies. Furthermore, environmental justice is committed to preserving natural resources and ensuring a sustainable, livable planet for future generations.

Eco-social justice connects environmental justice with broader social justice issues, emphasizing the interconnectedness of ecological health and human well-being. In parallel, environmental ethics examines human moral responsibility toward the natural world and how this intersects with justice for people. Ultimately, environmental justice acts as a bridge between environmental concerns and wider justice movements, advocating that a sustainable and equitable future necessitates addressing the interlinked social, racial, and economic inequalities.

For example, communities of color often experience higher exposure to environmental hazards due to systemic racism, including practices like redlining and industrial zoning. Environmental justice movements frequently align with racial justice campaigns to tackle these disparities. Additionally, environmental harm often correlates with economic inequality, as low-income communities are more likely to be located near polluting industries. Environmental justice calls for fair compensation and protections for those economically marginalized by environmental policies.

Moreover, environmental justice intersects with global justice, addressing the disproportionate environmental harm caused by wealthy nations while poorer nations bear the brunt of the consequences, such as climate change and resource exploitation. There are ongoing calls for equitable international agreements on matters like carbon emissions, climate adaptation, and resource allocation.

During Jesus's time, environmental justice was not a prominent issue, as society was primarily agriculturally based. Today, however, the environmental crisis, alongside climate change, is largely human-made, driven by greedy lifestyles and the unrestrained development of land and natural resources. People in the developed world bear significant moral responsibility due to their substantial contribution to rising greenhouse gas emissions.

According to a UN report in 2023, more than half of all global greenhouse gas emissions originate from the following countries: China, the United States, India, the European Union, the Russian Federation, and Brazil, while the forty-five least developed countries account for only 3 percent of global emissions.[1] In this critical time of ecological crisis and climate change, revisiting the parable of the Sower can inspire us to adopt more ecologically friendly attitudes and practices.

The Parable of the Sower

Mk 4:1-20 (cf, Mt. 13:1-23; Lk. 8:4-15)

Mk 4:1 Again he began to teach beside the sea. Such a very large crowd gathered around him that he got into a boat on the sea and sat there, while the whole crowd was beside the sea on the land. 2 He began to teach them many things in parables, and in his teaching he said to them: 3 "Listen! A sower went out to sow. 4 And as he sowed, some seed fell on the path, and the birds came and ate it up. 5 Other seed fell on rocky ground, where it did not have much soil, and it sprang up quickly, since it had no depth of soil. 6 And when the sun rose, it was scorched; and since it had no root, it withered away. 7 Other seed fell among thorns, and the thorns grew up and choked it, and it yielded no grain. 8 Other seed fell into good soil and brought forth grain, growing up and increasing and yielding thirty and sixty and a hundredfold." 9 And he said, "Let anyone with ears to hear listen!" 10 When he was alone, those who were around him along with the twelve asked him about the parables. 11 And he said to them, "To you has been given the secret of the kingdom of God, but for those outside, everything comes in parables; 12 in order that 'they may indeed look, but not perceive, and may indeed listen, but not understand; so that they may not turn again and be forgiven.'" 13 And he said to them, "Do you not understand this parable? Then how will you understand all the parables? 14 The sower sows the word. 15 These are the ones on the path where the word is sown: when they hear, Satan immediately comes and takes away the word that is sown in them. 16 And these are the ones sown on rocky ground: when they hear the word, they immediately receive it with joy. 17 But they have no root, and endure only for a while; then, when trouble or persecution arises on account of the word, immediately they fall away. 18 And others are those sown among the thorns: these are the ones who hear the word, 19 but the cares of the world, and the lure of wealth, and the desire for other things come in and choke the word, and it yields nothing. 20 And these are the ones sown on the good soil: they hear the word and accept it and bear fruit, thirty and sixty and a hundredfold."

Interpreting the Parable

The parable of the Sower is found in the Synoptic Gospels, and according to the theory of Markan Priority, Mark serves as a source for Matthew and Luke, who edited Mark independently. However, our goal is not to explore the theology of each evangelist but to examine the meaning of the parable as presented by Jesus in its context. While we do not have a copy of the original account, we consider the Markan version—the earliest we possess—to be the closest representation of the original.

The parable itself is found in Mk 4:3-8, which offers a vivid depiction of the sower performing his work in the field and anticipating a future harvest. Mk 4:9-20 includes additional commentary, with verses 4:9-10 acting as a transition to Mark's interpretation of the parable, which is elaborated upon in verses 4:11-20.[2]

In Mk 4:11-20, the evangelists (Mark, Matthew, and Luke) allegorize the parable of the sower for their communities. In this interpretation, the sower represents the one who teaches, the seed symbolizes the word, and the four types of ground correspond to four types of hearers: the path, rocky ground, among the thorns, and good soil.

Those on the path represent individuals who, when they hear the word, have it taken away immediately by Satan (Mk 4:15). Those on rocky ground hear the word and receive it with joy at first. However, they lack deep roots and endure only for a short time; when trouble or persecution arises due to the word, they quickly fall away (Mk 4:16-17). Those sown among the thorns hear the word, but it yields no fruit because they are distracted by the cares of the world, the lure of wealth, and the desire for other things (Mk 4:18-19). Lastly, those sown on good soil hear the word, accept it, and bear fruit (Mk 4:20).

However, Jesus's parable can be understood not merely as a simplified allegory focused on the word of God and human preparedness, as Mark's interpretation suggests, but rather as a reflection of the diverse conditions of agricultural life. The parable vividly portrays the sower working in the field. It is natural to observe the presence of paths, rocky ground, thorny ground, and fertile soil—conditions that may require preparation or plowing by the sower.[3] Given that this parable is grounded in agricultural realities, we should emphasize the sower's labor: scattering seeds and anticipating the harvest. In this context, the rule or reign of God is likened to the sower's diligent work. Though the sower is not omnipotent, he works tirelessly from sowing to harvesting.

The parable's significance becomes clearer when we closely observe the sower's actions. He scatters seeds broadly across the land, and his task is not to selectively choose the most promising locations but to sow widely and then plow the land afterward—a common and accepted practice.[4] If plowing follows sowing, the sower can confidently prepare the soil for growth. One-time sowing is insufficient; the sower's attention and efforts must continue until the harvest to ensure a bountiful yield.

The sower understands that some seeds will fall on paths, rocky ground, and among thorns. While these conditions are not inherently problematic, they are simply part of the natural landscape. The difference lies in their unsuitability for sowing. The sower does not intend to sow seeds in these locations and does not expect them to thrive there. Therefore, Mark's allegorical interpretation in 4:11-20 is out of context from an agricultural perspective. The three challenging soil conditions are natural occurrences, not inherently negative. Thus, they should not be equated with negative aspects of the human heart, as the allegory suggests.

The focus should not be on where the seed falls but rather on the sower's actions. The parable likely depicts a sower who scatters seeds widely, acknowledging that some will land on unsuitable ground. This loss of seed may be an unavoidable cost, as he cannot perfectly control where each seed falls. He sows widely because he intends to plow the land afterward; sowing is not the end of his work but the beginning. While fertile soil is a gift from God, the sower's responsibility is to prepare it, even if that preparation occurs after sowing. In agriculture, the sower's work continues daily throughout the growing season, including weeding and nurturing the plants. Good soil is not created all at once; it requires ongoing care until the harvest.

This parable implies that opportunities should be offered to all people equitably, regardless of their social standing or economic circumstances. It emphasizes both procedural fairness and equality of opportunity. The sower's act of scattering seeds indiscriminately across the land exemplifies procedural fairness.[5]

The parable assumes the use of high-quality seeds, even if it does not explicitly state this. In agricultural contexts, the importance of using quality seed is implicit. The sower understands that good seeds, when sown properly, yield a bountiful harvest. These seeds are not produced by the sower but are a gift from God. They may symbolize the inherent abilities and talents that individuals possess but cannot create themselves. Each person receives unique gifts that require identification and development. Families, schools, and communities play a vital role in nurturing and fostering these gifts.

Engaging Environmental Justice

The parable of the sower offers profound insights into environmental justice, highlighting the interconnectedness of ecological health and human well-being, and underscoring the crucial role of human moral responsibility toward the natural world. It provides a robust framework for environmental ethics, enabling us to advocate for a healthy planet and challenge the unsustainable practices of greed-based overconsumption and corporate exploitation of natural resources.

The parable's agricultural setting itself is a testament to the beauty and inherent sustainability of nature. We see fertile land, paths, wildflowers, thorny hills, rocky outcrops, trees, and mountains—a rich tapestry of life given by God. Humanity is positioned within this creation, not as its master, but as its steward. We have the power to cultivate and nurture the land, but we also bear the responsibility to avoid its exploitation and degradation. We can prepare good soil, but we must not deplete it. This understanding necessitates a shift from dominion over nature to a responsible partnership with it.

The sower's relationship with nature and God reveals a profound humility. His livelihood depends entirely on the bounty of nature, understanding that the quality of the seeds themselves, as well as the air, water, sunlight, and wind, are gifts from God. This dependence fosters a lifestyle characterized by simplicity, gratitude, and a lack of ambition for dominion. His worldview rejects the pursuit of limitless accumulation in favor of a life lived in harmony with nature's rhythms. He understands the intricate dance of sowing, waiting, and harvesting, respecting the natural limits of time and yield. This leaves ample space for reflection, family life, and communal engagement, enriching his life beyond mere material gain. His reliance on God and nature cultivates a deep sense of humility—a vital counterpoint to the hubris of environmental exploitation.

The sower's lifestyle and worldview resonate with Laozi's philosophy, as expressed in the adage, "Humanity follows the earth; the earth follows heaven; heaven follows the Dao; the Dao follows nature" (人法地, 地法天, 天法道, 道法自然, rén fǎ de, de fǎ tiān, tiān fǎ dào, dào fǎ zì rán).[6] This suggests that humanity should understand its origins on the earth, learn from nature, and live in harmony with its rhythms for prosperity. This path requires recognizing one's limitations and embracing humility. As Laozi observes, "Those who are content are rich" (知足者富, zhī zú zhě fù).[7]

The sower's approach to his work demonstrates an understanding of ecological diversity.[8] He sows broadly, accepting that some seeds will fall on paths, rocky ground, or among thorns. Crucially, he does not view these areas as worthless or something to be conquered. He acknowledges that these varied terrains, including the presence of wildflowers and trees, contribute to the overall health of the ecosystem. His focus is on maximizing the potential of fertile land while recognizing and accepting the inherent limitations and diversity of the wider landscape. The seeds that fall on unsuitable ground are not necessarily a failure; they are part of a natural cycle, providing nourishment for birds or illustrating the limitations of growth in specific environments. The rocky ground, the sun's intensity, and the presence of thorns are not inherently negative; they are integral components of a balanced ecosystem.

The parable implicitly advocates for a lifestyle that aligns with natural rhythms. The seasonal nature of sowing, tending, and harvesting promotes a balanced approach to work and rest, fostering self-contentment and strong community bonds. This rhythm counters the relentless pace of modern life, often at odds with ecological sustainability. This nature-based lifestyle is not merely practical; it is also crucial for robust mental and emotional health, which can, in turn, prevent the destructive behaviors that harm both nature and other people. The cyclical nature of life mirrored in the parable's agricultural setting, offers a potent antidote to the unsustainable demands of modern consumerism.

The parable underscores the profound interconnectedness of all life. Just as the seed's growth depends on healthy soil, water, and sunlight, our own lives are inextricably linked to the environment. The health of the ecosystem directly impacts our well-being. The parable, therefore, serves as a powerful reminder of our shared dependence on a flourishing environment and the urgent need for sustainable practices that ensure the continued health of both humanity and the natural world.[9]

In conclusion, the seemingly simple agricultural imagery of the parable offers a complex and deeply relevant message for our time. It encourages a reevaluation of humanity's relationship with the natural world, urging us toward a future defined by stewardship, sustainability, and a profound respect for the intricate web of life.

Contemporary Implications

The parable of the sower, while seemingly simple in its agricultural setting, offers a surprisingly rich framework for understanding contemporary environmental justice issues. Beyond its traditional theological interpretations focusing on the reception of the word of God, the parable reveals profound insights into humanity's relationship with the natural world and the ethical responsibilities inherent in that relationship. We will explore how the parable's core tenets illuminate key aspects of environmental justice today, highlighting the disproportionate impact on vulnerable communities and the urgent need for systemic change.

The parable's setting is deeply embedded within the rhythms of nature. The sower's actions, the broad scattering of seeds, and the acceptance of some seeds falling on unsuitable ground illustrate the inherent diversity of the natural world and the understanding that not all environments are equally conducive to growth. This recognition of ecological diversity directly challenges anthropocentric viewpoints that prioritize human needs above all others, ignoring the interconnectedness of life and the inherent value of all ecosystems. The sower's acceptance of loss—some seeds falling on paths, rocks, or thorns— suggests a humility that acknowledges the limits of human control and the importance of respecting natural processes. This perspective contrasts sharply with exploitative practices that prioritize short-term economic gain over long-term environmental sustainability.

Low-income communities and communities of color frequently bear the brunt of environmental hazards, from polluted water sources (as evidenced by the Flint water crisis) to proximity to polluting industries and inadequate access to green spaces. This unequal distribution is not accidental; it reflects systemic injustices rooted in historical and ongoing patterns of discrimination and power imbalances. The parable's depiction of the sower's acceptance of the limitations inherent in the land should not be misconstrued as passivity. Instead, it highlights the need for active intervention to address systemic inequalities that create environments more vulnerable to hazards for certain populations.

The parable also raises crucial questions about Indigenous rights and land sovereignty. Indigenous communities often possess intimate ecological knowledge accumulated over generations, which is vital for sustainable resource management. However, these communities frequently face threats to their lands and traditional ways of life from extractive industries and environmentally damaging practices. The parable's emphasis on respecting the diversity of the landscape mirrors the need to respect the diversity of human cultures and their traditional connections to the environment. The disregard for Indigenous rights and knowledge represents a profound failure of environmental justice, one that has far-reaching consequences for both the environment and human well-being. This necessitates a shift toward a more inclusive and participatory approach to environmental decision-making, where Indigenous voices and perspectives are central.

The parable's message extends beyond local contexts to encompass global environmental justice. The exploitation of resources in developing countries by wealthier nations and corporations creates profound inequalities and environmental devastation. Deforestation, mining, and pollution often disproportionately affect marginalized populations in the Global South, while the benefits accrue primarily to those in wealthier countries.

As seen above, the parable of the sower provides a powerful framework for analyzing and addressing environmental justice issues in the twenty-first century. By emphasizing the interconnectedness of all living things, the need for humility and respect for natural limits, and the importance of equitable resource distribution, the parable calls for a fundamental shift in human attitudes and actions toward the natural world. Addressing the complex challenges of environmental injustice requires acknowledging systemic inequalities, upholding Indigenous rights, promoting corporate accountability, and fostering a global commitment to sustainability and social justice. Only through such comprehensive action can we hope to create a world where all people can thrive in harmony with a healthy planet.

Conclusion

Our interpretation moves beyond traditional theological readings to explore the parable's profound implications for environmental ethics and the urgent need for a paradigm shift in our relationship with the natural world.

First, the parable establishes nature as the ultimate source and sustainer of life. The fertile soil, the sun, and the rain are not mere props but fundamental elements that determine the success or failure of the sower's efforts. This emphasizes humanity's inherent dependence on the natural world, a dependence often overlooked in anthropocentric worldviews that position humans as separate from and superior to nature. The parable implicitly critiques the human tendency to dominate and exploit nature, highlighting instead the need for a reciprocal and respectful relationship where humanity recognizes its embeddedness within, and dependence upon, the natural world. This understanding is crucial for addressing contemporary ecological crises, such as climate change and biodiversity loss, which largely result from human actions that disregard the limits and intrinsic value of natural systems. Further exploration might consider the implications of this dependence, such as the vulnerability of human societies to environmental changes and the necessity for sustainable practices that maintain the health of ecosystems.

Second, the parable explicitly highlights the diversity of the natural world. The seeds fall on paths, rocky ground, among thorns, and in fertile soil—a clear depiction of the varied conditions that exist within any ecosystem. This diversity is not presented as a problem to be overcome but as an inherent characteristic of nature. The sower does not attempt to alter this diversity, accepting that some seeds will fall on unsuitable ground and will not flourish. This contrasts sharply with human practices that often seek to homogenize and simplify natural systems, leading to ecological degradation. This section could delve into the ecological importance of biodiversity and the consequences of its loss, including reduced resilience of ecosystems, loss of ecosystem services, and decreased capacity to adapt to environmental change. A comparative discussion of monoculture versus polyculture and their relative impacts would further strengthen this point.

Third, the parable challenges the anthropocentric notion that humanity is the center of the world, separate from and superior to the natural world. While the sower actively engages in cultivating the land, he is also depicted as being at the mercy of natural forces. The success of his efforts depends on factors beyond his control, demonstrating a humble acceptance of humanity's place within the larger ecological framework. This understanding of humanity as a steward, rather than a master, is crucial for developing a sustainable relationship with nature. The implications for environmental policy and corporate practices are significant, calling for a shift toward practices that prioritize ecological integrity and intergenerational equity. A discussion on the historical shift from a stewardship model to one of dominion could provide valuable context.

Fourth, the parable suggests a path to human flourishing that is intricately linked to respecting and appreciating nature's gifts. The sower's dependence on the land fosters a sense of gratitude and a life characterized by simplicity and contentment. This contrasts starkly with consumer-driven societies that prioritize endless growth and material acquisition, resulting in ecological depletion and social inequality. This section could explore the link between simpler lifestyles and reduced environmental impact, examining the societal and economic implications of shifting toward more sustainable consumption patterns.

Finally, the parable underscores the importance of learning from nature and preserving its intrinsic value. The sower's actions, while human-driven, are deeply intertwined with natural processes. His success depends on understanding and working with, rather than against, these processes. This calls for a shift toward more holistic and integrated approaches to resource management and ecological restoration. This section could discuss Indigenous ecological knowledge and its crucial role in fostering sustainable practices, as well as the use of biomimicry—imitating nature's designs and processes—to develop more sustainable technologies and solutions. Specific examples of traditional ecological knowledge systems and successful biomimicry projects would strengthen this argument.

By examining the parable through the lens of environmental justice, we move beyond a simplistic reading to uncover a powerful call for ecological responsibility and sustainable living. The parable becomes a potent metaphor for the urgent need to reevaluate our relationship with nature, recognize our dependence on it, and embrace the diversity and intrinsic value of all living and nonliving things.

Questions for Discussion

1. What is the central focus of the parable of the Sower? Is it the sower's actions, the seeds themselves, the diverse types of soil, or the ultimate harvest?
2. If some seeds fell on rocky ground, a path, or thorny soil, does that necessarily mean the sower failed? How might we redefine success and failure within the context of this parable?
3. What constitutes "good soil" in the parable? Is it solely a gift of nature, or does it also involve human cultivation and stewardship?
4. What environmental insights or ethical considerations can we glean from the parable of the Sower? How does the parable inform our understanding of humanity's relationship with the natural world?

Notes

1 United Nations, "What Is Climate Change?" accessed April 19, 2025. https://www.un.org/en/climatechange/what-is-climate-change.
2 Yung Suk Kim, *Jesus's Truth*, 18. We find the evangelist's interpretation of the parable in the Wheat and Weeds in addition to the parable of the Sower. Otherwise, Jesus never explains his parable when he tells it because it is a story that must be interpreted by his audience.
3 Philip Payne, "Order of Sowing and Ploughing in the Parable of the Sower," *New Testament Study* 25, no. 1 (1978): 124.
4 Philip Payne, "Order of Sowing and Ploughing in the Parable of the Sower," 124.
5 Yung Suk Kim, *Reading Jesus' Parables with Dao De Jing*, 2–9. Dao De Jing emphasizes impartiality in human lives. For example, Dao De Jing 5 reads: "Heaven and earth are impartial. They treat all things as straw dogs. The wise are also impartial. They treat people as straw dogs. Heaven and earth are like a bellows. While empty, it is never exhausted. The more it is worked, the more it produces."
6 Dao De Jing 25, accessed March 23, 2025. https://drkimys.blogspot.com/p/dao-de-jing_22.html.

7 Dao De Jing 33, accessed March 23, 2025. https://drkimys.blogspot.com/p/dao-de-jing_22.html.
8 Much of this paragraph is a revision from my book, Yung Suk Kim, *How to Read the Gospels*, 166–7.
9 Elaine Wainwright, "Part Four: An Ecological Reading of Mark's Gospel," accessed Nov 24, 2024. https://hail.to/tui-motu-interislands-magazine/publication/430InQe/article/p9j2RGB.

13

Conclusion

Justice is multifaceted and influences various aspects of our lives. As we have seen, Jesus's parables challenge many forms of injustice found within individuals, institutions, and society as a whole. While these parables may not directly address our everyday concerns, they can still resonate with our experiences and perspectives.

We also need to know that parables extend beyond the limits of our imagination; they are ongoing narratives that require continual reflection and attention. This allows Jesus's stories to remain relevant and be retold in contemporary contexts.

While each parable highlights multiple aspects of justice, for heuristic purposes, this book associates specific parables with specific types of justice. However, it is essential to understand that each parable encompasses a range of justice elements. This approach enables readers to engage more deeply with the parables and enhances their understanding based on their contexts.

In particular, exploring Jesus's parables through the lens of political philosophy reveals the enduring power of storytelling and its profound implications in real-life situations. These parables invite us to grapple with persistent questions of justice and morality that resonate from Jesus's time to our own.

We have examined ten facets of justice and their impact on actions, decisions, and societal structures, both ancient and modern. From distributive to environmental justice, each parable challenges us to reevaluate our values, behaviors, and responsibilities. The central question—"What is the right thing to do?"—guides our discussion, reflecting the moral dilemmas of Jesus's ministry and the ethical challenges we face today. Through this lens, the parables expose inadequate moral frameworks and inspire deeper commitments to equity and compassion.

Acknowledging the insights of these teachings is only the beginning. As global inequality and societal divisions deepen, we must align our practices with the principles of justice found in these parables. This requires confronting the complexities of justice in diverse contexts and translating insights into concrete action through inclusive dialogue that fosters empathy and fairness.

Navigating the challenges we face today calls for sustained conversations that extend beyond academic circles. Jesus's parables serve not only as historical treasures but also as essential tools for shaping future narratives and actions. They urge us to build communities that prioritize restorative justice, advocate for the marginalized, and confront systemic injustices with courage. In our polarized world, finding common ground through humility, active listening, and collective action is paramount.

Summary of Justice and Parables

1. Distributive Justice (Fair Allocation of Resources)
   - The Vineyard Laborers (Mt. 20:1-16): Challenges meritocratic norms, highlighting equity and generosity in labor compensation. Sparks discussion on fair wages, economic justice, and income inequality.
   - The Rich Man and Lazarus (Lk. 16:19-31): Underscores the consequences of ignoring the poor and prompts reflection on wealth disparity, social responsibility, and the moral obligation to aid the less fortunate.
2. Attributive Justice (Fairness in Assigning Rewards and Punishments Based on Merit)
   - The Talents (Mt. 25:14-30): Emphasizes personal responsibility and ethical use of abilities and resources. Raises questions about contributing to community well-being and promoting equality.
   - The Treasure Hidden in a Field (Mt. 13:44) & The Pearl of Great Price (Mt. 13:45-46): Illustrate prioritizing justice and righteousness over material wealth, highlighting the true value of contributing to a just society.
3. Procedural Justice (Fairness in the Processes Used to Make Decisions)
   - The Seed Growing Secretly (Mk 4:26-29): Highlights the often unseen, gradual nature of positive social change and personal transformation, emphasizing patience and faith in the process of justice.
   - The Wheat and the Weeds (Mt. 13:24-30): Addresses the coexistence of good and evil, urging patience and discernment in addressing societal injustices.

4. Social Justice (Fairness in Social Structures and Institutions)
   - The Pharisee and the Tax Collector (Lk. 18:9-14): Emphasizes humility in pursuing justice, promoting an inclusive and empathetic approach.
   - The Leaven (Mt. 13:33): Illustrates the transformative power of small gifts and actions, highlighting the importance of incremental social change.
5. Racial Justice (Fairness in Addressing Racial Inequality)
   - The Good Samaritan (Lk. 10:25-37): Illustrates compassion transcending cultural boundaries, prompting discussions about racial divisions and humanitarian aid.
   - The Mustard Seed (Mk 4:30-32; Lk. 13:18-19; Mt. 13:31-32): Highlights the potential for transformative change from small beginnings, relevant to grassroots social justice movements.
6. Restorative Justice (Focus on Repairing Harm and Reconciliation)
   - The Father and Two Sons (Lk. 15:11-32): Focuses on forgiveness and reconciliation, relevant to discussions about restorative justice and community healing.
   - The Unmerciful Slave (Mt. 18:21-35): Emphasizes mercy and forgiveness as integral to restorative justice, highlighting the importance of healing over punishment.
7. Compensatory Justice (Fairness in Redressing Wrongs)
   - The Unjust Steward (Lk. 16:1-9): While seemingly unethical, it highlights shrewdness and resourcefulness in creating positive outcomes, prompting reflection on using resources wisely to foster justice.
8. Retributive Justice (Fairness in Punishment for Wrongdoing)
   - The Parable of the Tenants (Mt. 21:33-46; Mk 12:1-12; Lk. 20:9-19): Addresses stewardship, responsibility, and the consequences of failing to uphold commitments, raising questions about resource access and power dynamics.
   - The Parable of the Unjust Judge and the Widow (Lk. 18:1-8): Emphasizes perseverance in seeking justice, even in the face of systemic indifference.
9. Global Justice (Fairness in International Relations and Resource Distribution)
   - The Rich Fool (Lk. 12:13-21): Prompts reflection on the ethical use of wealth for a global community, emphasizing stewardship and responsibility.

- The Lost Sheep (Lk. 15:1-7; Mt. 18:10-14): Highlights the value of every individual, calling for community support and outreach to marginalized members globally.
10. Environmental Justice (Fairness in Access to Environmental Resources)
    - The Sower (Mk 4:1-20; Mt. 13:1-23; Lk. 8:4-15): Uses the metaphor of seed growth to illustrate the need for equitable access to healthy environments for all communities, addressing the impact of environmental neglect and promoting sustainable practices.

This book treats justice as a holistic concept that guarantees fair treatment for all individuals, free from biases and prejudices. It advocates for a restorative society that offers equal opportunities for everyone to reach their full potential. Equality is a fundamental aspect of justice, ensuring that all individuals have the same rights and freedoms. Moreover, justice requires that everyone be treated equally, regardless of gender, class, ethnicity, race, or other social determinants.

Humanity is an integral part of nature, and we can derive valuable lessons about the principles of justice from the natural world—essentially, "the right mode of living." First, plants and trees do not engage in aggressive competition for resources; they are content with what they have and do not seek to take more from others. In Mt. 6:25-34, Jesus teaches that humans should prioritize seeking God's reign and righteousness over concerns about what to eat, drink, or wear. Second, plants and trees flourish in diversity while maintaining their unique identities. For instance, although the mustard seed is the smallest of seeds, it possesses the potential to grow into something remarkable. This emphasizes realizing one's potential rather than competing to be the largest. Lastly, nature exemplifies inclusivity and diversity. No single entity dominates; instead, all elements coexist harmoniously, each finding its place within the natural order.

Diversity characterizes how nature survives and thrives. It is crucial for understanding a world where various people and cultures coexist. This implies that no race, culture, tradition, or religion should dominate others. Truth can be discovered across multiple aspects of human life and through diverse perspectives, even when they are difficult to express.

Mere differences between cultures do not automatically constitute diversity. We must learn to think collectively, respect one another, and collaborate to create a just society and a better world. Differences in cultures or religions should not be perceived as threats or taboos; instead, they should be viewed as opportunities for mutual engagement and shared learning experiences. Otherwise, cultural or religious arrogance may dominate our social and political landscapes. Ultimately, we need critically engaged diversity to foster global solidarity. While we are different, we also share a common humanity: our honor and duty to uphold and pass on to future generations.

Bibliography

"About Restorative Justice." Accessed Nov 15, 2024. https://law.wisc.edu/fjr/rjp/justice.html.

"Adam Smith's Moral and Political Philosophy." Accessed Oct 6, 2024. https://plato.stanford.edu/entries/smith-moral-political/.

Adams, Samuel L. "The Bible in Christian Nationalist Rhetoric." *Interpretation* 78, no. 4 (2024): 298–309.

Analects of Confucius. Accessed March 21, 2025. http://www.acmuller.net/con-dao/analects.html#div-16.

AP News. Accessed Nov 6, 2024. https://apnews.com/article/jd-vance-georgia-shooting-7d7727a1aff8491f66914a4d8a14cd8c.

Aristotle. *Nicomachean Ethics*, translated by David Ross. New York: Oxford University Press, 1925.

Aristotle. *The Politics*, edited and translated by Ernest Barker. New York: Oxford University Press, 1946.

Batten, Alicia. "Dishonor, Gender and the Parable of the Prodigal Son." *Toronto Journal of Theology* 13, no. 2 (1997): 187–200.

bell, hooks. *Feminism Is for Everybody: Passionate Politics*. New York: Routledge, 2014.

BibleGateway Blog. Accessed March 24, 2022. https://www.biblegateway.com/blog/2012/04/why-didnt-they-stop-martin-luther-king-jr-on-the-parable-of-the-good-samaritan.

"Black Lives Matter." Accessed Nov 12, 2024. https://blacklivesmatter.com.

Borg, Marcus. *Jesus: The Life, Teaching, and Relevance of a Religious Revolutionary*. New York: HarperCollins, 2008.

Braithwaite, John. *Restorative Justice & Responsive Regulation*. Oxford: Oxford University Press, 2002.

Buttrick, David. *Speaking Parables: A Homiletic Guide*. Louisville, KY: WJKP, 2000.

Calvin, John. *Commentary on a Harmony of the Evangelists: Matthew, Mark, and Luke*, Vol. 3. Edinburgh: Calvin Translation Society, 1846.

Carey, Greg. *Stories Jesus Told: How to Read a Parable*. Nashville: Abingdon, 2019.

Carlston, Charles. "Reminiscence and Redaction in Luke 15:11–32." *Journal of Biblical Literature* 94 (1975): 368–90.

Carpenter, John. "The Parable of the Talents in Missionary Perspective: A Call for an Economic Spirituality," *Missiology* 25, no. 2 (1997): 165–81.

Carson, D. A. "Matthew." In *The Expositor's Bible Commentary*, vol. 8. Grand Rapids, MI: Zondervan, 1984.

Carter, Warren. *Matthew and the Margins: A Socio-Political and Religious Reading.* Sheffield: Sheffield Academic Press, 2000.

"The Catholic Online." Accessed Mar 21, 2022. https://www.catholic.org/bible/book.php?id=17&bible_chapter=4.

Chrysostom, John. *Homilies on Matthew in Nicene and Post-Nicene Fathers,* Vol. 10. Grand Rapids, MI: Eerdmans, 1978.

Coates, Ta-Nehisi. "The Case for Reparations." In *The Atlantic,* 2014. Accessed Nov 20, 2024. https://www.theatlantic.com/magazine/archive/2014/06/the-case-for-reparations/361631/.

Cohen, Sheldon. "Social Relationships and Health." *The American Psychologist* 59, no. 8 (2004): 676–84.

Cole, Teju. *Open City.* New York: Random House, 2011.

Cone, James. *Black Theology of Liberation.* Maryknoll, NY: Orbis, 1990.

"Contemporary Approaches to the Social Contract." Accessed Oct 6, 2024. https://plato.stanford.edu/entries/contractarianism-contemporary/.

Cook, Michael. "Jesus' Parables and the Faith that Does Justice." *Studies in the Spirituality of Jesuits* 24, no. 5 (1992): 1–35.

Cranfield, Charles. "The Good Samaritan." *Theology Today* 11, no. 3 (1954): 368–72.

"Critical Philosophy of Race." Accessed Oct 6, 2024. https://plato.stanford.edu/entries/critical-phil-race/.

Crossan, John Dominic. *Finding Is the First Act: Trove Folktales and Jesus' Treasure Parable.* Eugene, OR: Wipf & Stock, 2008.

Crossan, John Dominic. *In Parables: The Challenge of the Historical Jesus.* New York: Harper & Row, 1973.

Crossan, John Dominic. *The Power of Parable: How Fiction by Jesus Became Fiction about Jesus.* New York: HarperOne, 2012.

Dao De Jing. Accessed March 19, 2025. https://drkimys.blogspot.com/p/dao-de-jing_22.html.

Davies, W.D and Dale Allison. *A Critical and Exegetical Commentary on the Gospel According to Matthew,* Vol. 3. London: T&T Clark, 1997.

De Boer, Martinus. "Ten Thousand Talents: Matthew's Interpretation and Redaction of the Parable of the Unforgiving Servant (Matt 18:23-35)." *Catholic Biblical Quarterly* 50, no. 2 (1988): 214–32.

Dobbin, Frank and Alexandra Kalev. *Getting to Diversity: What Works and What Doesn't.* Cambridge, MA: Belknap Press, 2022.

Dobrovolny, Mary Kay. "The Laborers in the Vineyard." In *Social Justice in the Stories of Jesus: The Ethical Challenge of the Parables,* edited by Matthew Gordley, 319–21. Pittsburgh, PA: Wiley Blackwell, 2024.

Dodd, C.H. *The Parables of the Kingdom.* Rev. ed. 1936. London: James Nisbet & Co, 1961.

Doty, William. "An Interpretation: Parable of the Weeds and Wheat." *Interpretation* 25, no. 2 (1971): 185–93.

Dryzek, John. *Politics of the Earth*. Oxford: Oxford University Press, 2022.

Duff, Nancy. "Luke 15:11-32." *Interpretation* 49, no. 1 (1995): 66–9.

Eckersley, Robyn. *The Green State: Rethinking Democracy and Sovereignty*. Cambridge, MA: MIT Press, 2004.

Eliade, Mircea. *The Sacred and the Profane: The Nature of Religion*. Orlando, FL: Harcourt, 1987.

Ernst, Van Eck and John Kloppenborg. *The Parables of Jesus the Galilean: Stories of a Social Prophet*. Eugene, OR: Cascade, 2016.

Esler, Philip F. *Community and Gospel in Luke-Acts: The Social and Political Motivations of Lucan Theology*. New York: Cambridge University Press, 1989.

Findlay, Alexander. *Jesus and His Parables*. London: Epworth Press, 1950.

Fitzmyer, Joseph. *The Gospel According to Luke*. New York: Doubleday, 1985.

Ford, Richard Q. *The Parables of Jesus and the Problems of the World: How Ancient Narratives Comprehend Modern Malaise*. Eugene, OR: Cascade, 2016.

Foucault, Michel. *The Order of Things*. New York: Pantheon, 1970.

Fox, Eric. "The Parable of the Lost or Wandering Sheep: Matthew 18:10-14; Luke 15:3-7." *Anglican Theological Review* 44, no. 1 (1962): 44–57.

Funk, Robert W. "Beyond Criticism in Quest of Literacy: the Parable of the Leaven." *Interpretation* 25, no. 2 (1971): 149–70.

Funk, Robert W. "The Good Samaritan as Metaphor." *Semeia* 2 (1974): 74–81.

Funk, Robert W. *The Parables of Jesus*. Oregon, CA: Polebridge Press, 1988.

Funk, Robert W., Bernard Brandon Scott, and James R. Butts, eds. *The Parables of Jesus: Red Letter Edition: A Report of the Jesus Seminar*. Sonoma, CA: Polebridge Press, 1988.

Getty-Sullivan, Mary Ann. *Parables of the Kingdom: Jesus and the Use of Parables in the Synoptic Tradition*. Collegeville, MN: Liturgical, 2007.

Gilligan, Carol. *In a Different Voice: Psychological Theory and Women's Development*. Cambridge, MA: Harvard University Press, 2016.

González, Gusto. *Tres Meses en la Escuela de Mateo*. Nashville, TN: Abingdon Press, 1996.

Gordley, Matthew. *Social Justice in the Stories of Jesus: The Ethical Challenge of the Parables*. Pittsburgh, PA: Wiley Blackwell, 2024.

Gospel of Thomas. Accessed Oct 27, 2024. https://www.gospels.net/thomas.

Gowler, David B. *What Are They Saying About the Parables?* New York; Mahwah: Paulist Press, 2000.

Grant, Robert and D. Freedman. *The Secret Sayings of Jesus according to the Gospel of Thomas*. London: Fontas Press, 1960.

Hanson, K. C. "Kinship." *Biblical Theology Bulletin* 24 (1994): 183–94.

Harrington, Brooks and John Holbert. *No Mercy, No Justice: The Dominant Narrative of America Versus the Counter-Narrative of Jesus' Parables.* Eugene, OR: Cascade, 2019.

Harrington, Daniel. *The Gospel of Matthew.* Collegeville, MN: Liturgical Press, 1991.

Hays, Richard. *The Moral Vision of the New Testament: Community, Cross, New Creation, A Contemporary Introduction to New Testament Ethics.* New York: Harper, 1996.

Heil, John. "Reader-Response and the Narrative Context of the Parables about Growing Seed in Mark 4:1-34." *Catholic Biblical Quarterly* 54, no. 2 (1992): 271–86.

Herzog, William R. *Parables as Subversive Speech: Jesus as Pedagogue of the Oppressed.* Louisville: Westminster/John Knox Press, 1994.

Herzog, William R. "Sowing Discord: The Parable of the Sower (Mark 4:1-9)." *Review and Expositor* 109, no. 2 (2012): 187–98.

"The History of Utilitarianism." Accessed Oct 6, 2024. https://plato.stanford.edu/entries/utilitarianism-history/.

Hultgren, Arland J. *The Parables of Jesus: A Commentary.* Grand Rapids, MI: Eerdmans, 2000.

Hunter, A.M. *The Parables: Then and Now.* London: SCM Press, 1971.

Jackson, Maggie. *Uncertain: The Wisdom and Wonder of Being Unsure.* Guilford, CT: Prometheus Books, 2024.

Javanbakht, Arash. *Afraid: Understanding the Purpose of Fear and Harnessing the Power of Anxiety.* Lanham, MD: Rowman & Littlefield, 2023.

Jeremias, Joachim. *Jerusalem in the Time of Jesus. An Investigation into Social and Economic Conditions during the New Testament Period.* Philadelphia: Fortress, 1969.

Jeremias, Joachim. *The Parables of Jesus,* translated by S.H. Hooke. New York: Charles Scribner's Sons, 1955.

Jeremias, Joachim. "Tradition und Redaktion in Lukas 15." *Zeitschrift für die neutesamentliche Wissenschaft* 62 (1971): 172–89.

Jeremias, Joachim. "Zum Gleichnis vom verlorenen Sohn, Luk. 15, 11-32." *Theologische Zeitschrift* 5 (1949): 228–31.

"Jeremy Bentham." Accessed Oct 6, 2024. https://plato.stanford.edu/entries/bentham.

Jerome. *The Letters of St. Jerome,* vol. 1, edited by Johannes Quasten and Walter J. Burghardt. Mahwah, NJ: Paulist Press, 1963.

Jiménez, Pablo. "The Laborers of the Vineyard (Matthew 20:1-16): A Hispanic Homiletical Reading." *Journal for Preachers* 21, no. 1 (1997): 35–40.

"John Locke." Accessed Oct 6, 2024. https://plato.stanford.edu/entries/locke/.

Johnson, Luke Timothy. *The Gospel of Luke.* Collegeville, MN: Liturgical Press, 1991.

"John Stuart Mill." Accessed Oct 6, 2024. https://plato.stanford.edu/entries/mill/.

Jones, J.R. "Love as Perception of Meaning." In *Religion and Understanding,* edited by D. Phillips, 141–53. Oxford: Blackwell, 1967.

Juel, Donald. "The Strange Silence of the Bible." *Interpretation* 51, no. 1 (1997): 5–19.

"Justice." In the *Stanford Encyclopedia of Philosophy*. Accessed Oct 6, 2024. https://plato.stanford.edu/entries/justice/.

Kant, Immanuel. *Groundwork for the Metaphysics of Morals* (1785), translated by H.J. Paton. New York: Harper Torchbooks, 1964.

"Karl Marx." Accessed Oct 6, 2024. https://plato.stanford.edu/entries/marx/.

Keddie, Anthony. *Class and Power in Roman Palestine: The Socioeconomic Setting of Judaism and Christian Origins*. Cambridge: Cambridge University Press, 2019.

Khatchadourian, H. "Compensation and Reparation as Forms of Compensatory Justice." *Metaphilosophy* 37 (2006): 429–48.

Kim, Yung Suk. *Jesus's Truth: Life in Parables*. Eugene, OR: Resources, 2018.

Kim, Yung Suk. "Justice Matters, But Which Justice? In the case of Jesus' Parables." *Currents in Theology and Mission* 46, no. 3 (2019): 41–3.

Kim, Yung Suk. *Reading Jesus' Parables with Dao De Jing*. Eugene, OR: Resources, 2018.

Kim, Yung Suk. *Resurrecting Jesus: The Renewal of New Testament Theology*. Eugene, OR: Cascade, 2015.

Kloppenborg, John S. *Q the Earliest Gospel*. Louisville and London: W/JKP, 2008.

Knight, George. "Luke 16:19-31: The Rich Man and Lazarus." *Review and Expositor* 94, no. 2 (1997): 277–83.

LaHurd, Carol Schersten. "Re-viewing Luke 15 with Arab Christian Women." In *A Feminist Companion to Luke*, edited by Amy-Jill Levine, 246–68. New York: Sheffield Academic, 2002.

Landry, David and Ben May. "Honor Restored: New Light on the Parable of the Prudent Steward (Luke 16:1-8a)." *Journal of Biblical Literature* 119, no. 2 (2000): 287–309.

Levine, Amy-Jill. *Short Stories by Jesus: The Enigmatic Parables of a Controversial Rabbi*. New York: HarperOne, 2014.

Livingston, Robert. *The Conversation: How Seeking and Speaking the Truth About Racism Can Radically Transform Individuals and Organizations*. New York: Crown Currency, 2021.

MacIntyre, Alasdair. *After Virtue*. Notre Dame, IN: University of Notre Dame Press, 1981.

MacIntyre, Alasdair. *Ethics and Politics: Volume 2: Selected Essays*. Cambridge: Cambridge University Press, 2006.

Malina, Bruce and John Pilch. *Social-Science Commentary on the Synoptic Gospels*. Minneapolis, MN: Fortress Press, 1992.

Marshall, Christopher D. *Compassionate Justice: An Interdisciplinary Dialogue with Two Gospel Parables on Law, Crime, and Restorative Justice*. Eugene, OR: Cascade, 2012.

Massaro, Thomas. *Mercy in Actions: The Social Teachings of Pope Francis*. Lanham, MD: Rowman & Littlefield, 2018.

McArthur, Harvey K. "The Parable of the Mustard Seed." *Catholic Biblical Quarterly* 33 (1971): 198–201.

McGaughy, Lane C. "The Fear of Yahweh and the Mission of Judaism: A Postexilic Maxim and Its Early Christian Expansion in the Parable of the Talents." *Journal of Biblical Literature* 94, no. 2 (1975): 235–45.

McIver, Robert K. "The Parable of the Weeds Among the Wheat (Matt 13:24-30, 36-43) and the Relationship Between the Kingdom and the Church as Portrayed in the Gospel of Matthew." *Journal of Biblical Literature* 114, no. 4 (1995): 643–59.

Meier, John. "The Parable of the Wheat and the Weeds (Matthew 13:24-30): Is Thomas's Version (Logion 57) Independent?" *Journal of Biblical Literature* 131, no. 4 (2012): 715–32.

Metzger, Bruce. *A Textual Commentary on the Greek New Testament*. New York: Hendrickson, 2005.

Mill, John Stuart. *On Liberty, Utilitarianism and Other Essays,* edited by Mark Philp and Frederick Rosen. Oxford: Oxford University Press, 2015.

Mills, Charles W. *Black Rights/White Wrongs: The Critique of Racial Liberalism*. Oxford: Oxford University Press, 2017.

Moltmann, Jürgen. *Ethics of Hope*. Minneapolis, MN: Fortress, 2012.

Mullen, Elizabeth and Tyler G. Okimoto. "Compensatory Justice." In *The Oxford Handbook of Justice in the Workplace,* edited by Russell Cropanzano and Maureen L. Ambrose, 477–96. New York: Oxford University Press, 2015.

Myers, Ched. *The Biblical Vision of Sabbath Economics*. LAB/ORA Press, 2023.

Myers, Ched. *Binding the Strong Man*. Maryknoll, NY: Orbis, 2008.

Neyrey, Jerome. "First-Century Personality." In *The Social World of Luke-Acts: Models for Interpretation*, edited by Jerome Neyrey, 67–96. Peabody, MA: Hendrickson Publishers, 1999.

Nixon, Rob. *Slow Violence and the Environmentalism of the Poor*. Cambridge, MA: Harvard University Press, 2013.

Nozick, Robert. *Anarchy, State, and Utopia*. New York: Basic Books, 1974.

NPR. Accessed Nov 23, 2024. https://www.npr.org/2024/11/19/nx-s1-5196056/new-zealand-maori-indigenous.

NPR On-Point. Accessed Nov 13, 2024. https://www.npr.org/2024/11/11/nx-s1-5184398/virginia-elected-its-first-indian-american-member-of-congressb.

Nussbaum, Martha. *Creating Capabilities: The Human Development Approach*. Cambridge, MA: Belknap Press, 2013.

Oakman, Douglas. "The Buying Power of Two Denarii." *Forum* 3 (1987): 33–8.

Oesterley, W.O.E. *The Gospel Parables in the Light of Their Jewish Background*. New York: Macmillan, 1936.

Okin, Susan. *Justice, Gender, and The Family*. New York: Basic Books, 1991.

O'Rourke, John. "Some Notes on Luke 15:11-32." *New Testament Studies* 18, no. 4 (1972): 431–3.

Park, Rohun. "Revisiting the Parable of the Prodigal Son for Decolonization: Luke's Reconfiguration of Oikos in Luke 15:11-32." *Biblical Interpretation* 17 (2009): 507–20.

Parsons, Mikeal. "The Prodigal's Older Brother: The History and Ethics of Reading Luke 15:25-32." *Perspectives in Religious Study* 23 (1996): 147–74.
Pateman, Carol. *The Sexual Contract*. Stanford, CA: Stanford University Press, 1988.
Payne, Philip. "Order of Sowing and Ploughing in the Parable of the Sower." *New Testament Study* 25, no. 1 (1978): 123–9.
Perrin, Norman. *Rediscovering the Teaching of Jesus*. New York: Harper & Row, 1967.
Peterson, William L. "The Parable of the Lost Sheep in the Gospel of Thomas and the Synoptics." *Novum Testamentum* 23, no. 2 (1981): 128–47.
Pogge, Thomas W. *World Poverty and Human Rights*. Cambridge: Polity, 2008.
Powelson, Mark and Ray Riegert, eds. *The Lost Gospel Q: The Original Sayings of Jesus*. Berkeley, CA: Seastone, 1996.
Powery, Emerson B. *The Good Samaritan: Luke 10 for the Life of the Church*. Grand Rapids, MI: Baker Academic, 2022.
"Racist Texts About Slaves and 'Picking Cotton' Sent to Black People as State AGs, Colleges and Police Probe their Origins." Accessed March 19, 2025. https://www.cnn.com/2024/11/07/us/racist-text-messages-post-election/index.html.
Räisänen, Heikki. "The Prodigal Gentile and His Jewish Christian Brother, Luke 15:11-32." In *The Four Gospels*, edited by F. Van Segbroek et al., 1617–36. Leuven: Leuven University Press, 1992.
Rawls, John. *A Theory of Justice*. Cambridge, MA: Belknap Press, 1971.
Rawls, John. *The Law of Peoples: With "The Idea of Public Reason Revisited"*. Cambridge, MA: Harvard University Press, 2001.
Rawls, John. *Political Liberalism*. New York: Columbia University Press, 1993.
Reid, Barbara. *Parables for Preachers, Year A. Matthew*. Collegeville, MN: Liturgical, 2001.
Reid, Barbara. *Year B. Mark*. Collegeville, MN: Liturgical, 1999.
Reid, Barbara. *Year C. Luke*. Collegeville, MN: Liturgical, 2000.
Rindge, Matthew S. "Luke's Artistic Parables: Narratives of Subversion, Imagination, and Transformation." *Interpretation* 68 (2014): 403–15.
Rodríguez, José. "The Parable of the Affirmative Action Employer." *Apuntes* 8, no. 3 (1988): 51–9.
Rohrbaugh, Richard L. "A Peasant Reading of the Parable of the Talents/Pounds: A Text of Terror?" *Biblical Theology Bulletin* 23, no. 1 (1993): 32–9.
Sandel, Michael J. *Justice: What's the Right Thing to Do?* New York: Farrar, Straus and Giroux, 2009.
Sandel, Michael J. *Liberalism and the Limits of Justice*. Cambridge: Cambridge University Press, 1987.
Sanders, Jack T. "The Parable of the Pounds and Lukan Anti-Semitism." *Theological Studies* 42 (1981): 660–8.
Sanders, Jack T. "Tradition and Redaction in Luke 15:11-32." *New Testament Study* 15 (1968-69): 433–8.

Schellenberg, Ryan. "Kingdom as Contaminant? The Role of Repertoire in the Parables of the Mustard Seed and the Leaven." *Catholic Biblical Quarterly* 71, no. 3 (2009): 527–43.

Schottroff, Luise. *The Parables of Jesus*. Minneapolis: Fortress, 2006.

Schüssler Fiorenza, Elisabeth. *In Memory of Her: A Feminist Reconstruction of Christian Origins*. Louisville, KY: WJKP, 1994.

Schweitzer, Albert. *The Quest of the Historical Jesus*. New York: Macmillan, 1968.

Schweizer, Eduardo. *The Good News According to Matthew*. Louisville, KY: WJKP, 1975.

Scott, Bernard. *Hear Then the Parable: A Commentary on the Parables of Jesus*. Minneapolis: Fortress Press, 1989.

Scott, Bernard. "The King's accounting: Matthew 18:23-34." *Journal of Biblical Literature* 104, no. 3 (1985): 429–42.

Scott, Bernard. "Lost Junk, Found Treasure." *The Bible Today* 26 (1988): 31–4.

Scott, Bernard. *Re-Imagine the World: An Introduction to the Parables of Jesus*. Santa Rosa, CA: Polebridge Press, 2001.

Sen, Amartya. *Development as Freedom*. New York: Anchor Books, 2000.

Shiva, Vandana. *Staying Alive: Women, Ecology, and Development*. Berkeley, CA: North Atlantic Books, 2016.

Snodgrass, Klyne R. *Stories with Intent: A Comprehensive Guide to the Parables of Jesus*. Grand Rapids, MI: Eerdmans, 2008.

Sobrino, Jon. *No Salvation Outside the Poor: Prophetic-Utopian Essays*. Maryknoll, NY: Orbis, 2008.

Stein, Robert H. *The Method and Message of Jesus' Teachings*. Louisville, KY: Westminster John Knox, 1993.

Strong's Greek: 4698. "σπλαγχνίζομαι." Accessed March 21, 2025. https://biblehub.com/greek/4697.htm.

Tannehill, Robert. *Luke*. Nashville, TN: Abingdon Press, 1996.

Taylor, Charles. "The Nature and Scope of Distributive Justice." In *Charles Taylor, Philosophy and the Human Sciences, Philosophical Papers*, vol. 2. Cambridge: Cambridge University Press, 2010.

Tevel, J. M. "The Laborers in the Vineyard: the Exegesis of Matthew 20:1-7 in the Early Church." *Vigiliae Christianae* 46 (1992): 356–80.

Thurman, Howard. *Jesus and the Disinherited*. Boston, MA: Beacon, 1996.

Ukpong, Justin. "The Parable of the Talents (Matt 25:14-30): Commendation or Critique of Exploitation?: A Social-Historical and Theological Reading." *Neotestamenica* 46, no. 1 (2012): 190–207.

"Virtue Ethics." Accessed March 15, 2025. https://plato.stanford.edu/entries/ethics-virtue/.

Wainwright, Elaine. "Part Four: An Ecological Reading of Mark's Gospel." Accessed Nov 24, 2024. https://hail.to/tui-motu-interislands-magazine/publication/430InQe/article/p9j2RGB.

Waller, Elizabeth. "The Parable of the Leaven: A Sectarian Teaching and the Inclusion of Women." *Union Seminary Quarterly Review* 35, no. 1–2 (1979-80): 99–109.

Walzer, Michael. *Spheres of Justice*. New York: Basic Books, 1983.

WAMU.org. Accessed Nov 13, 2024. https://wamu.org/story/24/11/07/suhas-subramanyam-virginia-congress-south-asian/.

Weder, Hans. *Die Gleichnisse Jesu als Metaphern: Traditions- und redaktionsgeschichtliche Analysen und Interpretationen*. Göttingen: Vandenhoeck & Ruprecht, 1978.

West, Audrey. "Preparing to Preach the Parables in Luke." *Currents in Theology and Mission*, December 1, 2009, 405–13.

Westermann, Claus. *The Parables of Jesus in the Light of the Old Testament*. Minneapolis, MN: Fortress, 1990.

"White Gunman Caught in Killing of 9 in Historical Black Church." Accessed Nov 22, 2024. https://apnews.com/article/politics-south-carolina-religion-charleston-arrests-8747b77ae03a426e864f042454cab603.

"Why Māori are protesting in New Zealand." Accessed Nov 22, 2024. https://theweek.com/world-news/why-maori-are-protesting-in-new-zealand.

Wilder, Amos. *Early Christian Rhetoric: The Language of the Gospel*. Eugene, OR: Wipf & Stock, 2014.

Wilder, Amos. "The Parable of the Sower: Naïvete and Method in Interpretation." *Semeia* 2 (1974): 134–51.

Williams, Eric. *Capitalism and Slavery*. Chapel Hill, NC: The University of North Carolina, 1994.

Wink, Walter. *The Power That Be: Theology for a New Millennium*. Manhattan, NY: Harmony, 1999.

Wolff, Jonathan. *An Introduction to Political Philosophy*, 4th ed. Oxford: Oxford University Press, 2023.

Yoder, John Howard. *The Politics of Jesus*. Grand Rapids, MI: Eerdmans, 1994.

Young, Brad. *The Parables: Jewish Tradition and Christian Interpretation*. Peabody, MA: Hendrickson Publishers, 1998.

Young, Iris Marion. *Justice and the Politics of Difference*. Princeton, NJ: Princeton University Press, 2022.

Zehr, Howard. *Little Book of Restorative Justice: Revised and Updated*. New York: Good Books, 2015.

Zimmermann, Ruben. *Puzzling the Parables of Jesus: Methods and Interpretation*. Minneapolis, MN: Fortress, 2015.

Zizek, Slavoj. "Neighbors and Other Monsters: A Plea for Ethical Violence." In *The Neighbor: Three Inquiries in Political Theology*, edited by Slavoj Zizek, Eric L. Santner, and Kenneth Reinhard, 134–90. Chicago, IL: The University of Chicago Press, 2005.

Index

Abraham   18, 45–6, 48, 88–9
absolution   149
accountability   23, 27–30, 59, 81, 83, 119–20, 126–8, 130–3, 137–8, 143, 146, 149–50, 154, 159–63, 177, 191
addiction   60
affirmative action   48, 100, 113–15
afterlife   45
agathos   40, 42, 49
agency   12, 27, 59, 88, 152
agent   6, 53, 104, 152
allegorical interpretation   102, 157, 186
Amos   5, 19–21, 65, 84–5, 93
Aristotle   17
attitude   26, 54, 56, 60–1, 73, 78, 86–9, 96, 111, 124, 131, 171, 178, 184, 190
Augustus (emperor)   3

basic income   16, 35, 40–4
basileia tou theou   5, 36
Bentham, Jeremy   14
biases   18, 26–7, 60, 90–1, 107, 162, 198
biodiversity   191
Black Lives Matter (BLM)   96
burning bush   62

capitalism   19, 21, 174
Carey, Greg   46
character development   17, 63
Christian nationalists   113
Civil Rights Movement   96
classism   85, 91
climate change   1, 8, 20, 31, 173–4, 178, 183–4, 167, 191, 193
Cohen, Sheldon   172
Cole, Teju   90
colonialism   19, 99–100
common assets   49
common good   14–17, 49, 111, 159, 163, 172
common humanity   11, 107, 111, 199

communitarianism   15, 35, 43, 48, 58–9
Confucius   15, 17, 58, 63, 89–90, 104–5, 126, 132
consumerism   189
contract   13–4
cosmopolitanism   167–68
creation   20–21, 110, 112
criminal justice system   27, 60, 119–20, 149
Critical Race Theory   20–21, 110, 112
Crossan, John Dominic   2

debts   130–146
differences   16, 21, 43, 60, 99, 109, 176, 179, 198
dikaios   40, 42
disabilities   49, 71
discernment   24–25, 63
discrimination   4, 16, 18, 25–6, 29, 59, 71, 89, 91–2, 96, 99, 105, 107, 179, 190
Dodd, C.H.   2

ecological crisis   184, 191
ecosystem   32, 80, 178, 188–9, 191
educational culture   76
egalitarianism: luck   16
    relational   16
elitism   85
employment   23, 27, 41–2, 53, 58
enlightenment   74, 111
environmental ethics   183, 187, 191
environmentalism   19
Esler, Philip   139
Ethics: Biblical   12
    economic   174
    environmental   183, 187, 191
    Kantian deontological   12
    moral   15
    Paul's   16
    sharing   50

value   68
virtue   63
eudaimonia   17
Exodus   19, 21

fair wages   53, 92, 180, 196
Father and Two Sons (parable)   121–28
fear   57–9, 152, 159
Fiorenza, Elisabeth Schüssler   6
flexibility   74, 89–90, 105, 127
Ford, Richard   7
forgiveness   28, 121, 126, 129–32, 134, 149, 155–6, 161–2, 197
France, R. T.   157
full employment   41–2, 53
Funk, Robert   93

global crises   2
Global South   100, 190
God's grace   58, 62–3, 78, 83
God's justice   2, 162
God's righteousness (or the righteousness of God)   5, 37
God's rule (or the rule/reign of God)   2, 5, 22–5, 36–41, 61–5
Good Samaritan (parable)   101–108
Gordley, Matthew   2, 6
Green, Barbara   2
gun laws   82

harmony   17, 20, 28, 67, 105–6, 126, 145, 188, 191
Herzog II, William R.   6, 38, 139, 152–3
hierarchical organism   4
higher education   48, 114
Hillel   15, 104, 131
honor-shame   139
Hultgren, Arland   2
human dignity   4, 12, 14, 18, 35, 133
human frailty   91, 130–1

identity   15, 53, 65, 67, 77–9, 89, 91, 99–100, 103–5, 114, 179
inclusion   6, 18–19, 93, 99–100, 112, 114, 183
individualism   12, 15, 44, 49, 77, 106
interconnectedness   20, 32, 100, 145–6, 169, 172, 174, 183, 187, 189–90
interdependence   106, 174

Intersectionality   7, 18, 100, 107
investment   57, 66

Jackson, Maggie   90
Jewish tradition   45, 93, 102
Johnson, Luke Timothy   174
Josephus   129
Judaism   37, 46, 87, 96, 131
justice: attributive   53–68
   compensatory   137–46
   distributive   35–49
   divine   5, 19, 35, 44, 144, 152, 163
   economic   4, 17, 21, 44, 50, 196
   environmental   183–98
   gender   92, 180
   global   167–81
   Marxist   21
   principles of   11, 167, 196, 198
   procedural   71–93
   racial   99–115
   restorative   119–34
   retributive   149–65
   social   85–97
   universal law of   12
   wage   92
justification   88

Kant   12, 15, 49, 106, 114–15

labor union   158
Laozi   15, 17, 75, 79–80, 89, 91, 95, 111–12, 126–7, 131–2, 188
Lazarus   44–48
leadership   92, 94, 96, 107, 157
Leaven (parable)   92–96
Levine, Amy-Jill   65, 100, 152
liberalism   12–13, 127
liberation theology   21
libertarianism   13–15, 35, 80
Locke, John   12, 155
Lost Sheep (parable)   175–180

Marshall, Christopher   7, 103, 105
Martin Luther King Jr   96, 103
Marxism   21–22
materialism   64, 168
melting pot theory   113
Mencius   145

mental health   60, 108, 172
meritocracy   13, 53
metanoia   2, 127
migration   100, 179
Mill, John Stuart   14
Mishna   102
Moltmann, Jürgen   174
Montgomery Bus Boycott   95–6
moral desert   59
moral duty   46–7, 106, 115, 167
Moses   45, 62
Mustard Seed (parable)   108–115
Myers, Ched   6, 174

nationalism   85
Nazareth   3–4
neighborliness   27, 100, 102
Nozick, Robert   13
Nussbaum, Martha   168

opportunity   8, 13, 16, 27, 40, 46, 57–8, 66–8, 72, 74, 92, 100, 133, 168, 171, 178, 187
oppression   6, 18–19, 21, 99–100, 130, 139, 142, 144, 153, 161, 163

parabole   2
Passover   93
Paul   14, 16, 18, 21, 93, 106
Pearl (parable)   64–67
Pharisee and Tax Collector (parable)   86–92
Philo   93
pity   15, 35, 43, 48, 58–9
Pogge, Thomas   167
political philosophy   1, 11–13, 32, 99, 167, 195
postcolonial theory   19
poverty   4, 6, 12–13, 19, 23–4, 30–1, 35, 44, 46–8, 50, 60, 69, 75, 85, 88, 92, 114, 156, 162, 167–9, 172–4, 178
prejudice   18, 26–7, 85, 90–1, 96, 100, 198
princeps   4

racism   8, 18, 27, 85, 91, 96, 99–100, 107, 113, 144, 160–2, 183
Rawls, John   13, 43, 49, 167

reciprocity   130, 132, 140
reconciliation   3, 22, 28, 72, 119–20, 122, 124–7, 130–1, 137–8, 156, 161, 163, 197
rehabilitation   28, 60, 133, 150, 163, 178
representation   100, 107, 185
resistance   21, 133, 141, 146, 152, 157
retribution   7, 29–30, 119, 121, 126, 130, 132, 134, 150, 158, 163–4
Rich Fool (parable)   169–175
Rich Man and Lazarus (parable)   44–48
rivalry   122
Rosa Parks   95
rule: God's   2, 5, 38
   Roman   1, 19

school discipline   81
school shooting   82
Scott, Brandon   93
security   41, 82, 92, 145, 150
Seed Growing Secretly (parable)   72–77
self-concept   76
self-confidence   77
self-esteem   67, 89
Sen, Amartya   167
Sepphoris   3
sexism   85, 91
shuv   127
slavery   29, 99, 129, 144
Smith, Adam   12
Snodgrass, Klyne   140
social capital   68
social ladder   48
social welfare   60
societal norms   2, 6, 18, 71, 80, 86, 149
solidarity   16, 27–8, 31, 42, 44, 48, 58, 82, 85, 89, 91, 96, 106, 111, 113, 130, 168–9, 173, 199
Sower (parable)   184–191
stewardship   7, 20, 32, 56–7, 173–4, 189, 192
Stoicism   4
systemic injustice   6, 19, 139, 146, 152–3, 157, 162, 178, 190, 196

Talents (parable)   54–60
Talmud: Babylonian   102
   Jerusalem   40

tektōn 3
Temple   45, 86–8, 102
Tenants (parable)   156–163
Thurman, Howard   6
transformation   17, 21, 26, 28, 65, 67, 78–9, 82–3, 87, 89–90, 93–6, 100, 109–12, 126, 196
trauma   29, 59, 68–9, 107, 127, 162
Treasure (parable)   60–64

Unjust Judge and Widow (parable)   151–156
Unjust Steward (parable)   138–145
Unmerciful Slave (parable)   128–133
utilitarianism   14–15, 35, 49, 80

value ethics   68
Vineyard Laborers (parable)   35–44
virtue ethics   63
virtue theory   17
vocation   4, 61, 67, 158
voter suppression   100

West, Audrey   93
Wheat and Weeds (parable)   77–82
white privilege   107
Wink, Walter   6
wisdom   17, 74, 79, 90, 104, 111, 127, 140, 142
work ethic   54, 67, 78–9
worldview   5, 78, 188, 191

xenophobia   85, 91

Yoder, John Howard   6, 10

Zacchaeus   46, 56, 89, 97, 170
zeteo   65

About the Author

Yung Suk Kim is a Full Professor of New Testament and Early Christianity at the Samuel DeWitt Proctor School of Theology, Virginia Union University. He has written nearly twenty books in the area of biblical interpretation, Pauline studies, and the Gospels, including *How to Read the Gospels* (2024), *Monotheism, Biblical Traditions, and Race Relations* (2022), *How to Read Paul* (2021), and *Resurrecting Jesus: The Renewal of New Testament Theology* (2015). He co-authored *Toward Decentering the New Testament* (2018) with Mitzi Smith. He has also edited four volumes, including *At the Intersection of Hermeneutics and Homiletics* and *Paul's Gospel, Empire, Race, and Ethnicity*. In 2019, he was named the Scott & Stringfellow Outstanding Professor Award recipient at Virginia Union University.